Principles of Corporate Communication

CEES B.M. VAN RIEL

Erasmus University Rotterdam

PRENTICE HALL

LONDON · NEW YORK · TORONTO · SYDNEY · TOKYO · SINGAPORE ·
MADRID · MEXICO CITY · MUNICH

First published 1995 by
Prentice Hall
Campus 400, Maylands Avenue
Hemel Hempstead
Hertfordshire, HP2 7EZ
A division of
Simon & Schuster International Group

Typeset in 10/12pt Baskerville
by Mathematical Composition Setters, Salisbury, Wilts.

Printed and bound in Great Britain by
T.J. Press (Padstow) Ltd

Library of Congress Cataloging in Publication Data

Riel, C.B.M. van.
        [Identiteit en imago. English]
        Principles of corporate communication/Cees B.M. van Riel;
    edited and adapted by Chris Blackburn.
        p. cm.
        Translation of: Identiteit en imago.
        Includes bibliographical references and index.
        ISBN 0-13-150996-9 (pbk.)
        1. Communication in management.   2. Corporations–Communication
    systems.   3. Public relations–Corporations.   4. Corporate image.
I. Title.
HD30.3.R5413   1995
658.4'5–dc20
94-48042
CIP

British Library Cataloguing in Publication Data

A catalogue record for this book is available from
the British Library

ISBN 0-13-150996-9 (pbk)
1 2 3 4 5   99 98 97 96 95

Dedicated to Hanneke

Contents

Foreword

Like most people involved in the communication business, I get visited by a stream (well, perhaps it's more of a trickle) of keen people who are looking for the ultimate book on corporate communication. Many of my interlocutors seem to be writing a thesis on some aspect of the communication activity. They are desperate for definitions. 'What's the difference between corporate image, corporate identity and corporate reputation?' And 'Where is the one book that will tell me everything that I need to know about corporate communication?'

Until now I have invariably failed them. I don't myself go in for definitions much and I certainly don't know all the books to read. But these good folk need seek enlightenment no longer. Now comes *Principles of Corporate Communication*. This is a work of considerable scholarship, which I can recommend with a clear conscience.

It has three great virtues. First, it defines the whole subject and breaks it down into clearly comprehensible areas. Second, it is full of definitions, a few of which I even find myself agreeing with. Third, it takes into account, at least so far as I can judge, almost everything sensible that has been written on this subject.

Naturally I don't agree with all of van Riel's conclusions; it is very tempting to become a bit academic and abstruse in what is, to me at least, essentially a practical and pragmatic area of activity. Nevertheless I am clear that the book is a considerable addition to academic thought on corporate communication. In its grasp of the totality of the subject and its analysis of the various over-lapping, even conflicting areas of which the communication activity is comprised it is masterly. Those people aspiring to doctorates in corporate communication need look no further.

But is it any use for the practitioner? Well yes, I believe it is, because van Riel's analysis of the total corporate communication process gives clarity and perspective. Van Riel's strengths of analysis and synthesis are to my mind impressive.

Wally Olins
October 1994

Preface

Principles of Corporate Communication arose from the educational and research-driven need to have a source of reference that integrates the existing knowledge of corporate communication. Corporate communication is, in my personal opinion, a framework in which all communication specialists (marketing, organizational and management communication) integrate the totality of the organizational message, thereby helping to define the corporate image as a means to improving corporate performance.

Academic and practical knowledge in this field is expanding prudently towards a mature stage. However, I have kept to a concise track from the variety of information available in working papers, articles and books; I limited myself to mostly English, German and, of course, Dutch sources. Making further contacts in the international network has convinced me that I did not study every possible relevant source. Nevertheless, one can assume that the majority of what can be seen as the dominant paradigms do integrate into the vision from which this book stems.

Principles of Corporate Communication consists of six chapters in which the central issues of corporate communication are dealt with. In the first chapter I present my personal views regarding the nature of the field. The second and third chapters administer the meaning and measurement of, respectively, 'corporate identity' and 'corporate image'. The fourth chapter presents a corporate communication strategy (based on theoretical evidence and practical experience) to be followed in order to prepare and implement an effective corporate identity programme. The fifth chapter deals with 'organizing corporate communication': who should do what, and how to organize the communication processes and integrate all corporate messages from a variety of specialized sources (marketing, public relations, investor relations, CEO communications, etc.). The final chapter presents four practical illustrations of the value of 'theoretical' notions in the field of corporate communication for international operating companies like Rabobank, Canon Europe, Akzo Nobel and Fortis.

As with most books, this one could not have come to fruition without the contributions of many people. Several representatives of the corporate world supplied me with information in order to be able to illustrate this, mostly academic, book with practical examples. Willem Lageweg equipped me with information regarding Rabobank; Richard Kok and Annemarie Hendriks did the same concerning the corporate communication policy of Akzo Nobel; Peter Kersten patiently provided me with all essential background information about Canon Europe; and finally, Jan van Heuverswyn entrusted me with the dynamic developments within the financial service supplier, Fortis. I am grateful for their personal support and naturally for the willingness of the companies they represent, in granting me permission to publicize actual developments in their global corporate communication policies.

Several people working within well-known international research agencies also offered support by formulating constructive criticism on concept versions of the manuscript: Sibolt Mulder (Motivaction), Stewart Lewis (Mori), Henk Oostenbrink (FHV/BBDO) and Peter van Westendorp (NSS), who offered help and counsel at various points.

Several colleagues of the Business School of Erasmus University in Rotterdam facilitated me in a significant way, directly or indirectly, in completing this book. I highly appreciated the support of Margot Barten, Onno Maathuis, Ad Pruyn, Daniël de Raaf, Fred van Raaij, Johan van Rekom, Ale Smidts and Berend Wierenga.

The main core of this book was originally written in Dutch and published in the Netherlands as *Identiteit en Imago* (Academic Service, Schoonhoven, 1992). The translation from Dutch into an updated English version could not have been done without the help of several people. I am much obliged to Jacquelien Bakker, Dusanka Pajcin, Anne Thomas and, last but not least, to my colleague Chris Blackburn, Subject Chair and Senior Lecturer in Marketing at Oxford Brookes University, who edited the final version of the manuscript.

Cees B.M. van Riel
Leiden/Rotterdam, October 1994

About the author

Cees B.M. van Riel is Professor in Corporate Communication at the Business School of the Erasmus University Rotterdam in the Netherlands. He is Director of the Corporate Communication Centre, a research institute at the same university. Van Riel has worked as a communication strategy consultant for several Belgian and Dutch companies.

Van Riel studied mass communication and economic history at the Catholic University of Nijmegen in the Netherlands. He has published several books and articles on corporate identity, corporate image and organization of communication, e.g. *Profiles in Corporate Communication in Financial Institutions; A comparison between Europe and the USA* (1989); *Handboek Corporate Communication* (1990); *Identiteit en Imago* (1992); *Management of Corporate Communication Profit Organizations* (with R. Adema and B. Wierenga, 1993); and *Organisational Identification and Employee Communication* (1994).

Chapter 1

Introduction

Organizations use three basic forms of communication. The most important is 'management communication', i.e. communication by (senior) managers with internal and external target groups. In order to expedite this task successfully, companies have engaged specialists in the field of marketing communication and organizational communication (public relations, public affairs, investor relations, labour market communication, corporate advertising, etc.). The wide range of internal 'sources' can lead to a fragmented, even contradictory, picture communicated by the company when viewed as a whole. Companies are aware of the dangers of fragmented communication and strive for an increase in mutual coherence between all forms of internal and external communication.

Corporate communication encompasses marketing communication, organizational communication and management communication. It may be seen as a framework in which various communications specialists – working from a mutually established strategic framework – can integrate their own communications input. The basic philosophy underlying this framework can be described as directing the company's communications policies from within the 'corporate strategy—corporate identity—corporate image' triangle. Representatives of the various communications specialities consult on the development of 'common starting points (CSPs)', directly linked to the agreed communications strategy for implementing the actual and desired corporate identity and supporting the company's image.

1.1 Evolution of organizational communication

Communication is increasingly gaining the status of a valuable, if not indispensable management tool, together with the obligations that such status carries. Compared with ten years ago, according to the results of a recent study by the Conference Board, communication managers are no longer seen as mere 'information conduits'; rather, they act as fully fledged strategic advisers to senior management (Troy, 1993). In common with financial management, production management and human resource management, communication

1

is expected to contribute to the achievement of company objectives. Communication's role in this process can be summarized briefly as follows: 'to professionally carry out the *window* and the *mirror function*'. The phrase 'window function' refers to the preparation and execution of a communications policy, resulting in messages that portray all facets of the organization in a lucid and appealing way. The anticipated outcomes of this portrayal are the changes desired by the company on a cognitive, affective and conative level in those target groups with which it is aimed to build and maintain a relationship. The 'mirror function' refers to the monitoring of relevant environmental developments and to the 'anticipation' of their consequences for the company's communications policy: for instance, the mapping of image-building among various relevant stakeholders, publication of actual achievements (e.g. market shares), evaluations of future trends (issue management) and, in particular, keeping up with changes in the internal organizational climate.

1.1.1   Corporate communication: integrating three forms of communication

It is possible to distinguish three main forms of communication in organizations that fulfil the aforementioned functions. The most important form of communication is *management communication*, i.e. communication by (senior) managers with internal and external target groups. 'Management', in this sense, refers to anyone who is authorized to exert influence on internal and external stakeholders, effecting access to resources that are essential for the company (Pfeffer and Salancik, 1978). An example of this in practice might be 'management by word of mouth', obviously directed at internal target groups; or again, the influence of the senior manager as the figurehead of the company as manifested through public lectures, interviews and the like.

Companies have engaged specialists in the field of marketing communication and organizational communication to supervise such functions. In companies the emphasis (especially financial) is often placed on *marketing communication*: advertising, direct mail, personal selling, sponsorship, etc. Equally a range of *organizational communication* forms may be discerned, depending on the size, the diversity of and the sensitivity to interdependent relationships with specific target groups: public relations (PR), public affairs, investor relations, environmental communication, corporate advertising, internal communication, etc.

Until recently communication was seen as the exclusive territory of the 'public relations' and 'marketing communication' departments. However, this era now seems to have come to an end, as witnessed particularly in the rise of 'new' forms of communication *within* functional management domains such as 'financial management' (investor relations), 'production management' (e.g. environmental communication) and 'personnel management' (labour market communication), which communicate with internal and external target groups apparently outside the scope of influence of the 'traditional' communication departments.

In practice, the large variety of internal communications 'sources' can lead to fragmented, sometimes even contradictory, external manifestations of the company as a whole. Organizations are only too aware of the dangers of fragmented communication. This is not only due to the fear of supervening 'incidents' which may harm their reputation, but also the desire to avoid compromising the effectiveness and efficiency of the total communication effort. It thus becomes clear why it is possible to observe a tendency to strive for increased mutual coherence between all forms of internal and external communication. The presupposition which underlies this striving for coherence is that a coherent communication policy positively contributes to the favourable image of each individual component, which in turn is working positively to contribute to the entire performance of the company. A favourable corporate reputation is not an isolated objective, but a vital condition (thus a means) to create a sound commercial basis from which the success (in the widest sense of the word) of the company will eventually stem. On this latter point, contemporary empirical evidence can be found in studies recently carried out on the relationship between a company's achievements and its reputation (Fombrun and Shanley, 1989; Maathuis, 1993). See Table 1.1.

Figure 1.1 shows forms of internal and external communication which might be used in a hypothetical company. It shows that communication as a management tool is used in many areas of the organization other than public relations

Table 1.1 Hypotheses in Fombrun and Shanley (1989) and Maathuis (1993)

Hypotheses	Fombrun and Shanley	Maathuis
1. The greater a firm's prior accounting profitability, the better its reputation	Confirmed	Confirmed
2. The greater a firm's prior accounting risk, the worse its reputation	Confirmed	Confirmed
3. The greater a firm's current market risk, the worse its reputation	Not confirmed	Confirmed
4. The greater a firm's current dividend yield, the worse its reputation	Confirmed	Not confirmed (indications for opposite)
5. The greater a firm's current media visibility, the better its reputation	Contrary confirmed	Not confirmed (indications for dependence on economic situation)
6. The more non-negative a firm's current media coverage, the better its reputation	Not confirmed	Confirmed
7. The larger the firm, the better its reputation	Confirmed	Confirmed
8. The greater a firm's advertising intensity, the better its reputation	Confirmed	Only confirmed for high-familiarity companies

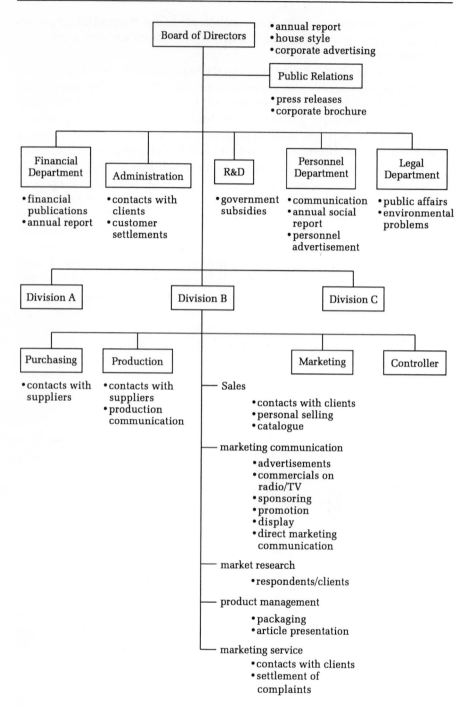

Figure 1.1 Organization chart of a hypothetical company

and marketing (advertising). However, this does not necessarily imply the recruitment of large numbers of communication specialists into different management areas. In practice various communication functions are assigned to staff in these departments as a specialized subsidiary task, perhaps even as a main task. Specialists in environmental communication, labour market communication or investor relations, for example, generally operate on an individual basis within their own functional management areas. Specialized activities such as these rarely lead to the creation of substantial new communication departments within the company.

The new communication specialities generally occupy few employees. However, that does not mean that their efforts are negligible in comparison with the company's other communication activities. On the contrary, the growing number of internal sources of communication seems to lead in practice to fragmentation of the company's total communication output, and sometimes even to contradictions. The various communication specialists are naturally inclined to consider their own departmental interests rather than the strategic interests of the total organization.

By sheer coincidence, or as a result of unfortunate combinations of circumstances, this can sometimes lead to awkward situations, such as those recently experienced by the Dutch companies Vendex and BAT. In both cases, contradictory messages were given about the company in the same newspaper (*Het Financieele Dagblad*) on the same day. In each case, the two conflicting messages were both likely to attract attention, one because it was newsworthy and the other because it made striking claims. The Vendex company, owner of the V&D chain of department stores, announced: 'The V&D of tomorrow offers you greater choice and quality', adding the words 'V&D is at your service'. Unfortunately, the front pages of all the national newspapers carried reports of substantial forthcoming reductions in the company's workforce, thus indicating that fewer employees would be available to put these promises into effect.

The tobacco company BAT placed an advertisement in *Het Financieele Dagblad*. The text of the advertisement is shown in Figure 1.2. Again, a less optimistic message appeared on the front page of the newspaper, namely that 123 employees of BAT Amsterdam were to be made redundant (Figure 1.3).

The inconsistent messages relating to Vendex and BAT just happened to catch my attention at about the same time. These companies are by no means the only ones to suffer such mishaps. The examples should be taken as an illustration of the fact that incidents of this kind happen more often than one might expect. If it is Vendex and BAT today, it could be any other company tomorrow. Contradictions of this kind can be avoided only if a conscious effort is made to harmonize communication from all sources within the company.

Organizations in increasing numbers are becoming aware of the dangers inherent in fragmented communication. They fear embarrassing incidents, and a reduction in the overall effectiveness and efficiency of their total communication.

We are right on course for our 1989 forecast: a pre-tax profit of two thousand million pounds, i.e. a 22% increase
Patrick Sheehy, President of Directors

Results up to and including third quarter, 1989

£ = $1.62 on 30.9.1989
£ = $1.81 on 31.12.1988

Up to & incl. 3rd quarter
(30th Sept)

	1988	1989	change 1988–1989
Pretax profit	£ 1.048 min.	£ 1.228 min.	+ 17%
Profit per share	40.77p	47.25p	+ 16%
Dividend per share	7.60p	19.60p	+ 158%

* Pre-tax profit rose by 17% over the first three quaters, and by 21% during the third quarter.

* Profit in the financial services sector shows a gigantic increase to £598 million, or 42% of the group total. Profit from tobacco trading rose to £587 million.

* Profit per share rose by 15%.

* Purchase programme for own shares already in progress.

* Reorganization proceeding according to plan, and will be completed mid-1990.

* Second interim dividend 10.30 pence, thus total interim dividend 19.60 pence. (1988: interim dividend 7.60 pence, whole year dividend 20.10 pence.)

More value from your shares

Shareholders will receive a copy of the full quarterly report by post. Copies can be obtained from: The Company Secretary, BAT Industries plc, Windsor House, 50 Victoria Street, London SW1H 0NL

Figure 1.2 Translation of an advertisement placed by BAT Industries in *Het Financieele Dagblad*, 25 November 1989

For reasons such as these, companies are clearly making efforts to reduce fragmented communications output, and to harmonize all forms of internal and external communication. This can only be achieved if the company develops a policy of producing all its communication within a consistent framework. The different forms of communication can only be coordinated if all the

BAT plans to close cigarette factory in Amsterdam

It has been confirmed that the management of the Dutch operation of the British conglomerate BAT Industries plan to close their Amsterdam cigarette factory, which employs 123 workers. The works council, which was officially informed of the plan on Friday, rejects it and is discussing possible action with the trade unions.

For some time now, rumours of imminent closure have been circulating within the company. After it became known in February 1989 that general director F. van Vliet had taken part in an international company-wide working group called "Europe 1992", the task of which was to study the implications of European unity, questions have been put to the directors about the possible consequences for the Amsterdam branch. Until yesterday, Van Vliet maintained the position that he was "neither willing nor able to give any information" to the personnel.

BAT wishes to concentrate cigarette production in Europe in fewer centres. The victims will be the cigarette factories in Amsterdam and Liverpool. In Amsterdam, this means that 123 people will have to look for other jobs. The marketing staff in Amsterdam, who number a little over a hundred, can continue with their work, since the concern plans to maintain sales.

The company wishes to transfer the Amsterdam production to Brussels. The production of the Liverpool factory, where 467 jobs are threatened, will be taken over by the Brussels and Southampton factories.

According to Van Vliet, cigarette production in Amsterdam is not sufficiently profitable in comparison with competing cigarette factories. The scale of production is too small, which means that costs are too high. "We are making a profit, but we do not know how long that will continue. We must avoid having to make a decision in a loss situation." Last year, BAT Netherlands made a net profit of 8 million guilders, compared with 6.5 million in the previous year. The company result fell from 9.3 million guilders to 3.5 million guilders. The net turnover amounted to 124 million guilders.

In addition to the small scale of the operation, the purchasing policy of the company has contributed to the situation. Sales of BAT's national brands Gladstone, Belinda and Montano are falling steadily, while the market share of the international brand Lucky Strike seems stuck at about .5%. Barclay, BAT's second world brand, with a market share in the Netherlands of over 4%, cannot compensate fully for the losses. In two years, the total market share in the Netherlands fell from 24.2% to 23%.

The works council rejects the closure plan. "For years we have wanted to extend production. That was never taken seriously, and now we are confronted with this plan," said J. Brugman, secretary of the works council.

According to Brugman, it looks as through the directors never managed to stomach the fact that they had to climb down in 1979. Then too, BAT wanted to close the Amsterdam factory and transfer production to Brussels. The enterprise board of the court of justice in Amsterdam overruled that decision on the grounds that the discussions with the unions had been broken off too soon. BAT was acting contrary to the OESO guidelines for multinational companies.

According to Van Vliet, the British-French financier Sir James Goldsmith's recent hostile bid for the mother company BAT Industries had no influence on the decision to close the Amsterdam factory. In Liverpool and in Amsterdam, BAT will make efforts to help the affected employees to find fresh employment, through retraining, mediation and active job searches. In Brussels, 70 new jobs will be created, for which employees from Amsterdam will be considered. BAT plans to negotiate with the unions a "very good" financial package for workers who opt out.

The food unions FNV and CNV reject the planned closure of the cigarette factory. "It is unimaginable that a company which made a profit of 7.9 million guilders last year should have to close", commented the spokesperson for the FNV.

Figure 1.3 Translation of the report on forthcoming redundancies among BAT employees (*Het Financieele Dagblad*, 25 November 1989)

employees involved have the necessary freedom and motivation. In practical terms, this means that representatives from marketing and public relations departments, and communication specialists from the different management areas, must agree upon a policy framework within which coordination is possible. The move towards harmonization proceeds from the basic assumption that a coherent communication policy facilitates the process of creating a favourable image of the company in the eyes of its major target groups.

The increasing interest in corporate communication should be viewed in the context of the developments described above. This book offers a framework based on corporate communication concepts and analyses. These will be described in detail. An attempt will be made to show how the framework can be used to harmonize all forms of internal and external communication, with the aim of improving the company's chances of creating – and maintaining – a favourable image in all the appropriate quarters.

1.2   Three main forms of corporate communication

1.2.1   Introduction

In practice, communication takes many forms. In industry, 'public relations' and 'advertising' are the oldest terms denoting particular forms of communication, and they are still the most frequently used. However, they are no longer the only ones that appear in the job titles of communication staff. The desirability of this trend is open to question; empirically, it appears that the original areas of operation of both public relations and marketing have been increasingly split into specialized subdivisions.

It seems at first sight that, as far as marketing communication is concerned, subdivision into specialized areas is not especially far-reaching in its consequences. This is because all elements in the promotional mix are ultimately the responsibility of the marketing director. However, the subdivision of what was originally public relations can have adverse effects. Here, there is no one person – outside central management – who bears ultimate responsibility both for communication policy and for communication in practice, except in the case of sales promotion. This hampers the resolution of internal conflicts.

In this book, the three main forms of corporate communication are described as 'marketing communication', 'organizational communication' and 'management communication'. 'Marketing communication' is used as a general term to cover advertising, sales promotions, direct mail, sponsorship, personal selling and other (communications) elements in the promotional mix. 'Organizational communication' covers public relations, public affairs, investor relations, labour market communication, corporate advertising, environmental communication and internal communication.

The following sections contain a brief sketch of these three main forms of corporate communication.

1.2.2 Management communication

Managers fulfil key functions in organizations. Management is often described as 'accomplishing work through other people'. Typically this includes functions like planning, organizing, commanding, coordinating and controlling (Fayol, 1949). Management is only possible with the consent of the managed. In other words, we cannot really manage anyone who does not want to be managed. As a consequence, one of the manager's roles is to continuously persuade individual subordinates that the goals of the organization are desirable. Communication, therefore, is vitally necessary to an organization, not only to transmit authority, but also to achieve cooperation (Timm, 1986).

The responsibility for communication stretches across all levels of an organization. Senior management, but also middle and junior management, use communication to achieve desired results such as:

1. developing a shared vision of the company within the organization;
2. establishing and maintaining trust in the organizational leadership;
3. initiating and managing the change process; and
4. empowering and motivating employees (Pincus, Robert, Rayfield and DeBonis, 1991).

Externally, management (especially the CEO) has to be able to communicate the vision of the company in order to win support of external stakeholders.

Several authors tend to be critical about the effectiveness of communication by managers (Rice, 1991). Nevertheless more and more people are convinced that organizational success often depends upon good communication

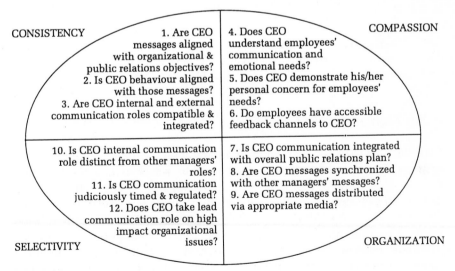

Figure 1.4 Four principles of CEO internal communications strategy (Pincus *et al.*, 1991)

by managers. As a consequence there is a growing need for better communication.

Most authors, both in academic and in management literature, underline the figurehead role of the CEO. The American Pincus has defined four principles of (internal) communication for the CEO (see Figure 1.4).

In addition to the 'symbolic' role of the CEO, middle and junior management play an important role in communication.

> They must understand how those above them are likely to act because of their organisational position and how those below them are similarly motivated and limited by their placement in the organisational space. The critical task of middle and lower management is to interpret organisational goals, or guide subordinates to do so, in ways which optimise organisational functioning. Once the goals are determined and the principles understood, management (in discussion with communication specialists) must develop and decide upon a more specific set of communication strategies. (Allen, 1977)

Communication appears to be too vital for organizational success to leave it solely to managers. Experts both in marketing and in organizational communications are necessary to support managers in improving the effectiveness of their communication responsibilities, by supplying developed programmes which increase the involvement of employees and elicit the support of external stakeholders. General managers should never consider hiring communication experts as the panacea of organizational communication:

> such a communication specialist quickly becomes the resident expert and a feeling seems to creep over the rest of the management team that they no longer need worry about the problem. The danger is, of course, that it is patently absurd to expect one person (or department) operating out of one position, to solve a problem that is organisationally pervasive. This kind of lip service to remedy of organisational ills will not relieve anyone in the organisation of their own proper communication role, any more than the presence of a training executive relieves individual managers of their responsibility for training. (Allen, 1977)

1.2.3 Marketing communication

In the familiar works on marketing communication, a distinction is often drawn between the promotional mix and the public relations mix (Verhage and Cunningham, 1989). Floor and van Raaij (1993) and Gusseklo (1985) make a distinction between the corporate communication mix and the marketing communication mix. Marketing communication consists primarily of those forms of communication that support sales of particular goods or services.

Almost every writer on the subject regards advertising as the dominant element in the marketing communications mix – or, at least, as the most salient. Rossiter and Percy (1987) regard advertising as a process of relatively indirect persuasion, based on information about product benefits, designed to create favourable impressions that 'turn the mind toward' purchase. Sales promotion is often regarded as 'additional activities to above-the-line media advertising which support sales representative and distributor' (Jefkins, 1983). Direct mail is currently one of the growth sectors in marketing expenditure. Knecht and Stoelinga (1988) describe it as 'any form of direct advertising distributed by addressed mail'. The same authors describe sponsorship as

> an activity in which an institution (the sponsor) gives material (usually financial) support to (a) an association or individual for the presentation of sporting or artistic performances, or other performances of a kind interesting to a particular public, or (b) the organisers of a cultural or sporting event, in exchange – as a minimum – for mention of its brand name.

The element in the promotional mix to which by far the greatest share of money is devoted is personal selling, or the directly related activity of sales management. The distinguishing feature of this form of marketing communication is the direct personal contact between the seller and the prospective buyer, which facilitates adjustment to the needs of the individual client. Personal selling is defined by Kotler (1988) as 'oral presentation in a conversation with one or more prospective purchasers for the purpose of making sales'.

A number of authors regard marketing-oriented public relations – or, to use Kotler's term, publicity – as an instrument of marketing communication. Kotler defines publicity as 'non-personal stimulation of demand for a product, service or business unit by planting commercially significant news about it in a published medium or obtaining favourable presentation of it upon radio, television or stage that is not paid for by the sponsor' (Kotler, 1988).

By far the largest share of a company's total communication budget is devoted to marketing communication. Considering the enormous sums of money involved, it is inevitable that a great deal of information has now become available on both qualitative and quantitative aspects of marketing communication. This information includes financial data (e.g. advertising expenditure), information on target groups (e.g. patterns of media consumption) and data on the quality of external agencies (e.g. advertising agencies) which provide companies with services relating to various forms of marketing communication.

The topic of marketing communication is of direct interest to academic circles throughout the world, not so much as an independent discipline, but more as a logical component of marketing within business education courses, e.g. business administration. Large numbers of researchers are working in this field, so it comes as no surprise to find that expertise in marketing communication has reached a highly 'scientific' level. Indeed, contributions to periodicals such as the *Journal of Advertising, Journal of Advertising Research, Journal of Marketing Communication* (new journal) or the *Journal of Consumer Research* are often so specialized that few of those engaged in the practice of marketing communication seem able or willing to read them!

1.2.4 Organizational communication

'Organizational communication' is used here as a general term to cover public relations, public affairs, investor relations, labour market communication, corporate advertising, environmental communication and internal communication. It denotes a heterogeneous group of communications activities which have only a few characteristics in common. (See Box 1.1.)

Their most important shared characteristic is without doubt the fact that all forms of organizational communication are directed primarily at so-called 'target groups', i.e. groups with which the organization has an interdependent relationship, usually indirect. Unlike marketing communication, the various forms of organizational communication are less obvious in their attempts to influence the behaviour of groups on which the organization depends. Examples of such relationships are those with, say, public authorities (which may exercise the power to implement regulations unfavourable to the organization) or with financial journalists. When dealing with such groups (civil servants or financial journalists), it is unwise to employ styles that are, say, generally accepted in other areas of marketing communication activity, e.g. expansive references to product benefits. A business-like approach is much more likely to be effective. It will nevertheless be clear to all concerned that whatever forms of communication the company uses, it should strive to create for itself the most favourable position possible.

Another characteristic of all forms of organizational communication, in the sense in which the term is used in this book, is the fact that the different forms of communication manifested remain firmly rooted within the organization. It is obvious that they will not all fall within the functional management area of marketing. From this point of view, organizational communication could be described as 'all forms of communication used by the organization, other than marketing communication'. In many companies, most of the forms of organizational communication already mentioned fall within the sphere of activity of the public relations department. Companies differ greatly in the ways in which organizational communication is incorporated into the organizational structure. The organization chart of an imaginary company (Figure 1.1) shows how, in practice, many forms of organizational communication can develop outside the PR department. This can happen when the need arises in a particular functional management area for a special form of communication directed at an identifiable 'organization-related target group'. The immediate cause of this 'external development' is the undesirability, on grounds of content or strategy, of incorporating the newly recognized communication requirement into the existing PR department. It might, for example, be strategically important to service a new organizational target group by means of a special department created specifically to serve its needs. As regards content, it is often said that a given mode of communication can be better exploited if it is anchored within a relevant (knowledge-generating) functional management area.

Investor relations, for example, may be conducted from the finance department, or labour market communication may be linked with human resource management. Another content-based argument is the necessity for harmonizing the total mix of management tools available, including communication, within a functional management area, in order to further company goals as effectively as possible.

In contrast to the state of affairs in marketing communication, there is a

---

Box 1.1 Organizational communication

Public relations: 'Public relations is the management function that establishes and maintains mutually beneficial relationships between an organisation and the publics on whom its success or failure depends.' (Cutlip, Center and Broom, 1994)

Public affairs: 'the strategic approach to situations which constitute either an opportunity for the company or a threat to it, and which are connected with social and political changes, formation of public opinion, and political decision-making' (Leyer, 1986).

Environmental communication: 'the policy instrument aimed at realising the organisation's environmental strategy, by informing, convincing ant motivating internal and external target groups, and securing their participation. This means on the one hand, enabling internal target groups to contribute to environmental care within the company; and on the other, it means establishing the desired environmental image amongst external target groups, by coordinating communication activities.' Stichting Milieu Educatie (SME); Association for Environmental Education, annual report, 1991)

Investor relations: 'IR is a corporate marketing activity combining the disciplines of communication and finance, providing present ant potential investors with an accurate portrayal of a company's performance and prospects. Conducted effectively, investor relations can have a positive impact on a company's total value relative to that of the overall market and company's cost of capital.' (USA National Investor Relations Institute)

Labour market communication: 'a management instrument which utilises planned integration and application of various communication disciplines to control and direct the flow of communication both towards potential employees and towards persons or institutions which play an important part in attracting them' (Thomas and Kleyn, 1989)

Corporate advertising: 'paid-for corporate communication designed to establish, develop, enhance and/or change the corporate image of an organisation (Bernstein, 1986)

Internal communication: 'the communication transactions between individuals and/or groups at various levels and in different areas of specialization that are intended to design and redesign organizations, to implement designs, and to coordinate day-to-day activities' (Frank and Brownell, 1989)

dearth of hard figures on organizational communication at an aggregated level. In some commercial companies and non-profit organizations, this holds true even domestically, at the individual microlevel of the organization itself. Such figures as are available should therefore be viewed in perspective. First and foremost, it is clear that figures relating to organizational communication are much lower than those relating to marketing communication. This applies both to finance and to personnel.

At a rough estimate, figures for both expenditure and personnel are at most about a fifth of those for marketing communication.

In academic circles worldwide, organizational communication receives at least as much attention as marketing communication. There is, however, one important difference. Fragmentation in the practice of organizational communication has led to a fragmented approach in different academic disciplines. In Anglo-Saxon universities, the emphasis is on public relations, often in the form of a course element in journalism; or on organizational communication, as part of a social science course.

The major periodicals in the field of organizational communication are devoted primarily to public relations and to communication science. Relevant periodicals include *Public Relations Review*, *Public Relations Quarterly*, *Journal of Business Communication* and *Management Communication Quarterly*. However, important articles may also be found in academic 'management' periodicals, such as *Long Range Planning*, *Journal of Business Strategy* and *Sloan Management Review*.

1.3   From fragmentation to harmonization

1.3.1   Introduction

Organizations are becoming increasingly aware of the fact that communication as a function is not being fully exploited. The growth of various 'new' forms of communication has resulted in a tendency for the sum of communication activity to be certainly no greater than its constituent parts. Many companies are realizing indeed that the sum of all their internal and external communication activities creates a fragmented impression, with the inevitable consequences for the company's image. Companies are therefore making understandable efforts to improve the coordination of their communication.

This problem has been approached in various ways. The roots of developing a policy aimed at conveying a consistent image of the company to the target groups started in the 1930s with the introduction of 'housestyle manuals' which offered clear and consistent guidelines about corporate design. Among specialists in marketing communication, it has led to discussion of the need for integrated communication.

PR specialists approached the problem by reconsidering the nature and limitations of their own sphere of activity. This process led to the claim that every element of communication not directly aimed at promoting sales forms part of the (coordinating) function of public relations.

1.3.2 The pursuit of integration in marketing communication

Attempts have been made since the 1950s to achieve an 'integration of effort' within marketing communication. The pursuit of integration relates not only to those four elements that constitute the marketing mix (the familiar Four Ps), but also to the elements that constitute the communication mix within each of the Four Ps (integrated communication). Central to the concept of marketing is the need to operate in a customer-oriented fashion. This is only possible if each function within the whole company makes its contribution. According to the classical interpretation of marketing, 'integration' meant integration of all marketing instruments. The notion was subsequently extended to include the requirement that the relevant activities of all functional management areas should be integrated as far as possible, to achieve the best possible customer orientation.

Floor and van Raaij have pointed out that, although pronouncements on integrated marketing communication may have a modern ring, the pursuit of coordination and integration has in fact long formed the basis of communication policy. The historical picture supports this view; the real question is, to what extent has the situation which is theoretically desirable been realized in practice? The view of the Dutch marketing specialist Knecht is not optimistic. He has carried out a study of integrated communication on behalf of the Union of Advertisers and the Dutch Association of Recognized Advertising Agencies. On the basis of his practical experience, he distinguishes five stages in the move towards integrated communication. He reaches the interesting conclusion that only a few agencies (and perhaps companies?) have progressed beyond stage 3. A summary of the five stages is given in Box 1.3. The fifth phase is remarkably similar to the descriptions of corporate communication; this will be discussed at a later stage.

Integrated marketing communication

Until the latter half of the 1960s, marketing communication really only meant advertising. The German author Meffert (1979) played a leading part in achieving broad acceptance of the idea that there ought to be greater coherence and unity in the communication mix of an enterprise. Subsequent writers used the term 'integrated marketing communication', and advocated uniformity of text and illustration across all modes of communication, to achieve an optimal cumulative effect.

From the 1960s onwards, following design specialists, marketing communications managers advocated integration of all messages by a company by

Box 1.2 Knecht's five phases of integrated marketing communication (Knecht, 1989a)

1. Integrated media advertising
   This means achieving the best and most comprehensive mix of the media available for transmitting the message.
2. Integrated advertising
   This term denotes the integration of media advertising, direct advertising and packaging.
3. Integrated media communication
   The aim at this stage is optimal coordination of media advertising, direct advertising, editorial publicity, product placement and promotion of the brand or product name by means of sponsorship.
4. Integrated marketing communication
   This phase involves optimal integration of elements of the marketing mix additional to the communication and media modes mentioned in stage 3. According to Knecht, the most vital element is personal selling, although price and distribution are also important.
5. Integrated communication
   In the fifth phase, the application of communication elements primarily adapted for marketing is extended to the other functions of the enterprise. At this stage, communication must be coordinated across enterprise functions and target groups so as to prevent the emergence of contradictions which could harm the corporate image.

bringing them to the attention of all relevant target groups. In the 1990s this concept still appears to be relevant from the numerous books (for example Schultz, Tannenbaum and Lauterborn, 1994) and journal articles covering the subject. A new abbreviation in marketing literature has even appeared: IMC, 'integrated marketing communication', which means integration of content and form of all commercial messages of a company, aimed at enlarging the effectiveness and efficiency of the company's total communication activity.

It is generally accepted that an effort must be made to integrate marketing communication. Initially, 'integration' was taken to mean 'unification', or 'making uniform'. This interpretation was subsequently reduced to the requirement that the final picture created in the mind of the recipient must be consistent, and must not be marred by internal contradictions (Floor and van Raaij, 1993). This can only be achieved if the different elements of the communications mix are carefully coordinated during initial planning. Staff responsible for those elements must hold intensive consultations, otherwise there is great danger of inconsistencies and internal contradictions arising.

The timing of these consultations is as important as their content and form. The initial approach described in the literature on 'diffusion of innovation' (see for example Rogers, 1983) – in which a mass-media campaign is aimed at establishing awareness and knowledge of goods, services or companies – should be followed in due course by a more personal approach to the target group.

An integrated marketing communication strategy offers the company great advantages. An integrated approach is supposed to lead to a situation in which the whole is greater than the sum of the parts. In other words, synergy is created.

1.3.3 *The pursuit of coordination in organizational communication*

Coordination between different forms of internal and external communication is being pursued in the field of organizational communication, just as it is in marketing. The approach has been shaped in two different ways. First, an attempt was made to connect internal and external communication policies by the introduction of a common symbolism. There was already a long-standing tradition of unification of corporate symbolism as set down in a 'house style manual'. This produced a uniform image in terms of logos, house style, company clothing, office and shop fittings, and company architecture. Indeed, the house style manual might be regarded as a precursory example of the concept of integrated organizational communication.

Less recent and less obvious is the move towards integration and adjustment between the different forms of communication generated by the organization as a whole. There are several reasons for this slow evolution. The first is the historic process of division of organizational communication into a range of forms which are not always ready for coordination, or capable of it. Second, there may be conflicts of interest, both at a personal level (career prospects) and at a business level. However, there is recent evidence of change, and attempts are increasingly being made to coordinate the activities of different communication specialists. The Finnish writer Aberg states that 'all communication activities within the organisation must be integrated in order to support the achievement of the organisation's aims and goals' (Aberg, 1990). According to Aberg, communication has four functions within an organization: 'supporting internal and external core operations' (to regulate), 'organisation and product oriented profiling' (to persuade), 'informing internal and external audiences' (to inform), and 'socialising individuals into a good organisational citizen' (to integrate). According to Aberg, 'total communications' means that all these four forms of communication must be coordinated if communication is to make an effective contribution to realizing the goals of the organization. Figure 1.5 is Aberg's representation of the 'total communications' sphere.

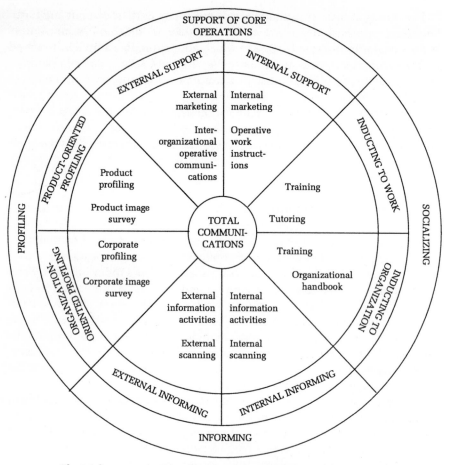

The total communications domain (Aberg, 1990)

1.3.4 Orchestration of all forms of corporate communication through 'common starting points'

Striving for more coordination in total communication originates from special-ists in the field of design (unambiguity *qua* company logo) and, somewhat later, from specialists in the field of marketing communication. In effect, since the 1950s, the latter have been emphasizing the necessity to create more coher-ence in the total communication of companies with the help of 'integration of content and form of all commercial messages of the company' (Knecht, 1989a; Schultz *et al.*, 1994, Floor and van Raaij, 1993). Organizational commun-ication specialists, particularly specialists in the field of public information, aim to achieve this coherence by means of an improvement in the coordination of the company's objectives and communication objectives (van Woerkum, 1984).

From the corporate communication perspective (van Riel, 1992; van Rekom and van Riel, 1993) all forms of communication are taken into consideration for potential orchestration into a coherent whole. The basic philosophy which underlies this notion could be described as *directing the company's communications policies from within the 'corporate strategy-corporate identity-corporate image' triangle*. Representatives of the various communications specialisms jointly develop the *'common starting points'* (CSPs), derived directly from the chosen communications strategy, itself a consequence of the company's actual and desired corporate identity and the company's image (see Figure 1.6).

Although differences will exist as to how detailed these CSPs will be in various companies, each company will be able to identify 'common starting points': in other words, individual areas established by all relevant internal parties concerned in the company's communications and not by a kind of 'head office'. Such 'starting points' exist in any organization and can be used as a basis for the achievement of communication policy objectives, even within individual and specific areas of communication expertise. Moreover, working within the mutually determined parameters or 'wavelengths' set by no means implies absolute uniformity. It should be possible to deviate from the determined 'wavelength' if good reasons arise. Action in the case of such eventualities should, of course, be mutually agreed upon in advance.

CSPs could be considered as central values which function as the basis for undertaking any kinds of communication envisaged by an organization. Establishing CSPs is particularly useful in creating clear priorities, e.g. to facilitate

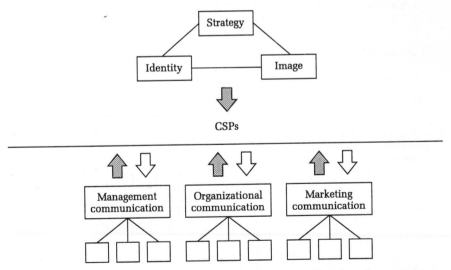

Figure 1.6 Directing the whole of the communications activity through common starting points

an eventual control and evaluation of the total communication policy. A successful balance of communications between the corporate and the business unit (BU) level on one side and among BUs themselves on the other, does not occur by strictly adhering to the CSPs, but by adapting the CSPs on which the various company divisions wish to base the starting points of their own communication policy. On the basis of recent company experience, following this procedure allows the development of guidelines for overall company communication activity. To create such guidelines to enable clear 'transmission' on the communication policy 'wavelength' at BU and at corporate level, three steps need to be taken:

1. Translation of strategy into CSPs at a general level.
2. Delineation of the CSPs by the representatives of each BU with respect to their own organization level by indicating what they wish to *Promise* to the most important categories of target groups; how they wish to *Prove* this; and, in which *Tone* of voice they wish to communicate the message (PPT).

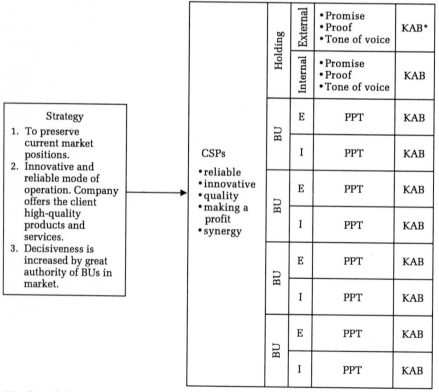

*K = knowledge, A = attitude, B = behaviour

Figure 1.7 From strategy to CSPs

3. Subsequently making the plan more specific, by indicating per division for the different kinds of target groups: what that division wants target groups to know (*Knowledge*), to feel (*Attitude*) and to do (*Behaviour*), both with respect to the entire company and with respect to the individual BU. This is termed the KAB section of CSP implementation.

See Figure 1.7.

1.4 Focus of interest of corporate communication

1.4.1 The nature of the field

Corporate communication takes into account both the total of marketing communication and the large range of forms of organizational communication and 'management communication'. Corporate communication is mainly an approach that the various communication specialists – working from a mutually established strategic framework – could adopt to streamline their own communication activities. The purpose behind this is not that a(nother) new communication department should be added or that an existing department should be replaced. The corporate communication philosophy does, however, imply that the 'Chinese walls' between (and sometimes even 'within') the three aforementioned forms of communication should be removed. Corporate communication is primarily 'corporate'; it only subsequently encompasses 'communication'; that is to say, communication specialists must focus initially on the problems of the organization as a whole (corpus) and only subsequently should they look at implicit and explicit functions of communication with respect to contributing to the realization of the company's objectives.

During the past fifteen years the philosophy of corporate communication has increasingly been accepted, first by the senior management and latterly by communication specialists. However, the concrete consequences of this increased degree of acceptance differed considerably in its early stages (at the end of the 1970s) than from the present. In the initial phase, corporate communication was mainly seen as an 'invention' of consultants. Strongly inspired by British examples, firms of (inter)national consultants came into being offering corporate communication services. Their offer particularly found ready buyers in large companies and later in large government institutions. Nine times out of ten, however, their advice led to a corporate image campaign, followed by advice on how to bring about more uniformity in their communication policy. For this reason, corporate communication at first became synonymous with promoting the corporate image and making a standard plea for the introduction of a 'monolithic identity' (see Chapter 2).

Gradually, both advisers and clients gained insight into the antecedents of corporate image, namely the nature of the corporate strategy, the corporate identity and the heterogeneity of the context of the environment in which the organization operates. This soon led to an awareness that it is not always desirable nor practical to stimulate 'uniformity' in overall communication policy.

From the outset, advisers fell victim to the power of persuasion of their own arguments. After their views were reasonably widely accepted in organizations and the Chinese walls between marketing and organizational communication diminished (for instance, leading to steering committees in which a common communication policy is developed), clients correctly concluded that it was they who should play first fiddle in the orchestration of total communication. This by no means implies that advisers no longer have any significance. However, their part, just as that of other internal specialists in companies, should never be a solo performance. The current and future activities in the field of corporate communication will by definition have to be executed by an ensemble of specialists. The management of such an ensemble will have to be vested formally in the client at all times.

Viewed in such a light, there has been a clear shift in emphasis with respect to the consequences of accepting the corporate communication philosophy. In the 1990s not only 'simple' (emphasis on external orientation) image improvement is involved, but also a number of more internally directed tasks, which are aptly described by Luscuere (1993) as possessing the 'diagnostic and alteration capability' to stimulate all those involved internally to cooperate and to work on the basis of the company's general interest, rather than merely attending to their own subsector.

1.4.2 *Focal responsibilities of corporate communication*

The focal responsibilities of corporate communication can be summarized as follows:

A. to develop initiatives in order to minimize non-functional discrepancies between the desired identity and the desired image, taking into account the interaction of 'strategy-image-identity';
B. to flesh out the profile of the 'company behind the brand';
C. to indicate who should perform which tasks in the field of communication, to formulate and execute effective procedures in order to facilitate decision-making about matters concerning communication.

Corporate communication should be regarded as a new vision of the role of communication both within the organization and in the interrelationships between the organization and its environment. It does not imply the need for yet another communication department in the organization, and the aim is certainly not to replace existing communication departments, such as public relations. This would in fact be illogical in the light of the reasons behind the emergence of corporate communication in the form discussed.

My own view is that corporate communication is not a new profession, but a new way of looking at communication. Equally, it is desirable that the existing communication profession should benefit from the recent insights developed by corporate communication. It would undoubtedly be beneficial if all existing communication specialists were to try to apply the basic ideas of corporate communication in their own fields. This would mean taking greater account of each other's insights than in the past, whether in the realm of scientific theory or in that of practical methods and techniques. There must be a greater readiness to approach communication questions from an interdisciplinary viewpoint. The original foundations on which the communication specialists built their expertise were marketing and the science of communication. They will soon be obliged to draw on a broader range of specialities. Particular attention will have to be paid to the sciences of organization, psychology and strategic management, and to the development of an interdisciplinary framework for tackling communication problems.

The holistic perspective of corporate communication pre-eminently makes it an area for special attention, which can be meaningfully positioned within the interdisciplinary research and educational field of management. For decades, international 'business administration' training has covered the central topics of the field in passing and under a number of different titles. Together with 'corporate communication', 'business communication' and 'organizational communication' are frequently coined concepts. The various designations show that there are differences in emphasis with respect to the way in which research and education are shaped in this area. The difference is mainly in the choice between placing the emphasis on (a) skills, which are necessary to execute communication tasks successfully, or on development of theories, and (b) on a holistic approach, or on an accentuation of a specialist branch of communication within an organization. Should one (as Shelby, 1993, has tried recently) draw up a positioning figure and name the x-axis and the y-axis in accordance with the two above-mentioned pairs, then, in my opinion, the academic practice of corporate communication should be classified holistic rather than specialistic and as the formulation of theories rather than as the training of skills. The latter classification in particular raises critical questions for people with practical experience.

1.4.3 The 'tension' between theory and practice

The need for and the knowledge of corporate communication has come about primarily through commercial practice. Alongside Blauw's (1986/1994) pioneering work in the Netherlands, attention should be drawn in particular to the important role of Olins (1978) in the United Kingdom and of the Germans Birkigt and Stadler (1986) in the German-speaking countries. Only in their wake has the subject matter been taken up by researchers. The researchers' need for the deepening of insight and the need for concrete support in solving problems by people with practical knowledge on a daily basis do not necessarily complement each other. A similar phenomenon has occurred in the fields of public relations and marketing. Through this precedent, one could have predicted that something similar would also happen in the field of corporate communication. Basically, in such cases a natural tension (in both senses of the word) inevitably arises. In my opinion, mutually critical attitudes can only yield profits for both parties. Researchers will have to redouble their efforts to demonstrate the practical relevance of their research. People with practical knowledge will have to make efforts to put to wider use the numerous insights available as a consequence of research into their own companies' situations.

I take the view that it is necessary to keep research progressing at full speed, yet never to lose sight of the connection with practice. Problem-oriented research, in my opinion, will have to serve as the guideline for future research in the field of corporate communication. With that I hope for and expect some patience of people with practical knowledge with respect to the period of time it takes to make the results of such research available.

The field – as an academic discipline – is still in its infancy. This is in spite of the fact that Rebel (1993), for instance, has demonstrated that from the beginning of the twentieth century attention has been paid to topics connected with 'image', in particular by psychologists (stereotypes, schemata theory and 'cognitive maps'), by political scientists (image-building of one's enemy) and by communication researchers (e.g. agenda-setting). Nevertheless, the confusion concerning the central concepts of corporate communication has not yet been resolved and, in particular, little thorough empirical research has been done on the basis of which structural, explanatory models might be established.

However, there are several indications that one may be able to face the future with confidence. In the first place, a greater depth can be observed in the studies of several authors, remarkably many of whom are European, particularly on the forming of the concept and the realization of the two notions of 'corporate identity and corporate image'. In addition to this, another development observed in the past ten to fifteen years is that both above-mentioned concepts have been studied in relation to each other on the one hand and in connection to 'corporate strategy' on the other.

Some examples of the many studies recently carried out should illuminate this point. One of the first such emanates from Johannsen (1971, company image and product image). Later, the publication of Birkigt and Stadler (1986, relation identity-image) became very well known. These authors had a considerable impact, not only in the Netherlands, but especially in their native German-speaking regions. Their publications have proved to have been invaluable sources for scholars in Germany (Wiedmann, 1988; Kammerer, 1988; Tanneberger, 1987; Merkle, 1992), Austria (Hinterhuber, 1989) and Switzerland (Fenkart and Widmer, 1987; Tafertshofer, 1982), especially in respect of the transformation of the corporate strategy into corporate communication policy. In this connection French authors (Ramanantsoa, 1988; Reitter, Chevalier, Laroche, Mendozá and Pulicani, 1991; Kapferer, 1992) and the Italian author Gagliardi (1990) are of great relevance. Other international academic authors who have significantly contributed to the body of knowledge of corporate communication are Selznick (1957); Kennedy (1977); Dowling (1986); Abratt (1989, in particular image measuring); Higgins and Diffenbach (1989); Sobol and Farrelly (1988, influence of disclosure of the corporate strategy on the image) and Fombrun and Shanley (1989, impact of corporate performance on image); Poiesz (1988); Verhallen (1988); Pruyn (1992); and Scholten (1993), in particular through their respective publications in the field of the forming of concepts and realization of images. Van Rekom (1992) is notable because of his approach of establishing the identity of a company by means of means-end analysis, and van Riel, Smidts and Pruyn (1994) by measuring the identification with the organization in relation to internal communication.

The majority of the studies carried out until now can be classified under the heading 'strategy-identity-image'; in other words they can be ranged under the A of the focal tasks of corporate communication. Fortunately, research has recently started in order to acquire insights into the B (profiling of the company behind the brand) and the C (organization of the communication) as well. Much progress has been made, especially in the field of the latter subject. In this connection attention could be drawn, for instance, to the studies of Knapper (1987), Verbeke, Mosmans and Verhulp (1988) and Adema, van Riel and Wierenga (1993). However, in comparison to the studies on 'identity' and 'image', these are mainly explorative studies, with a specifically Dutch focus.

1.4.4 Definition of corporate communication

Few writers have had the courage to try to define corporate communication. Welcome exceptions are the Dutch publications of Blauw, and Thomas and Kleyn (1989), whose definition has already been quoted. Blauw describes corporate communication as: 'the integrated approach to all communication produced by an organisation, directed at all relevant target groups. Each item of communication must convey and emphasise the corporate identity' (Blauw, 1994).

The following definition, formulated by Jackson, is one of the first to appear in the international literature: 'Corporate communication is the total communication activity generated by a company to achieve its planned objectives' (Jackson, 1987).

In contrast to the description that I gave in a previous publication (van Riel, 1990), I am now inclined to lay greater stress upon the ultimate goal of corporate communication, which is the creation of a positive basis for relationships with the groups upon which the company depends. I therefore favour the following formulation:

> Corporate communication is an instrument of management by means of which all consciously used forms of internal and external communication are harmonised as effectively and efficiently as possible, so as to create a favourable basis for relationships with groups upon which the company is dependent.

Following Jackson's example, I prefer 'corporate communication' without an 's'. With an 's', it implies integration of methods; without an 's', it denotes the integrated communication function. Jackson remarks:

> Incidentally, note that it is corporate communication – without a final 's'. Tired of being called on to fix the company switchboard, recommend an answering machine or meet a computer salesman, I long ago adopted this form as being more accurate and left communications to the telecommunications specialists. It's a small point but another attempt to bring clarity out of confusion. (Jackson, 1987)

It goes without saying that it is not the term itself that is important, but the meaning that one attaches to it. However, a 'label' has to be chosen, and for the purposes of this book, the term 'corporate communication' has been adopted. The term is internationally recognized and it occurs regularly in the literature. There are certain disadvantages in the use of this term, including the impression which it may create that corporate communication is only relevant to corporations. As with terms such as 'corporate culture' and 'corporate strategy', the use of the word 'corporate' in 'corporate communication' merely indicates the attempt to link up with the substantial international literature on the subject. The term 'corporate' should therefore not be taken as the adjective corresponding to 'corporation'; it should be interpreted in this context in relation to the Latin word 'corpus', meaning 'body', or, in a more figurative sense, 'relating to the total'.

The point is that the ideas basic to corporate communication are relevant both to private companies and to public and not-for-profit organizations. For obvious reasons, companies have become aware in recent times of the need to create a favourable image. This has resulted in a tendency for corporate communication to be associated primarily with enterprises. However, pressure is now increasing on subsidized institutions and government bodies to give a good account of themselves, so their need to pay attention to these matters is at least equal to that of commercial enterprises.

1.5 Identity and image: two concepts central to corporate communication

In section 1.4, reference was made to a number of authors who have published books on corporate communication during the last decade. The great majority of these authors chose titles in which the term 'corporate image' was prominent. This is also true for contributions of the majority of academic authors (see section 1.4.3).

Despite the popularity of the term, there is a lack of clarity about the precise meaning of the term 'corporate image'. Furthermore, many people seem to confuse the concept of 'image' with the closely related concept of 'identity'. However, in spite of their relationship, there is a fundamental difference between them. In general terms, 'corporate image' can be described as the picture that people have of a company, whereas 'corporate identity' denotes the sum total of all the forms of expression that a company uses to offer insight into its nature. The following more scientific definitions form the basis of discussion in this book.

Corporate identity will be defined in Chapter 2 as 'the self-portrayal of an organisation, i.e. the cues or signals which it offers via its behaviour, communication and symbolism' (van Rekom, van Riel and Wierenga, 1991). Corporate image will be discussed in Chapter 3, where it is defined as follows:

> an image is the set of meanings by which an object is known and through which people describe, remember and relate to it. That is, the net result of the interaction of a person's beliefs, ideas, feelings and impressions about an object. (Dowling, 1986)

In part, the corporate image can be seen as reflecting the identity of an organization. The good or bad reputation of an organization is determined to a considerable degree by the signals that it gives about its nature. No matter how frank and open these signals are, there is no guarantee that they will create a positive image in the minds of most members of the target group. Nine out of ten for diligence does not automatically lead to a high image rating. There are various other external factors which also influence the image of an organization. These include the (negative) influence of the conduct of certain company members; rumour formation; and, most of all, the rational and (apparently) irrational ways in which members of the target groups select signals from those put out by the organization. 'The public' often turns out to be more obstinate than envisaged (Bauer, 1964).

1.6 Reader's guide to the rest of the book

The remaining five chapters cover the following material. The concept of corporate identity is central to Chapter 2; a theoretical discussion is followed by an overview of the key practical methods of measurement. Corporate imagery is covered in a similar fashion in Chapter 3. In Chapter 4, a plan for developing a corporate identity programme is presented. The plan is based on theoretical developments. It involves a systematic long-term approach to the use of all communication elements with the aim of creating a positive impression among target groups with whom the organization has an interdependent relationship. Chapter 5 presents a perspective on the organization of communication. Chapter 6 contains some practical case histories illustrating the foregoing principles.

Chapter 2

Corporate identity

This chapter sets out to define the concept of corporate identity, and to show how it may be put into operation. A view of the concept of corporate identity is presented in sections 2.2 to 2.5. Section 2.6 contains a discussion of alternative methods of measuring corporate identity.

The four sections devoted to the conceptual definition of corporate identity cover several issues. Section 2.2 deals with the relevance of corporate identity. From section 2.3 onwards, an argument will be developed leading to the presentation of my own definition of corporate identity. Section 2.4 is concerned with the function of symbols in strengthening the links with an organization. Section 2.5 presents several methods of classifying different types of corporate identity. These include Olins' widely known classification; Kammerer's fourfold division; and van Riel's typology. From section 2.6 onwards, methods currently available for measuring corporate identity are considered. The chapter ends with a short evaluation.

2.1 Introduction

The terms 'image' and 'identity' are frequently used in descriptions of company communication strategies. It has become generally accepted that image is 'the picture of an organization as perceived by target groups', while identity is associated with 'the way in which a company presents itself to its target groups'.

Originally, corporate identity was synonymous with logos, company house style, and other forms of symbolism used by an organization. The concept has gradually been broadened and become more comprehensive, and is now taken to indicate the way in which a company presents itself by the use of symbols, communication and behaviour. These three elements constitute the so-called corporate identity (CI) mix. All elements in the CI mix can be used both internally and externally to present the personality of an enterprise, according to an agreed company philosophy.

2.2 The relevance of corporate identity

A company that has a strong, convincing corporate identity can achieve much more with its various target groups. A strong corporate identity is effective in the following ways:

- *Raising motivation among employees*
  Keller (1990) refers to 'the internal effect of corporate identity'. A strong corporate identity creates a 'we—feeling'. It enables employees to identify with their company. Their increased commitment to the company affects their behaviour, which then has an external impact. This leads to better use of the company's 'human capital'.
- *Inspiring confidence among the company's external target groups*
  When a company presents a powerful corporate identity, the various external target groups can develop a clear picture of it. A purposefully deployed corporate identity, based on consistent signals, is essential, since a company that conveys conflicting messages risks losing credibility. This is true in relation to all the company's target groups, but those mentioned in the next two points in particular receive special attention in the literature.
- *Acknowledging the vital role of customers*
  Many companies see their customers as their most important target group, since they ultimately justify the existence of the company. The use of a well-defined corporate identity to inspire customer confidence establishes the basis of a continuing relationship, thus securing the future of the company.
- *Acknowledging the vital role of financial target groups*
  Suppliers of capital are often perceived as a company's second most important target group. They must have confidence in the company, because they usually take the highest risks in supplying potentially considerable sums of money.

We may picture corporate identity as a kind of adhesive. A powerful corporate identity enhances the likelihood of identification or bonding with the organization. This applies both to internal and to external target groups.

2.3 Definition of corporate identity

The more people write about corporate identity, the more definitions there seem to be. A small selection is given in Box 2.1, to illustrate the diversity. It appears that the same confusion reigns in practice, as can be seen from a MORI survey commissioned by Henrion, Ludlow & Schmidt (London, 1993) to study the meaning of the term 'corporate identity' in different European countries. In the United Kingdom, corporate identity was most often defined as corporate communication or design; in Germany and Austria, as the total internal and external image; in Spain and Scandinavia, as external image and corporate

---

Box 2.1 Definitions of corporate identity

1. Corporate identity is the strategically planned and operationally applied internal and external self-presentation and behaviour of a company. It is based on an agreed company philosophy, long-term company goals, and a particular desired image, combined with the will to utilise all instruments of the company as one unit, both internally and externally. (Birkigt and Stadler, 1986)

2. Corporate identity is the sum of all methods of portrayal which the company uses to present itself to employees, customers, providers of capital, and the public. According to organisational units, CI is the sum of all the typical and harmonised methods of portrayal of design, culture and communication. (Antonoff, 1985)

3. ... identity means the sum of all the ways a company chooses to identify itself to all its publics. (Margulies, 1977)

4. Corporate identity reflects the distinctive capability and the recognisable individual characteristics of the company. Identity in this sense also includes the distinction and recognition of parts of the whole company, and the attribution of those parts to the whole. (Tanneberger, 1987)

5. Corporate identity is the total of visual and non-visual means applied by a company to present itself to all its relevant target groups on the basis of a corporate identity plan. (Blauw, 1994)

6. Corporate identity is the tangible manifestation of the personality of a company. It is the identity which reflects and projects the real personality of the company. (Olins, 1989)

7. Corporate identity is the expression of the personality of a company, which can be experienced by anyone. It is manifested in the behaviour and communication of the company, and in its aesthetic, formal expression; it can also be measured as the perceptual result amongst internal and external target groups. (Lux, 1986)

8. Corporate identity embodies, besides all visual expressions, also all non-visual expressions and behaviour in the social, economic and political field. (Henrion, 1980)

9. The corporate identity is the firm's visual statement to the world of who and what the company is – of how the company views itself – and therefore has a great deal to do with how the world views the company. (Selame and Selame, 1975)

10. Corporate identity is the strategy which helps to increase the economic performance and the efficiency of a company. It coordinates achievements, values and information, and leads to integration in the sense of cooperation. (Hannebohn and Blöcker, 1983)

---

culture. The findings are shown in Table 2.1. They are the result of telephone interviews with 160 people who bore ultimate responsibility for corporate identity in companies that numbered among the top 500 in the countries

Table 2.1 Definition of corporate identity in several European countries (percentage) (MORI, 1993)

	Total	Britain	France	Germany	Scandinavia	Austria	Benelux	Spain
Pu... e...								
Expression of culture/values/ philosophy	20	4	20	40	13			
Internal projection/ behaviour of staff	18	7	13	38	10	45	15	5
Advertising/ communications support	4	2	5	5	5	0	0	5
Product/brand support	4	5	8	5	8	0	0	0

Note: The target audience was defined as the 'senior persons responsible for corporate identity' in major companies, which led to a mix of director functions. The sample consisted mainly of those in Public Affairs (35%), Corporate Communications (31%) and Marketing (19%). Corporate identity is primarily described in terms of external image and projection. The concept of external image and projection features in half of the spontaneous definitions of corporate identity. It is the leading theme in all countries, and is especially prevalent in the Benelux countries and among Chairmen (59%). Just over a quarter spontaneously mention visual elements of presentation, and specifically logos. This varies considerably by country, with strong emphasis in Britain and Scandinavia, but relatively little in France and Benelux. The Public Affairs and Marketing functions (30% and 31% respectively) are most likely to focus on visual presentations. In contrast, a total of 38% are internally-oriented in their definitions, stressing identity as an expression of culture/values/philosophy, or projection to and via employees. This internal orientation is pronounced in Germany (78% in total) and Austria (80%), compared to 11% in Britain. Half of the CEOs surveyed also mention internal factors.

concerned. The interviewees were asked: 'How, briefly, would you define corporate identity?' It is clear that virtually no-one knew exactly what 'corporate identity' meant, and that this confusion greatly hampers communication of the concept. The fact that many people also believe that corporate identity is the same as image (see MORI survey) does not help matters.

According to Bernstein (1986), the word 'identity' is derived from the Latin *idem* (meaning 'same'). There is probably also a connection with the Latin *identidem*, meaning 'repeatedly', or 'the same each time'. The interpretation of identity derived from dictionary definitions, e.g. 'the characteristic or condition of complete agreement, absolute or essential similarity, unity of being', provided design specialists with a strong argument to press for consistent use of symbols by companies. Viewed in this light, corporate identity was associated primarily with 'design', e.g. logos, house style and staff clothing. Carter (1982) describes corporate identity as 'the logo or brand image of a company, and all other visual manifestations of the identity of a company'. The emphasis on a suitable visual symbol relates to the necessity of creating a favourable (first) impression on prospective and existing clients. A combination of visual symbols is a quick and penetrating way of conveying a simple idea about a company, or its emotional value. However, if one limits oneself to what Wathen (1986) calls 'logomotion', one underestimates the other factors that influence the formation of an image of a company. Most writers thought initially that 'other factors' meant communication campaigns: 'communicating long-range goals and strengths to the public' (Wathen, 1986). The influence of several German writers has led to the inclusion of behaviour, which has also been termed 'communication in the broadest sense of the word'.

It is almost impossible to communicate only in symbols, because members of target groups, whether consciously or unconsciously, use all their senses to form a total picture of the object in question, and to make a judgement about it. This means that it is extremely risky to concentrate all one's attention on visual means of communication, and leave the rest more or less to chance. No company can achieve individuality and attract confidence solely by means of design (Tanneberger, 1987). If the management of a company wishes to do something purposeful with its corporate identity, it must take account of all aspects of the company, including-communication and behaviour (Tanneberger, 1987).

The traditionally narrow meaning of the term 'corporate identity' has been broadened, largely under the influence of the German writers Birkigt and Stadler (1986), towards a concept in which 'corporate strategy' on the one hand is clearly linked with 'communication in the broad sense' on the other. These writers speak of 'the planned and operational self-presentation of a company, both internal and external, based on an agreed company philosophy'.

The self-presentation of a company can be developed in three ways, i.e. the media that management may use to convey corporate identity are of three kinds. In fact, any action or expression of a company can be classified under one of these three headings:

1. *Behaviour* By far the most important and effective medium through which corporate identity is created is the behaviour of the company. Ultimately, target groups will judge the company by its actions. However, it is possible to emphasize particular aspects of company behaviour by means of communication and/or symbols.

2. *Communication* By 'communication in the narrow sense', Birkigt and Stadler mean the sending of verbal or visual messages. This is the most flexible CI instrument, and it can quickly be put to tactical use. The flexibility of communication lies in the fact that more abstract signals can be transmitted directly to target groups. A company can, for instance, inform its target

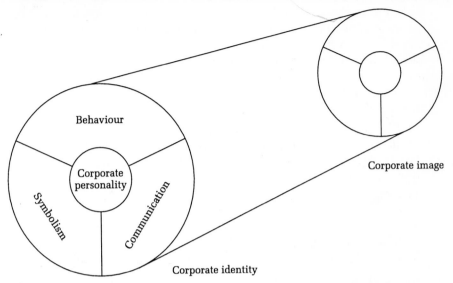

Figure 2.1 Corporate identity in relation to corporate image (adapted from Birkigt and Stadler, 1986, p. 28)

group directly that it is innovative. If the same message were to be conveyed only by the behaviour of the company, the process would be much longer and more laborious. At the same time, there is no point in telling the target group things that are not also apparent in the company's behaviour.

3. *Symbolism* According to Birkigt and Stadler, this tool should harmonize with the other expressions of corporate identity. It gives an implicit indication of what the organization stands for, or at least what it wishes to stand for.

These media together constitute the corporate identity mix (analogous to the marketing mix). They are the means by which the personality of a company manifests itself.

4. *Personality* is described by Birkigt and Stadler as 'the manifestation of the company's self-perception'. This implies that the company must know itself well, i.e. it must have a clear picture of its real situation, in order to present itself clearly through its behaviour, communication and symbolism. To Birkigt and Stadler's description may be added van Rekom's (1992) statement that the personality of a company includes its intentions, and the way in which it reacts to stimuli from the environment.

The communication, behaviour and symbolism of a company are in fact the concrete forms into which the company's personality crystallizes. The CI media described above may be seen as the outer forms of expression, while the personality is the deeper element which lies behind them.

Birkigt and Stadler see the image of a company as a projection of its corporate identity. They illustrated this by means of the diagram in Figure 2.1 (p. 33).

Birkigt and Stadler's model is useful considering didactic values; the model clearly shows the main issues in (a) the corporate identity mix and (b) the interaction between identity and image. However, from a strictly academic point of view the model is less useful, because of the following:

1. The model does not take into account that image is not just a reflection of identity. Corporate image can also be influenced by environmental aspects (local characteristics, competitors' behaviour, sociodemographic trends within the main stakeholder groups, etc.).
2. Image is not an end in itself, rather a 'mere' means to achieve better performance.
3. The model does not allow for the reciprocal effects of changes in behaviour, communication and symbolism on the personality of the organization, itself being, in turn, the driving force of these three corporate identity mix elements.

Corporate identity involves all the forms of expression (symbolism, communication and behaviour) by means of which an organization reveals its personality. The identity of an organization is expressed in 'what the organization really is' (Thomas and Kleyn, 1989). Following Bavelas (1960), Bernstein (1986) describes personality as 'the uniqueness of a company'.

The unique character of a company is not easy to determine. What makes Company X different from Company Y? The management will have a particular view of this, as will the employees. Employees of long standing will mention less striking items in this connection than employees who have recently transferred from another company. If the company is old enough, it will have developed patterns 'that are highly predictable and highly repetitive' (Bernstein, 1986). Some of these patterns will be unique to the company. Companies reveal these characteristics, whether deliberately or not, and they make the unique character of the company visible and even tangible to the relevant target groups. Unique characteristics are revealed in the company's products and buildings, in the nature and scale of its communication, and in its behaviour.

The work of Birkigt and Stadler (1986), described above, provides an important basis for developing the concept of corporate identity. Their definition of corporate identity appears to contain two crucial elements:

1. *... the strategically planned and operationally applied self-presentation of the company*
    The strategically planned self-presentation of the company can be described as the identity considered to be ideal under prevailing circumstances, i.e. a 'desired-identity'. There is no guarantee that the operationally applied self-presentation will coincide 100 per cent with that which was strategically planned. In practice, the two will often differ considerably. By analogy, one may conceptualize two identities, a 'desired-identity', towards

which the company strives, and an 'actual-identity', which is what the company is really like in practice.

2. *... on the basis of a desired image*
The object of all corporate identity policies is to create a certain desired image, or 'should-image'. This is the ideal, the desired reality, towards which management wants to work, but it is not necessarily the same as the image that the public has of the company, i.e. the 'actual-image'.

2.3.1 *Towards a definition of corporate identity*

It was suggested above that the phrase 'the self-presentation of the company' may be seen as central to Birkigt and Stadler's definition. Corporate identity may therefore be regarded as the manifestation of a bundle of characteristics which form a kind of shell around the organization, displaying its personality.

2.3.2 *Characteristics*

In this context, characteristics may be described as 'abstractable and relatively constant features by means of which one individual can be distinguished from others' (Tanneberger, 1987). This definition corresponds with Guildford's description of a 'trait' (see Tanneberger, 1987; Lux, 1986). An attribute is a concrete behavioural feature. The difference between an attribute and a characteristic is that an attribute is less abstract. A characteristic can be attributed to a person or to a company on the basis of their/its actual behaviour.

Lux states that 'the distinguishing features of personality form the core of the underlying characteristics through which a company gains its non-exchangeable identity'. These are the characteristics that say something about someone's behaviour (Lux, 1986). Similarly, Williams (1989) suggests that descriptions of identity are only significant if they contain a verb or a verb clause. To obtain a complete picture, the journalist's questions 'who, what, when, where, how, and why?' (Walsh and Ungson, 1991) should be asked in relation to every activity. The questions 'where, when and how?' yield a concrete description of the activity; the question 'why?' leads to deeper values, and permits us to construct a 'ladder' of attributes, characteristics, objectives and values.

If one thinks of corporate identity as a bundle of characteristics by means of which an organization is distinguished from others, then attention must be paid when defining the concept to the 'signals' or 'cues' that the organization offers, whether consciously or not, in the forms of communication, behaviour and symbolism. These signals or cues originate in values which are deeply rooted in the personality of the organization. Proceeding along these lines, corporate identity may be defined as follows:

> Corporate identity is the self-presentation of an organisation; it consists in the cues which an organisation offers about itself via the behaviour, communication, and symbolism which are its forms of expression. (Van Rekom, van Riel and Wierenga, 1991)

The signals may be concrete, for example the colour of the logo, or the delivery period; or they may be abstract, as for example when the company demonstrates its sense of social responsibility by making donations to worthy causes.

2.4 Symbolism as a binding agent

Having clarified the question of what corporate identity is, we may proceed to a deeper investigation of its functions in strengthening the links between an organization and its internal and external target groups. According to Olins, it is primarily visual elements that can increase short-term attachment to an organization. 'The question is, how the visual style of a company influences its place in the market, and how the company's goals are made visible in its design and behaviour' (Olins, 1989). The identity of a company can be traced through the names, logos, colours and rites of passage that the company uses in order to distinguish itself, its brands and its associated companies. In a sense, these serve the same purpose as religious icons, heraldry, national flags and other symbols: they encapsulate collective feelings of belonging, and make them visible. They also offer, to some extent, a guarantee of consistent quality standards, and contribute to the loyalty of customers and other target groups (Olins, 1989).

Organizations do not automatically have such symbols at their disposal: 'Sometimes names and symbols need to be created, traditions and rites of passage have to be invented and reinvented for corporations, in the same way as they have always been invented for different regimes in different countries.' Olins calls this 'the invention of tradition', and gives several examples of political and military leaders who tried to create a sense of grandeur by using symbols taken from a historical period of which most people were proud. One can find examples of symbolism used in 'state art', both in European capitals and in Third World countries. The underlying strategy has penetrated the business world too. It is apparent in the tendency to locate corporate headquarters in impressive buildings, usually tall and stylish. Attempts to gain prestige in the world outside, and to stimulate loyalty within the company, are made using a 'sophisticated approach' backed up by symbolism: flags, company museum or exhibition area, books about the (glorious) history of the company, and house style, including furnishings and matching staff outfits (Olins, 1989).

2.4.1 House style

House style is the best-known application of symbolism for promoting the unity and recognizability of a company. A unified visual presentation creates a coherent picture, and a well-designed house style contributes to the establishment and maintenance of corporate identity. The introduction of a house style initiates a process of self-awareness within the company. The visible signs of belonging together increase the 'company pride' of the employees, and produce a demonstrable increase in the readiness of different parts of the concern to cooperate (Olins, 1989; Carter, 1982).

Careful supervision and detailed programming of the house style are essential. After an introductory period during which various possibilities are tried out and modified, a house style manual is compiled. If the style fails to materialize, then repeated explanations must be given to the staff involved (Olins, 1989).

The intensity of use of symbolism can differ. If the most important function of the house style is to promote recognizability, i.e. if it is primarily pragmatic in nature, then Kammerer's term 'indicative identity' is appropriate (Kammerer, 1989). In this situation, the house style manual becomes something of a 'recipe book' to be consulted by the designers; it emphasizes superficial characteristics, without touching on the deeper elements of corporate identity. Kammerer speaks of an 'aesthetic frame', which elicits instant recognition among customers. The danger is that nothing more than this will be achieved.

At the other end of the spectrum from 'indicative identity', Kammerer describes 'thematic identity', which is an expression of the strategic principles of the company. The symbolism of thematic identity is not pragmatic, but dogmatic, since the company now wishes to give substance to its symbolism and to transmit values. The style of the company is being used not just to identify it, but to give expression to its identity (Kammerer, 1989). 'Thematic' and 'indicative' identity are not mutually exclusive; they can be connected, both implicitly and explicitly, A good example is the product design of Bang & Olufsen; this company strives for a radically simplified functional design (Kammerer, 1989).

Van Nelle provides a good example of house style. This company was the first in the Netherlands to design its factory, in 1934, in the brand-new glass-architecture style, thus providing its employees with abundant light and space in the workplace. The design specifications contained an explicit statement that at least as much attention must be paid to the human factor as to mechanical aspects (Bantje, 1981). The style of the Van Nelle factories and offices thus conveyed a social attitude. The same attitude was expressed in the fact that Van Nelle was the first company in the Netherlands to introduce a pension fund of the kind familiar to us today for all its employees (Bantje, 1981).

2.4.2   *Choice of the company name*

One of the most basic symbols of a company is its name. Sometim
changes so much that it is desirable to choose another name. A g
is the former Standard Oil of Ohio, which operated under the name SOHIO.
Although this company was one of the four largest oil companies in the United
States in about 1984, it had the image of a small, sleepy, Midwest oil company,
and some people even thought that SOHIO was a subsidiary of a Japanese electronics firm. In order to give the company more substance, the old name Standard Oil was revived, by means of an extensive programme. Within a short
time, the 'new' Standard Oil established a good, solid reputation (Muir, 1987).

The attitude of the employees is a critical factor in a company name change.
If the change is not communicated carefully to the employees, the whole
campaign may founder on their scepticism (Muir, 1987). Employees need to
have a feeling of belonging, and of being part of a shared culture. They need
to be proud of their company, and of everything connected with it. These
matters cannot be left to chance in a large organization. In order to arouse
feelings of loyalty, the organization must create symbols, such as flags, rituals
and names. The organization must make use of rituals and ceremonies to cele-
brate what it is, and the reason for its existence. Beliefs must be constantly
confirmed (Olins, 1989). If this does not happen, the company can begin to
stagnate.

This happened to British Airways, which was created in 1973 as the result
of a merger between BOAC and BEA. There was no basic preparation, and no
careful introduction of the new company. Employees failed completely to identify with the company, and ten years after the merger, some of them still had
the flags of the old companies on their desks. The company was managed in
a military fashion, and its service had a bad reputation. In the early 1980s, a
start was made on rectifying the situation. A new management team introduced
a new company policy; the employees were trained to give good service. A new
logo was introduced to draw attention to the changes, and to the 'reborn' British
Airways. In this way, the company managed to lose its sobriquet 'worst airline
in the world' (Diefenbach, 1987).

The symbolism of an organization consists of the images which strengthen
and support its actions and communication. These are visual images:
photographs, illustrations, non-verbal graphics, brand marks, logos, house
style.

Symbols are signs that people use to communicate with each other. At a very
early age, children become familiar with the signs and shapes that are most
commonly used in communication. People react to signs in different ways.
Many reactions are cognitive: meaning, in this context, that one thinks
consciously, then acts in a certain way. In other cases, one reacts unconsciously
to a signal. Reactions of this kind have been learned over a period of time.

Reactions are not always cognitive: people may also have an emotional

is. Such reactions are often to signs that evoke a certain warmth ne minds of members of target groups. According to Franzen and (1987), a sign that evokes a certain feeling may be described as a symbol. In these cases, symbols are signs with an emotional loading.

The power of a symbol lies in the increased attention that it attracts to the communication output of the organization. It is the key that sets the short-term memory working, without the need for a long exposition on the company and what it has to offer. A good symbol reduces the redundancy in communication to a minimum. This is one of the purposes for which companies use a brand mark (logo). In many cases, the logo is accompanied by a vignette. The two together function as a signal. They should have a direct association in people's minds with everything that the company is trying to communicate.

In many cases, this is effective. Signs in shopping streets are an example. Even in strange cities, people quickly recognize internationally used symbols, especially when they are in familiar colours, for example the well-known Kodak signs, which indicate to tourists the presence of a film and camera retailer.

2.5 Types of corporate identity

In addition to the company name and the company logo, the brand names of products also play a crucial part in distinguishing them from those of competitors. It is especially important for companies that offer different goods or services under different names to have a clear corporate identity policy. An important element in the corporate identity policy is the brand policy, which is the responsibility of the marketing department. Readers who require more detailed information on this are strongly recommended to consult Aaker (1991), Kapferer (1992) and de Chernatony and McDonald (1992).

The classifications provided by Olins and Kammerer are useful for discussing corporate identity in a broad sense, i.e. one that goes beyond brand policy. In their classifications, the choice of corporate identity proceeds directly from company structure or company strategy. Adapting Chandler's well-known remark, we may say that 'communication follows structure as structure follows strategy', and can take this as our guide in choosing the outlines of a corporate identity policy.

Olins distinguishes three kinds of corporate identity (Olins, 1989). In other words, there are three possible kinds of 'corporate shell':

1. *Monolithic identity* (Shell, Philips, BMW), in which the whole company uses one visual style. The company can be recognized instantly, and it uses the same symbols everywhere. Such companies have usually developed as a whole entity within a relatively narrow field.
2. *Endorsed identity* (General Motors, L'Oréal), in which the subsidiary companies have their own style, but the parent company remains

recognizable in the background. The different divisions can be recognized, but it is clear which is the parent company. These are diversified companies, the parts of which have retained parts of their own culture, traditions, and/or brands.

3. *Branded identity* (Unilever), in which the subsidiaries have their own style, and the parent company is not recognizable to 'the uninitiated'. The brands appear to have no relation to each other or to the parent company. The separation of the brand from the identity of the parent company limits the risk of product failure, but it also means that the brand cannot benefit from any favourable reputation which the parent company may enjoy.

Kammerer (1988) indicates how these identity structures are related to the goals of the parent company. The form of the company's 'shell' is ultimately determined by its strategy. At the widest, 'corporate' level, he distinguishes four types of identity strategy, which he names 'action types':

1. *Financial orientation* The subsidiaries are viewed as purely financial participants. They retain their own full identity, and the management of the parent company does not interfere in the day-to-day running or in the strategy of the subsidiary.

2. *Organization-oriented corporate identity* The parent company takes over one or more management functions of the divisions. In Kammerer's view, the sharing of organizational rules by the parent company and the subsidiaries is of central importance. In this situation, the parent company influences the culture of the subsidiaries to a far greater extent than in the case of functional orientation. However, the functioning of corporate identity at the level of the whole organization is strictly internal, and not directly visible to the outside world.

3. *Communication-oriented corporate identity* The fact that the subsidiaries belong to one parent company is clearly expressed in advertising and symbolism. One of the most important reasons for choosing this kind of corporate identity is to convey to the target groups the size of the concern. This can increase confidence in the subsidiaries, or respect for the whole company. It also means that goodwill achieved by one subsidiary can be exploited by others.

Communication-oriented corporate identity can proceed from organization-directed corporate identity, but this does not necessarily have to be so. It may be that nothing more than a common façade is created.

4. *Single company identity* The unity of action goes much further than with the other types. It is really monolithic identity: all actions, messages and symbols come across as one consistent whole.

Kammerer illustrates this by means of a diagram (see Figure 2.2).

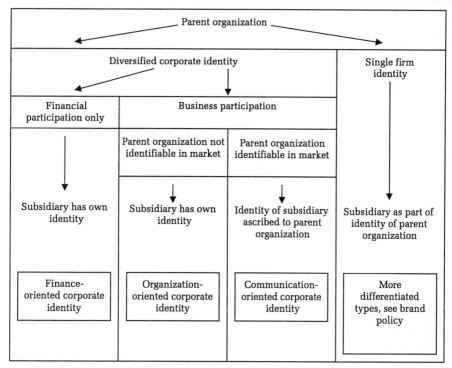

Figure 2.2 Kammerer's classification of corporate identities (1988)

2.5.1 Parent company visibility and effect on 'content management'

In my opinion three 'poles' of corporate communication can be identified: the uniformity model (position and corporate profile, analogous to BU and product level), the variety model (all three different) and the endorsement model (a compromise between the two previous models). Reproduced in Figures 2.3, 2.4 and 2.5 is a hypothetical demonstration of the three models in action, using the Belgium company AVEVE. AVEVE is active across the agricultural sector.

In the uniformity model, tight guidelines with respect to communication are imposed from the top of the organization. Unambiguity is chosen rather than specific naming, symbolism and sometimes rather than content (what should be communicated) or design/style (how it should be communicated).

In the variety model (also classifiable as financial holding model), the company chooses to leave the communication (how and what) completely free at the BU level. Communication with financial target groups will take place only at the holding level and then most circumspectly. In practice, this leads to a multiform brand policy within the various product market combinations (PMCs) on BU level. This model often occurs within financial holdings.

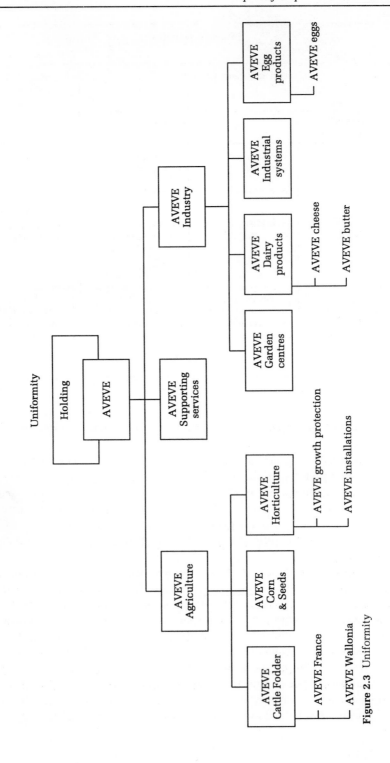

Figure 2.3 Uniformity

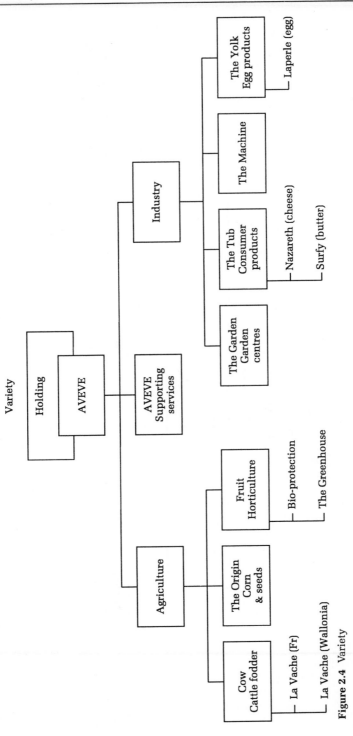

Figure 2.4 Variety

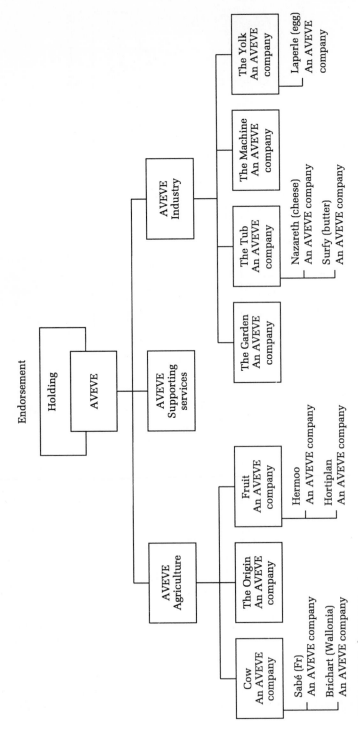

Figure 2.5 Endorsement

In the endorsement approach the company chooses a subtle balance between emphasizing the security-providing power of the 'parent behind the brand', i.e. the holding company in the background, together with a profile of the individual BU operating within a specific area.

It goes without saying that this threefold division is purely theoretical, since no company, including AVEVE, could or would even want to strictly conform to the categories of this typology. Indeed it may be better to speak of a company's selected 'major route' (i.e. as opposed to form of identity) and of the parallel routes to be chosen for the BUs, thus allowing them to be distinguished within the whole enterprise.

In the current literature a similar classification is employed (Olins, 1989; Kammerer, 1988; Biggar and Selame, 1992). The existing typologies, in particular the well-known threefold division of Olins, in my opinion has the drawback that too great an emphasis is placed on purely visual identity, especially on the choice of the name and the logo with which the company as a whole wishes to present itself externally. The impression is thereby created that the choice of the corporate communication policy of a company depends on the extent to which one wishes to reveal the 'parent behind the brand'. I term this 'parent visibility'.

In fact we have a continuum with maximum parent visibility at one extreme and, at the other, effective concealment as to who is the (financial) owner of the BU or the product.

Corporate name similar to BU and/or product name	Strong endorsement of corporate name	Weak endorsement of corporate name	Endorsement of corporate name towards financial stakeholder	Autonomy

Degrees of parent visibility

At least as important as the criterion of visibility of the 'parent', I feel, is the degree, within its overall communication policy, to which a company wishes to exert influence on the question as to *what* will be communicated about a number of basic matters. By this I mean the crucial role that 'common starting points' could play in determining the 'wavelength' within which a company can and should communicate with various types of target groups. I will designate this criterion 'content management'.

In practice companies can apply strong variations in the degree to which they both wish and are able to supervise the content of their overall communication policy. Again we have a continuum, with at one end a high degree of content management (tight planning and control) and, at the other, complete freedom for the BUs and the product managers with respect to how they exercise their own communication strategy.

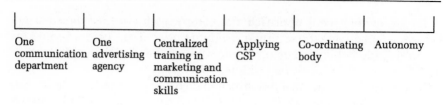

| One communication department | One advertising agency | Centralized training in marketing and communication skills | Applying CSP | Co-ordinating body | Autonomy |

Degrees of 'content guiding'

As has been stated above, the choice in favour of tight content management or complete freedom is of course determined to a considerable extent by whether one is able to find an appropriate cohesive proposition. For instance, one might select the core competence of a company, as manifested in all the BUs, which could serve as the common starting point in the overall communication strategy. However companies are often so diverse in nature that it may be impossible to find a proposition which applies throughout the total organization. In such instances, the usual conclusion is that it would be better to play down the parent behind the brand as much as possible. In my opinion this conclusion is incorrect, since one thereby ignores the possibility of using several profiles which actually proceed from one consistent positioning, as is made clear in Figure 2.6.

This figure shows that, by combining the two aforementioned scales with gradations in the field of parent visibility and content management, four quad-

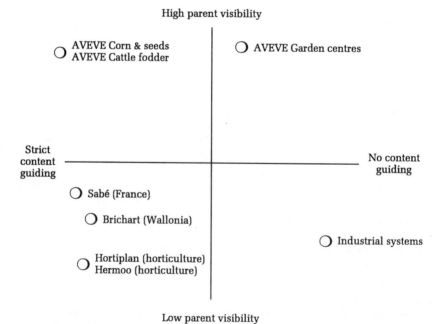

Figure 2.6 Combination of 'parent visibility' and 'content management' in elaborating corporate communication policy

rants can be established within which a company may choose its position with respect to the corporate communication policy. Thus, it is in principle possible for one company to position divisions in all four quadrants. In Figure 2.6 an example is given of the way in which the various BUs of the Belgian company AVEVE are actually profiled.

As can be seen in Figure 2.6, this could mean that some BUs could be placed within the monolithic model both visually and with respect to content, while other BUs in the same company might be placed within an endorsed or branded type of model.

Once a company chooses to profile one or more BUs within the first and second quadrants, it becomes necessary to make clear who and what is the 'parent behind the brand'. In other words, it is important to establish central values which can be used as a starting point to let the chosen and preferred values sink into the minds of the company's relevant target groups through communication and behaviour. In choosing such values it is advisable to search for a combination of internal 'ideal' objectives and driving forces and the actual perceptions and preferences existing in external target groups.

Striving for coordination by no means implies that the totality of communications employed by a company has to be uniform. It would be advisable to organizations with complex organizational structures and great differences in the nature of their product/market combinations to structure the corporate communication policy of their company (which need not necessarily be large itself) in a balanced manner. In other words, although the mutually agreed communications 'wavelength' should be strictly adhered to, there should be present the ability to cater for potential exceptions. It must be remembered, however, that it is this wavelength in which the 'parent behind the brand' should be primarily profiled, with a 'diffusion' effect down through the BUs and even down to product level by means of 'vertical brand stretching'.

2.6 Methods of measurement

2.6.1 Introduction

In section 2.3, corporate identity was described as 'the cues which an organisation offers about itself via the behaviour, communication, and symbolism which are its forms of expression'. The source of these cues is the personality of the organization.

Descriptions may be found in the literature of various methods of determining the actual nature of these different forms of expression. Methods of assessing the behavioural element in the CI mix include instruments to measure 'organizational climate' studies, like OCIPO (Organizational Climate Index for Profit Organizations) developed by de Cock *et al.* (1984, Catholic University of Leuven, Belgium) and the Rotterdam Organizational Identification Test (van Riel, Smidts and Pruyn, 1994).

The 'organizational climate' method, especially as described by Downs

---

Box 2.2 Methods of analyzing corporate identity

1. Methods of analysis for overall study of corporate identity
   1.1 Cobweb method (Bernstein; see pages 48–50)
   1.2 Star method (Lux; see pages 50–1)
   1.3 Laddering (van Rekom; see pages 51–5)
   1.4 Keller's Mannheimer CI test (Keller; see pages 55–7)
2. Methods of analysis for individual elements of the CI mix
   2.1 Behaviour: Organizational climate studies
                                   (see pages 57–9)
                            ROIT (see pages 59–65)
   2.2 Communication: Organizational climate studies
                            Communication audits (see pages 65–71)
   2.3 Symbolism: Facilities audit
                            Graphic design audit (see pages 71–2)

---

and Hazen (1977), can also be used in part for analyzing communication. This is because it is suitable for studying the quality of interpersonal communication. Auditing techniques are obviously also relevant. They can be used additionally to study symbolism, although it should be pointed out that the relevant audits (facilities and graphic design) are of a primarily descriptive nature.

In addition to the methods of evaluating elements of the CI mix, there are also a few techniques for studying corporate identity from a wider perspective. As a starting point for the analysis of corporate identity, we may consider two methods which are more or less identical, and which may be universally applied. They are Bernstein's cobweb method, and Lux's star method. A more thorough instrument is the analysis of the structure of meaning, recently developed by van Rekom (1992). Using a 'laddering' technique, one traces the cues that the company offers via concrete behaviour. This offers an overview of what the organization really does or, better, what employees do. It also provides insight into the relationships between the different 'motivation profiles'. Knowledge of these profiles will obviously increase certainty in formulating a promise for external communication.

Another method for analyzing overall corporate identity is Keller's Mannheimer CI method (1987). In my opinion, this method provides a measure not so much of corporate identity, as of its effect on the company's own employees.

The various methods of analysis may be grouped as in Box 2.2.

2.6.2 *Methods of analysis for overall study of corporate identity*

Cobweb method

In his book *Company Image and Reality*, the British author Bernstein (1986) describes a simple technique for reaching a management consensus on the desired company identity. He suggests that all members of the company management, together with others who may be involved, should hold a session to work through a programme aimed at simplifying the decision process.

At the beginning of the session, the participants are asked to name those attributes which, in their opinion, have played a decisive role in the development of the company, and which may also be important for its future development. The list must include all company values which seem relevant, even if some of them have perhaps fallen out of favour. After discussions, participants have to choose eight attributes which are considered to be relevant. Bernstein recommends the use of an overhead projector to show a diagram in which these attributes appear in the form of a wheel with eight spokes (see Figure 2.7). Each spoke is a nine-point scale, with the zero point at the centre and the nine at the outer extremity.

The participants must indicate on the nine-point scales how, again in their opinion, the company is rated by the public on each of the values. The participants are then asked to give their own personal rating. The differences between the collective view of the participants and their estimation of the public view are compared. The results of both 'investigations' can be shown quickly and easily with the aid of an overhead projector. The resulting 'cobweb' is shown in Figure 2.8.

The diagrams are intended to stimulate a discussion which should lead to agreement on the main principles for constructing or modifying the corporate identity.

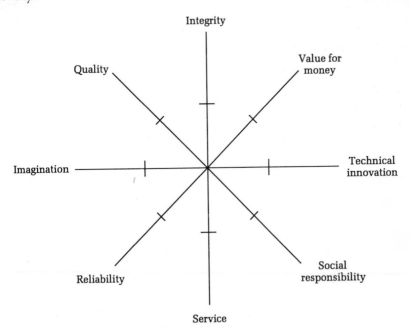

Figure 2.7 Cobweb method: before discussion

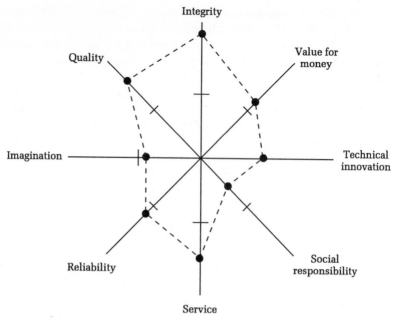

Figure 2.8 Cobweb method: after discussion

Bernstein's cobweb method is useful for putting managers' ideas into an explicit form. Areas of conflict within the management team may also be exposed. The most important function of the method is to bring out into the open the terms in which the managers are thinking, and to arrive at an unambiguous statement of the corporate identity desired by the management.

This method measures in the first instance the picture that the managers have of their company, which is not necessarily the same as the view of the company held by other employees or members of target groups. This in fact constitutes the weakness of the method: it does not actually measure the existing identity of the company. It should perhaps mainly be considered as a method for initiating discussion of the goals of the organization.

Lux's star method

This is similar to Bernstein's cobweb. In my opinion, the value of this method also is limited to the stimulation of discussion among senior management about the line that corporate identity should be following. This does not mean that it is not a useful practical device.

The main difference between the two methods is that in the Lux method, the distinguishing attributes of the company are predetermined. Lux maintains that there are seven dimensions which always underlie the personality of a company. He derives this view from a study by Guilford (1954), who found that there are seven dimensions along which individuals can be characterized. Lux believes that he has adjusted these seven dimensions to fit a company context, and has created a checklist on which a corporate identity character construction can be based. The dimensions are as follows (Lux, 1986):

1. *Needs: internal and external motivation*
   Needs are the central elements in the corporate personality. They are essential for the survival of the company, and provide the basic motivation for its actions. Examples are growth, security and a healthy working atmosphere.
2. *Competences*
   These are the special skills and the competitive advantages of the company.
3. *Attitude*
   The philosophical and political background of a company. This is the dimension in which the company views itself and its environment.
4. *Constitution*
   The physical, structural and legal working space of a company. This includes buildings, locations, organizational structure, etc.
5. *Temperament*
   The way in which a company achieves something (or fails to achieve it). This is the dimension that measures the strength, intensity, speed and feeling of the company's actions.
6. *Origin*
   In this dimension we see the relationship between the present personality of the company and its past. It is primarily concerned with the attributes that have shaped the company in the past.
7. *Interests*
   These are the concrete objectives of the company in the medium and long term. This dimension is concerned with what the company wants to do in the future.

This checklist is used for interviewing company employees, for carrying out research about the company, and during observation of the actions of the company. On the basis of the data gathered in this way, the dimensions are filled in, and the actual identity of the company is described. (See Figure 2.9.)

Lux uses the method himself in his consultancy work, when the culture of a company needs to be changed in a particular direction. Central to the method is the checklist, which is based on the literature on the psychology of personality. It should be regarded as an aid to measurement rather than as an actual measuring instrument.

Laddering

A completely different approach from those described above may be found in a method of corporate identity measurement developed by van Rekom,

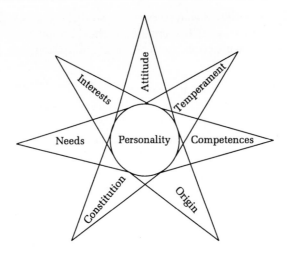

Figure 2.9 Lux's star

using the 'laddering' technique (see Box 2.3). 'Laddering' is described by
Reynolds and Gutman (1984) as 'an individual depth-interview technique which
is used to gain insight into the way in which consumers translate product attributes into meaningful associations relating to themselves'. In the classical
'laddering' interview (Reynolds and Gutman, 1984), concrete attributes are
generated by means of the Kelly Repertory Grid. This is a procedure in which
three different alternatives are offered to the respondent, who must then say
which of the three is different from the other two, and give scores to each of
the alternatives. The key question in the laddering technique is 'Why is that
important to you?' This question is repeated at every stage until a chain of
meanings is built up which leads through levels of increasing abstraction from
the concrete attribute, via its consequences, to the underlying values. All the
chains relating to a particular product can be combined in a hierarchical value
map (HVM), which charts the associations across the different levels of abstraction. (This is also referred to in the Dutch literature as 'meaning structure';
see IPM, 1989.)

This technique was originally developed to determine the image of products

---

Box 2.3 Questions in laddering interviews

I   What is your job?
II   What exactly do you do?
III Why do you do it in this way?
IV   Why is that important?

                                                        (van Rekom, 1992)

and brands, or, more precisely, to determine those aspects of the image that are relevant to a respondent who is considering buying or using the product. Laddering exposes the meaning structure that the respondent uses to decide upon an action, viz. purchase or use of the product in question. However, the laddering technique can also be used to determine the identity of a company. The signals that a company sends out to its environment are a result of the actions of its employees. If a company acts, this means that people are acting. The actions may be ascribed to the company itself if they are specified by the organization to such an extent that very different people can contribute to the process, and that it can continue as it is when individual employees are replaced. In the Western world, the activities of individuals in organizations are specified by means of job descriptions. In so far as employees act within the framework of their job descriptions, they are regarded as representatives of the organization.

A factor that is of decisive importance for the identity of the organization is the interpretations that employees place upon their own job descriptions (van Rekom, 1992). A counter clerk who works by the book will make a very different impression from one who adds their own personal flavour, for example by being more friendly than the rules require. In this way, the meanings that employees attach to the performance of their jobs are passed on as signals to the target groups. An organization is distinguished by its collective set of meanings, and by the ways in which they relate to each other. According to van Rekom, the measurement of identity is the detection of the structure of the collective meanings of the organization.

This method resembles that of Reynolds and Gutman (1984) in that it begins with the generation of attributes, but it then proceeds to the interpretations attached by respondents to their functions. The respondent is asked, for example, how quickly he or she assembles the parts of a mechanical device. Then comes the question: 'Why is this aspect important?' This question is aimed not at the results of using the product, as in product research, but at the intended consequences of the action, i.e. the objective. The answer to the question why a certain objective is important throws light on the underlying values of a company. In other words, we start with the concrete actions of an organization, and proceed to penetrate its personality. The company Overtoom, for example, guarantees to deliver office furniture anywhere in the Netherlands within twenty-four hours of ordering. The fulfilment of this promise is extremely important for the image of speed and reliability which the company wishes to create.

Van Rekom recommends that the aspects revealed during the laddering interviews should be put into a questionnaire, which can then be used to test the representativeness of the structure revealed during laddering. This questionnaire is the final instrument for measuring corporate identity. It contains all the attributes, characteristics, goals and values that appear in the HVM drawn up for the company. With the help of the questionnaire, scores are

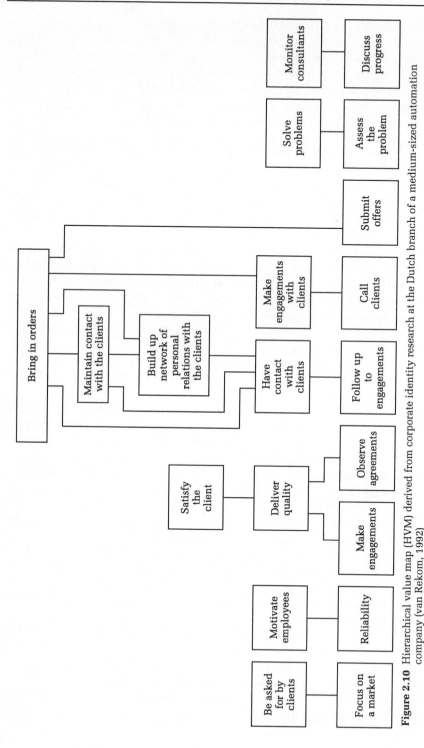

Figure 2.10 Hierarchical value map (HVM) derived from corporate identity research at the Dutch branch of a medium-sized automation company (van Rekom, 1992)

obtained for all these aspects, and the correlations among them are calculated. The results of the questionnaire indicate the degree to which the qualitative preliminary examination is representative of the organization as a whole. The original (qualitative) HVM (see, for example, figure 2.10) can then be corrected.

This procedure yields the final HVM of the company. It reflects the characteristics that constitute the company's corporate identity. Since the interviews start with individual function descriptions, the characteristics shown in the map have implications for the concrete behaviour of the company. A sketch of the company is produced which, according to van Rekom, forms a legitimate basis for constructing communication aimed at the various target groups and for company symbolism, thus ensuring that they are tied to the behaviour of the company. If the culture of the organization needs to be changed, it is clear which aspects of the culture are directly conveyed to outsiders via behaviour.

This method of measurement enables us to construct an overview of all the activities that a company directs towards its target groups, the values and objectives that lie behind these activities, and the relationships between them. This can be done not only for the company as a whole, but also for individual departments, and we can then compare the pictures that we have of the different departments with each other, or with the picture of the company as a whole. This comparison of images makes it possible to determine which aspects of the company's identity correspond with aspects of the image of the company held by various target groups (van Rekom, van Riel and Wierenga, 1991).

Keller's Mannheimer CI test

The Mannheimer CI test measures the internal effect of corporate identity. The test is based on the Mannheimer corporate identity model (see Figure 2.11),

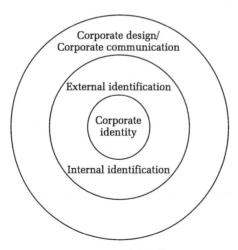

Figure 2.11 Mannheimer corporate identity model (Keller, 1990)

in which a particular corporate identity evokes identification reactions in the members of internal and external target groups. These identification reactions in turn affect the culture of the company, and thus have an indirect effect on its behaviour (Keller, 1990). The culture of the company is influenced by the scores on various dimensions (free interpretation of Keller, 1990).

The Mannheimer CI test distinguishes five dimensions which in combination measure employee identification:

- Identification skill: the ability of employees to identify with something.
- Performance: the readiness to achieve, both in general and in the particular work situation.
- Satisfaction: the level of satisfaction with the working situation; this is subdivided into work satisfaction and task satisfaction.
- Company climate: a mix of elements relating to information behaviour, leadership style, and company atmosphere.
- Example function: the extent to which people find it worthwhile to identify with the company.

Knowledge of these matters is extremely important, not only because of the crucial role of employees in shaping the external image (Kennedy, 1977), but also because of the decisive part played by motivated employees in the success of a company providing services in a strongly competitive market.

Keller (1990) has developed a questionnaire which checks the dimensions listed in Table 2.2 and their determinants individually, and gives a score for each factor, as in a psychological test. These scores can then be compared with averages for the industry.

This test includes a kind of 'thermometer', for checking whether all is well. If the interaction factors are significantly lower than the corresponding personal characteristics of the employees, then there is a problem. This 'thermometer' function is fulfilled by the dimensions 'satisfaction' and 'performance'.

Table 2.2 Dimensions and determinants in Mannheimer CI test

Dimensions	Determinants
Identification skill	– Need to identify – Willingness to identify – Fear of identifying
Performance	– Willingness to perform – Motivation to perform in this specific company
Satisfaction	– Career satisfaction – Satisfaction with job in this specific company
Corporate climate	– Information behaviour – Style of leadership – Atmosphere in the company
Example function of company	– Evaluation of company

If the general motivation to achieve is lower in the company than the personal desire for achievement, something is wrong. The same is true when satisfaction with the work in a given company is lower than satisfaction with the type of specific task. In such cases, comparison of the scores with industry averages constitutes a useful diagnostic tool. If differences are found, one can see immediately where the problem lies. It may be related to any of the following:

- The characteristics of the company itself, the climate of the company, and the extent to which it wishes to serve as an example to its employees.
- The personal characteristics of the employees:
  - to what extent are they inclined to identify with something or someone?
  - to what extent are they satisfied or dissatisfied with their choice of career?
  - to what extent are they generally motivated to high achievement?
- The interaction between personal characteristics and aspects of the company:
  - satisfaction with this particular work in this particular company;
  - motivation to achieve in this particular company.

The Mannheimer CI test measures not identity itself, but the effects of identity. Its primary use is as a diagnostic instrument when management has the feeling that something is wrong, without knowing exactly what. This test can expose many 'cultural' factors which would otherwise remain hidden.

2.6.3 Methods for analyzing individual elements in the CI mix

Behaviour

Organizational climate studies: the OCIPO method

Organizationl climate enjoys a long tradition in English language publications. Tagiuri (1968) defines organizational climate as 'a relatively enduring quality of the internal environment of the organisation that (a) is experienced by its members, (b) influences their behaviour, and (c) can be described in terms of the values of a particular set of characteristics (or attributes) of the environment'.

This was subsequently extended by other writers specifically in the direction of communication and/or of corporate culture. An intermediate form which is much used in Europe is the Organizational Climate Index for Profit Organizations (OCIPO), developed at the Catholic University of Leuven (de Cock *et al.*, 1984). A more compact version of this is the SOCIPO (Shortened Organizational Climate Index for Profit Organizations).

The SOCIPO method is based on the proposition that an organization is continually confronted by two questions:

1. Do people have the opportunity to develop within the organization (people-oriented), or do the objectives of the organization take priority (organization-oriented)?

2. Is the organization flexible in its relations with its environment, or does it try to control the current situation?

This is depicted in Figure 2.12.

The people-oriented/organization-oriented dimension and the flexibility/control dimension are used as coordinates to yield four areas within which the four main characteristics of internal organization are located:

1. The people-oriented/flexibility quadrant represents 'support'.
2. The people-oriented/control quadrant represents 'respect for rules'.
3. The organization-oriented/control quadrant represents 'effective information flow'.
4. The organization-oriented/flexibility quadrant represents 'innovation'.

A written questionnaire is used as the basis for determining where the organization lies with respect to these coordinates, i.e. whether it has a supportive climate, an innovative climate, a climate characterized by respect for rules, or a climate characterized by effective information flow. More details of the four types of climate are given in Table 2.3.

The SOCIPO model has been standardized by researchers at the Catholic University of Leuven on a large sample of companies. The scores on the four

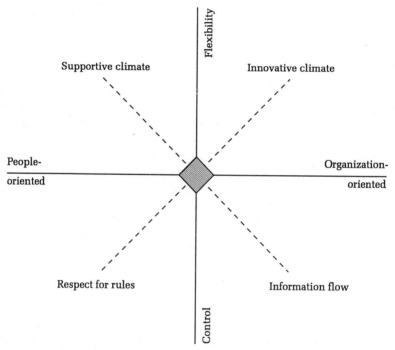

Figure 2.12 Dimensions for classifying types of organizational climate (de Cock *et al.*, 1984)

Table 2.3 Description of the four types of organizational climate (de Cock *et al.*, 1984)

Name	Characteristics	Main focus of attention
Supportive climate (1)	People oriented Value oriented	Cooperation, tolerance, support, maximization of human involvement
Innovative climate (2)	Change, adaptation, individual initiative, variety, competition	Growth and risk, stimulation of initiative, individual responsibility, optimal use of human resources, keeping track of scientific findings
Respect for rules (3)	Safety, continuity, uniformity, confirmation of the existing	Structure, formalization, centralization and standardization
Information flow	Planning, clear policy, efficiency	Productivity, efficiency, workload, development of logical guidelines, organization

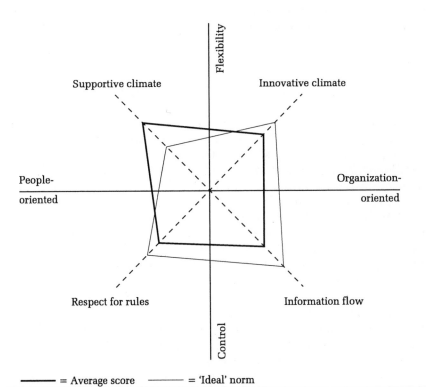

——— = Average score ─ ─ ─ = 'Ideal' norm

Figure 2.13 SOCIPO result for a medium-sized company

climate types for a large Dutch business-to-business company with a divisional structure were as follows:

- support   5
- innovation   15
- respect for rules   10
- effective information flow   15

One can thus compare the results for one's own company with those for more or less comparable companies. Figure 2.13 contains a diagrammatic representation of this process. It is based on research carried out by a consultancy agency on a large Dutch company which has a divisional structure.

The importance of the SOCIPO method derives, in my opinion, from the fact that it offers a relatively quick and cheap way of asking a large group within a company – not just senior managers – about their views on a number of company matters of crucial importance. It forms a good starting point for a process of internal change. As with similar methods of measuring corporate culture, too much importance should not be attached to the absolute values obtained. The main function of the procedure is to initiate discussion and to serve as a barometer which registers the changes in climate taking place within a company over time. Periodic use greatly increases the value of the method, and permits much more far-reaching conclusions with regard to the corporate identity policy of the organization.

Rotterdam Organizational Identification Test (ROIT)

When employees identify strongly with an organization, they are more likely to show a supportive attitude towards it (Mael and Ashforth, 1992), or to accept the organization's premises and make decisions that are consistent with organizational objectives (Littlejohn, 1989). Organizational identification is assumed to be influenced by antecedents like 'employee communication', 'perceived organizational prestige', 'job satisfaction', 'goals and values' and 'corporate culture'. The impact of these antecedents on organizational identification can be measured with the help of the so-called ROIT (Rotterdam Organizational Identification Test) scale (van Riel, Smidts and Pruyn, 1994). The preliminary model of the ROIT scale consists of the focal points shown in Figure 2.14.

The central focal point on the ROIT scale is the identification of an employee with his or her organization. Based on the concept of social identity (Ellemers, 1991) together with other propositions in the relevant literature (Ashforth and Mael, 1989; Mael and Ashforth, 1992; Cheney, 1983; Mowday, Steers and Porter, 1979), a fifteen-item organizational identification scale was constructed, including affective elements, but excluding behavioural intent. In order to determine an individual's strength of identification with an organization, it needs to be established whether an individual experiences the following:

- perception of belonging;
- congruence between goals and values;

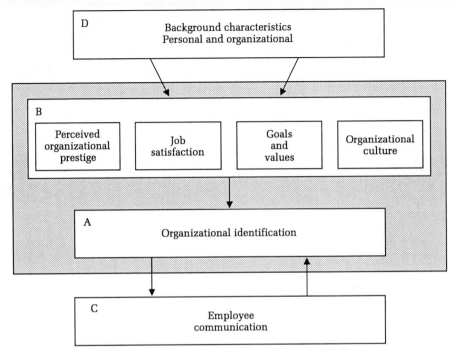

Figure 2.14 Preliminary model ROIT scale

- positive evaluation of membership;
- need for affiliation;
- perceived benefits of membership;
- perceived support;
- acknowledgement;
- acceptance;
- security.

These aspects were used to construct a scale that measures, in fifteen items, 'organizational identification'.

The complete ROIT questionnaire consists of 225 Likert statements for which the respondents have to indicate their degree of agreement or disagreement (on five-point scales). The questionnaire is divided into four modules (see Figure 2.14). It commences with the measurement of organizational identification (15 items), module A. In module B, consisting of 80 items, the antecedents of organizational identification are measured (perceived organizational prestige, job satisfaction, the perceived organizational goals and values, the means to attain these goals, and the perceived organizational culture). In module C, employee communication is assessed by means of 122 items, e.g. the quantity and usefulness of the information received and sent out on personal performance and on the performance of the organization, the communication climate, etc. For each of the employee communication media used by the organization, employees' opinion is measured with respect to the perceived organizational effort per medium, the reliability and accuracy of the employee communication messages, the usefulness of the media and, finally, the reported effort to process information from the media. In module D, personal and organizational background information such as age, tenure and organizational unit is measured. The self-administered questionnaire takes about 35 to 45 minutes for respondents to complete. The questionnaire has been extensively pretested in several types of organization.

Results of ROIT research

A ROIT survey enables organizations to develop indicators of the degree to which employees identify either with their company as a whole (IBM Worldwide) or predominantly with only the part of the firm in which they are operating (e.g. IBM France, sales and marketing department). In other words, ROIT data enable management to make a comparison between identification with the whole and with the individual business unit (see Figure 2.15).

Organizational identification, originally measured by means of fifteen items, is reduced by factor analysis to three dimensions: pride and involvement, acknowledgement and perceived opportunities, and likemindedness and congruence.

The ROIT survey makes it possible to detect 'weak spots' in the organization, creating or avoiding a supportive attitude towards the specific organization. The survey results in data that enable management to learn about the impact of five 'clusters' (several interrelated dimensions) on organizational identification:

- impact of employee communication on organizational identification;
- impact of perceived organizational prestige on organizational identification;
- impact of job satisfaction on organizational identification;
- impact of goals and values on organizational identification;
- impact of organizational culture on organizational identification.

		Identification with BU	
		Low	High
Identification with the whole	Low	1	3
	High	2	4

Figure 2.15 Identification at business unit and organizational level

Box 2.4 Example of impact of employee communication on organizational identification

One example can illustrate the type of information that can be acquired in this respect. Figure 2.16 shows the impact of employee communication on organizational identification, based on a survey in a large not-for-profit organization in the Netherlands.

Identification is explained quite well ($R^2 = 0.55$). In particular the identification dimensions 'pride and involvement' and 'acknowledgement and perceived opportunities' are explained by employee communication. To a much lesser extent, though statistically significant, 'likemindedness and congruence' is related to employee communication variables. Identification appears to be influenced mainly by the communication climate (regression coefficient 0.55, correlation $r = 0.72$). Apparently, in an open climate in which the employees feel accepted and are taken seriously by (top) management and co-workers, and in which they are involved in the organizational decision-making, the identification with the organization is stronger. The communication climate in its turn is affected by all the remaining three latent variables. Taken together they explain the 58 per cent of the variance of the perceived communication climate (see R^2). The amount and usefulness of the information that the employee receives about personal performance affects identification mainly through the communication climate. However, a direct effect on identification also exists. The total effect is 0.35 (see Table 2.4).

The amount and usefulness of the information that the employee receives about the organization substantially influences the communication climate, and thus indirectly identification. Surprisingly, however, no significant direct effect on identification exists. The total effect (0.20; see Table 2.4) is therefore smaller than the effect of information that the employees receive about themselves. One should notice, however, that the information received on personal performance is correlated significantly with the information received about the organization (correlation coefficient is 0.37, $t = 9.44$). Consequently, information on personal performance and the organization often appear to go hand in hand and together they influence the communication climate and eventually identification. Apparently though, some part of the identification is very specific to the individual in that information on personal performance does exert an extra effect on identification. Finally, the reliability, accuracy and

Table 2.4 Standardized total effects of employee communication on communication climate and identification, respectively

	Communication climate	Organizational identification
Info on own performance	0.31	0.35
Info about organization	0.36	0.20
Communication climate	–	0.55
Communication channels	0.23	0.22

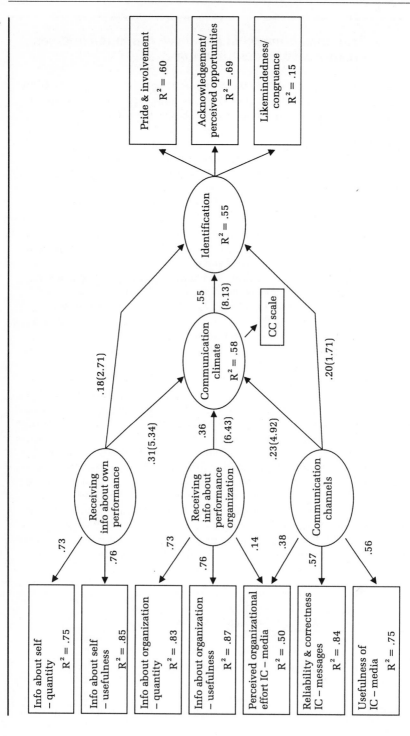

Figure 2.16 The impact of employee communication on organizational identification

usefulness of the information sent by the organization through the employee communication media, and to a lesser extent the amount that is sent, mainly indirectly influence identification through the communication climate (total effect is 0.22). The direct effect is small ($p = 0.09$).

Communication

Communication audit as an aid in investigating company communication

Following the trend in financial management, the use of audits in communication has become increasingly important. The term 'audit' derives from the Latin verb *audire* (to hear), and is often used in the sense of 'method of periodic review'. The review may be of a particular department or function.

The term 'audit' is also closely related to the Latin word *auditor*, which means 'judge'. An audit is not merely a descriptive process; it is also evaluative. One must remember that a communication audit does not happen in a vacuum; it is usually a preliminary to making changes in the way in which the company is managed. If the auditing technique is applied with care, there is usually little resistance to it, and it can lead only to improvements in communication and/or use of symbols.

There are different kinds of communication audits. The simplest ones involve compiling an inventory of the existing items of communication, and lead to a subjective evaluation of their consistency and impact. More fundamental reviewing methods have also been in existence since the beginning of the 1970s. These audits are concerned with 'overall organizational communication' (Goldhaber, 1986). In this section, a description will be given of several complex – and useful – auditing techniques of the kind described in the English-language literature on 'organizational communication'. Brief mention will then be made of the more simple inventory methods in the fields of (symbol) design.

Communication audits

In the English-language literature, communication audits have been shown most interest by psychologists and tend to be subsumed under 'organizational climate' studies (Falcione, Sussman and Herden, 1987). Communication audits have also received much attention from authors located in liberal arts and speech communication departments.

Within the framework of organizational climate studies, the work of Redding (1972) has been important in creating a focus on the 'ideal communication climate'. Redding distinguishes five dimensions which are important for the attainment of an ideal communication climate in an organization. These are defined as (1) supportiveness; (2) participative decision-making; (3) trust, confidence and credibility; (4) openness and candour; and (5) high performance goals (Falcione *et al.*, 1987). Various authors have built upon this, including Roberts and O'Reilly (1973), who have developed the Organizational Communication Questionnaire (OCQ), based on Redding's work. Another method that is in the Redding tradition, but which places greater emphasis on communication satisfaction, is the Communication Satisfaction Questionnaire (CSQ), a communication audit developed by Downs and Hazen (1977).

However, the best-known communication audit is without doubt that developed by the American International Communication Association (ICA). Initially, it bore the name of the organization, and was called the ICA Audit. It was subsequently adapted by Goldhaber and Rogers (1979), and after that it was called the Communication Audit Survey (CAS) questionnaire.

Finally, much space is devoted in the international literature to a valuable study initiated by the Finnish government and aimed at improving the communication climate in working relationships (Wiio and Helsila, 1974). They called their measurement method the LTT Communication Audit Questionnaire. Later, the revised version was named the Organizational Communication Development Questionnaire (OCD).

In order to give the reader a general idea of the subject matter covered by the four types of audit, and of the approaches adopted by them, a short description of each type is given below.

Organizational Communication Questionnaire (OCQ)

The questionnaire developed by Roberts and O'Reilly is intended primarily for making comparisons between organizations with respect to communication. It includes thirteen explicit communication variables and three implicit ones:

1. desire for interaction
2. directionality upward
3. directionality downward
4. directionality lateral
5. accuracy
6. summarization frequency
7. gatekeeping
8. overload
9. satisfaction
10. written communication
11. face-to-face communication
12. telephone communication, and
13. other channels of communication.

In addition, there are three other communication-related variables: trust in superior, influence of superior, and mobility aspirations.

Table 2.5 Summary of main elements in Organization Communication Questionnaire

Dimensions description and number of items in dimension		*Illustrative item and response format on 7-point scale*
1.	Trust (3 items)	How free do you feel to discuss with your superior the problems and difficulties you have in your job without jeopardizing your position or having it held against you later? (completely free to very cautious)
2.	Influence (3 items)	In general, how much do you feel that your immediate superior can do to further your career in this organization? (much to very little)
3.	Mobility (2 items)	How important is it for you to progress upward in your present organization? (not important to very important)
4.	Desire for interaction (3 items)	How desirable do you feel it is for your organization to be in contact frequently with others at the same job-level? (very desirable to completely undesirable)
5.	Directionality upward (3 items)	While working, what percentage of the time do you spend in contact with superiors? (fill in percentage)
6.	Directionality downword (3 items)	While working, what percentage of the time do you spend in contact with subordinates? (fill in percentage)
7.	Directionality lateral (3 items)	While working, what percentage of the time do you spend in contact with others at the same level? (fill in percentage)
8.	Accuracy (3 items)	When receiving information from sources listed below (superior, subordinates, peers), how accurate would you estimate it usually is? (completely accurate to completely inaccurate)
9.	Summarization (3 items)	When transmitting information to your immediate superiors, how often do you summarize by emphasizing aspects that are important and minimizing those that are unimportant? (always to never)
10.	Gatekeeping (3 items)	Of the total amount of information you receive at work, how much do you pass on to your immediate superior? (all to none)
11.	Overload (1 item)	Do you ever feel that you receive more information than you can efficiently use? (never to always)
12.	Satisfaction (1 item)	Express how you feel about communication in general, including the amount of information you receive, contacts with your superiors and others, the accuracy of information available, etcetera.
13–16.	Modalities of communications (4 items)	Of the total time you engage in communications while on the job, about what percentage of the time do you use the following methods? written ... %, face-to-face ... %, telephone ... %, other ... % (fill in percentage)

In an article by Greenbaum, Clampitt and Willihnganz (1988), the most important elements in the questionnaire are summarized in a table (see Table 2.5).

Communication Satisfaction Questionnaire (CSQ)

In the questionnaire developed by Downs and Hazen (1977), eight communication satisfaction variables, six career satisfaction variables and five more general demographic variables are scored on a ten-point scale. The eight communication satisfaction variables are as follows:

1. *communication climate* – deals with the general satisfaction with the perceived effectiveness of the communication atmosphere;
2. *supervisory communication* – measures satisfaction with upward and downward communication with the respondents' supervisors;
3. *organization integration* – involves the extent to which employees receive information about the immediate work environment;
4. *media quality* – focuses on the extent to which meetings are well organized, written directives are short and clear, and the degree to which the communication is about right;
5. *co-worker communication* – relates to satisfaction with horizontal communication relationships in the organization;
6. *corporate information* – deals with information about the organization as a whole, such as information about the corporation's financial standing;
7. *personal feedback* – concerns what workers need to know about how they are judged and how their performance is appraised; and
8. *subordinate communication* – consists of items only answered by supervisors, including 'extent to which subordinates initiate upward communication' (Greenbaum *et al.*, 1988).

Communication Audit Survey Questionnaire (CAS)

The CAS, which is much better known under its earlier name, the ICA Audit, makes a continuous comparison between the perceived actual situation and the desired situation. The questionnaire deals with the following topics: judgement of the amount of information to be received; judgement of the amount of information to be sent to others; and judgement of the feedback received on the information sent. Items include: 'In respect to information I send to my immediate supervisor, this is the amount of follow-up NOW ...'; and the same question, ending with '... this is the amount of follow-up NEEDED'. This is used to measure the difference between the actual situation and the desired situation ('current condition' and 'ideal condition'). Other items elicit judgements on the quantity of information ('the amount of information I receive'); the time-span within which it is received ('To what extent can you say the information is usually timely?'); the communication climate ('To what extent can you say, I trust my co-workers?'); career satisfaction; and the channels used by the organization. Finally, demographic variables are covered.

Organizational Communication Audit Questionnaire

The only well-known international European audits described in the international literature are of Finnish origin. Wiio in particular played a leading role in the development of this audit (Wiio and Helsila, 1974). It was originally called LTT, then OCD, and sometimes it is called OCA.

The changes of name indicate that in the course of time, a number of significant changes have been made to Wiio's audit. The following twelve communication variables are central to the current version of the Finnish audit:

1. overall communication satisfaction;
2. amount of information received from different sources – now;
3. amount of information received from different sources – ideal;
4. amount of information received about specific job items – now;

Topics of information	Supervisor/ management	Shop stewards	Fellow employees	Bulletin boards	Newsletter (house organ)	Staff meetings	Rumours	Memorandums	Other	(Additional up to 15)
Economic situation of the organization										
Employment situation										
My own work										
Changes in production										
Training and courses										
Employee benefits										
Sales										
Organization specific										

Figure 2.17 Testing audit results (Wiio and Helsila, 1974)

5. amount of information received about specific job items – ideal;
6. areas of communication that need improvement;
7. job satisfaction;
8. availability of computer information system;
9. allocation of time in a working day;
10. respondent's general communication behaviour;
11. organization-specific questions; and
12. information-seeking patterns.

The Finnish researchers developed a compact tool for measuring point 12, as shown in Figure 2.17.

The information collected in the communication audit on the quality of communication in a particular organization gains extra value if it can be tested against outside standards.

The most obvious comparison is against norms for other areas within the same commercial sector, where a similar audit has been carried out. This can be done both with the CAS audit and with the OCD audit, since extensive data-bases of audit results are available both at the International Communication Association in the United States and at the Institute for Human Communication in Finland. Goldhaber (1986) offers another possibility, which is also attractive. Based on the work of Greenbaum, who developed the CAS audit, he has produced a protocol against which a company can test its own results. Table 2.6 contains the basic elements of criteria for internal communication.

Table 2.6 Standards for internal communication (Goldhaber, 1986)

Area of performance criteria	Procedural instruction	Performance standard
Content Direction Criteria	Provide for the general orientation of new employees – within the department and relative to the entire organization	Within five working days of hiring
Feedback Content Timing	Encourage new employees to indicate problems promptly so that difficulties may be overcome quickly	Formal once-a-week brief interview for minimum of first three weeks
Initiation Content Controls Timing	Arrange for self or senior skilled personnel to train new employee in job details. Employ procedure charts as a guide and reference	Orient in two weeks Train in sixty days
Initiation Participation Interaction conditions Timing	Introduce employee to individual members of the group and do everything possible to ensure that new member is socially accepted by the group. Utilize methods appropriate to position	Immediately on date of start

Reliability and validity of audits

The audits are almost always carried out by external experts. This at least implies that there will be a well-considered and systematic approach, leading to a legitimate judgement. Hopefully, such judgements will be based on rigid criteria. All the audits discussed in this section are known to have been tested for reliability and validity by various authors. Table 2.7 taken from a previously mentioned publication by Greenbaum *et al.* (1988), contains a summary of judgements made about the audits.

Symbolism

Making an inventory of all symbols

To compile an inventory of the symbolism of an organization, the facilities audit and the graphics design audit (Napoles, 1988) may be used. The facilities audit is an inventory of all the means of communication where symbolism could be

Table 2.7 Comparative Instrument Assessment Schedule (Greenbaum *et al.*, 1988)

	OCQ	CSQ	CAS	OCD
General structure				
Items: total	35	51	134	76
communication items	27	40	109	54
demographics	–	5	12	7
outcome variable items	–	6	13	7
comm.-related items	8	–	–	–
org.-specific items	–	–	–	8
Dimensions	16	10	13	12
Response format:				
type of scale	7-point	7-point	5-point	5-point
open-ended	none	limited	extensive	limited
multiple choice inc.				
demographics	–	5 items	12 items	16 items
Administration				
ease of administering	high	high	high	moderate
ease of tabulating	high	high	moderate	moderate
past use of instrument	moderate	moderate	high	high
norms availability	none	yes	yes	yes
Psychometric data				
reliability overall	.70	.94	.838	n/a
inter-item within scale	.84 to .53	.86 to .75	.90 to .70	n/a
item to total				.39 to .22
				(LTT items only)
Validity				
face validity	high	high	high	high
discrimination valid.	high	high	high	n/a
factor stability	moderate	moderate	low	moderate
Evaluated by other				
researchers	yes	yes	yes	yes

used. The graphic communications audit is an inventory of all its current applications in printed matter produced by the company.

The facilities audit is an inventory of objects that might be used to carry visual messages, e.g. logos, slogans, etc. Buildings, interiors, equipment – virtually all objects that could carry a company logo – are important means of expressing the identity of a company. The average lorry, for example, is capable of delivering 7.9 million visual impressions per year, or about sixty per kilometre. This gives an indication of the importance of the company fleet, since the visual impression is a means of communication, and therefore an indirect sales method.

The researcher should be informed about all the company's locations, taking account of which target groups they serve, and how space, colour, lighting and symbolism are used in the locations to express the identity of the company.

Photographs of all the locations can be used to compile an overview, and missed opportunities can then be identified.

Graphic communications audit

The graphic communications audit produces an overview of all visual symbolism used in printed matter. If a complete picture is to be obtained, all the forms of written expression used by the company must be reviewed. They should then be compared for consistency and impact.

2.7 Conclusions

In this chapter, the concept of corporate identity has been examined in detail. It first appeared in the field of design, and gradually attained its present scope following, for example, the work of Birkigt and Stadler. One must, unfortunately, accept that at a conceptual level, there is no unambiguous, generally accepted definition of corporate identity, and therefore there is no corresponding instrument of measurement.

The measuring instruments that are reviewed in section 2.6 all have their merits in certain areas of corporate identity, for example company communication, design or personality. Some are useful for measuring the effects of corporate identity, e.g. the Mannheimer CI test. However, there is as yet no instrument for measuring company identity in its entirety. A combination of the Cobweb method of Bernstein and the Laddering method of van Rekom is, at this stage, probably the most acceptable approach for obtaining a clear view of the (desired and actual) corporate identity of an organization.

It is likely that the coming years will see considerable development in this area, until the various different views converge to yield a single definition of corporate identity, and a single instrument for measuring it in its entirety.

Chapter 3

Corporate image

This chapter will deal with the various levels of image analysis (3.2) and the importance of corporate image (3.3) before discussing a number of definitions. The subsequent majority of the chapter is devoted to the presentation of three trends discernable in corporate image literature (3.4). This consists of a review of the 'social criticism' approach (3.4.1), a discussion from the perspective of more analytically oriented authors (3.4.2) and ends on a consideration of 'utility'-oriented authors (3.4.3). After having considered the most important theoretical developments, section 3.5 reviews various image measurement methods used in practice. The following methods will be discussed: the corporate image barometer, the CIPA Motivation method, the CS technique, natural grouping and the photosort method.

3.1 Introduction

In the previous chapter, corporate identity was described as the self-presentation of a company; it consists of the cues offered by an organization via its 'behaviour', 'communication' and 'symbols'. Such signals are ultimately received by key people with whom the organization needs to interact to varying degrees. As more signals are received and the interest and involvement of the 'receiver' increase, a clearer picture or *image* of a certain object will appear. This object could be a product, a retailer, an organization or company or even a country.

An image might be considered as a photographic film which is on the point of 'developing' in people's minds. It provides the receiver (an individual) with a means by which to simplify the reality of objects through concepts such as 'good-bad' and 'pleasant-unpleasant'. The image of an object develops through a set of impressions that individuals experience when they directly or indirectly, are confronted with that object.

As a consequence, the following definition of image will be used in this book:

> An image is the set of meanings by which an object is known and through which people describe, remember and relate to it. That is the result of the

73

interaction of a person's beliefs, ideas, feelings and impressions about an object. (Dowling, 1986)

The great interest in 'images' primarily stems from the assumption that a positive image is the basic prerequisite for building a direct or indirect commercial relationship with various kinds of target group. Initially, that interest centred on images focused primarily on selling products/brands (brand image). Gradually, the focus widened and, particularly over the course of the last decade, there has been an explosion in publications about *corporate image*.

Interest in the concept of image, both theoretical and practical, mainly originated in the field of marketing. This is just as true of the academic literature as it is of the achievements and publications of image practitioners (for example, Ogilvy in the 1950s). During the last five to ten years, basic ideas about image originally developed in the marketing area at a product level have extended more towards the organizational level (corporate image).

There are significant differences between 'brand' and 'corporate' images. These differences become crucial when a company has to solve its 'image' problems (i.e. targets, goals). With respect to their conceptual development and operationalization, there are no fundamental differences in the core meaning of the terms. However, the literature can hardly be said to present a clear and consistent concept of the meaning of 'image' or of the ideal method of measuring images. Indeed, the opposite appears to be the case.

In order to provide the reader with a basis from which to evaluate the various points of view present in the literature, this chapter offers an outline of the most important views relating to the concept and the operationalization of corporate images.

In respect of *concepts* of imagery, attention will be focused on well-known marketing publications of a primarily sociopsychological origin, together with sociology-based concepts of image (Alvesson, Morgan, Boorstin *et al.*) and publications originating from the organizational communication field (Dowling, Abratt *et al.*).

In respect of *measurement* techniques, a similar aim is pursued, namely to offer the reader an overview of the methods (as currently practised) with which (corporate) images can be measured.

3.2 Image levels

The objects with which an image may be associated are of various kinds. Knecht (1986) uses this as a basis for distinguishing seven levels of image: product class image, brand image, company image, sector image, shop image, country image and user image. At product level, a distinction can be drawn between the image of a product class, such as beer, and the image of a particular brand, such as Heineken. At organizational level, distinctions should be made between the image of a company within a subsidiary, the image of the company, and the image of an industrial sector. This last is what Knecht calls the corporate image.

However, in this book, the term 'corporate image' is used to mean the image of an organization, since this would appear to be more in line with generally accepted ideas. In order to indicate the image of an industrial sector, the terms 'industry image' or 'sector image' can be used. The image of Akzo Nobel is thus a corporate image, while the image of the chemical industry is the sector image. The company image can be the image of a subsidiary; with regard to Akzo Nobel, this would be the image of Organon. An example of an image on a retail level would be the image of the local Tesco store. However, the overall image of 'Tesco's' is a corporate image. Images at national and international level are important for companies that also operate abroad. Images that people have of a country can wield great influence in international trade. The image that people have of solid, reliable German quality has a favourable influence on sales of German products. Finally, there is the user image. Many people think of the average owner of a BMW, for instance, as a middle-aged man with a pot belly and a cigar! Images at different levels influence each other. People form a picture of an object by means of chains or networks of associations, which are built up over a period of time as a result of slowly accumulating stimuli. This leads to the formation of a mosaic of impressions, which as a whole constitutes the image. Indeed, an image might well be compared to a classical Roman mosaic. Over two thousand years or so several of the small red, yellow or blue stones from the mosaic that originally formed a cohesive artistic expression will be lost. Nevertheless, the onlooker continues to appreciate the artist's general idea behind the creation of the mosaic, and hence to appreciate its artistic value. In other words, a 'receiver' does not have to have a highly elaborate image of an object to be able to describe, remember and relate to it.

According to Holzhauer, it often happens that we develop

> the knowledge which we have of a company as a result of being confronted by forms of advertising. We know nothing about the company which owns the Marlboro cigarette brand. However, we should not be surprised if the company strongly resembled the cigarettes. We often develop a company image on the basis of the image we have of its products, i.e. the brand image. The brand image is formed on the basis of the only information we have about the company, namely, brand advertising. In other words, brand advertising can determine the image of the company. Conversely, the picture we have of a company (Woolworth, Philips, Braun) can determine what we think of the products of that company. (Holzhauer, 1991)

3.3 The importance of the corporate image

In recent years, the importance of the corporate image has been recognized by increasing numbers of companies (see Box 3.1). One of the reasons behind

Box 3.1 The importance of a favourable image

A positive corporate image is a condition for continuity and strategic success. It is no longer solely the field of attention of marketing, but rather a strategic instrument of top management. (De Soet (CEO Dutch KLM), in Blauw, 1994)

A sound corporate image is an incentive for the sale of products and services. It helps the company recruit the right employees, it is important to the financial world and to investors and it generates faith among internal and external target groups. A sound corporate image provides a company with authority and forms the basis for success and continuity. (Blauw, 1994)

A sound corporate image creates emotional added value for a company which ensures that a company is always one step ahead of its competitors. A sound corporate image is competitive, which means distinctive and credible. (Brinkerhof, 1990)

A good image helps a company attract the people necessary for its success: analysts, investors, customers, partners, and employees. Identity management can secure that good image. (Chajet, 1989)

Image is a representation in the mind. It affects attitudes which in turn affect behaviour. No company can afford to ignore image. The impression it creates – consciously or unconsciously, whether it wishes to or not – inevitably affects people who do business with it. (Bernstein, 1986)

Research has found 9 out of 10 consumers reporting that when choosing between products that are similar in quality and price, the reputation of the company determines which product or service they buy. (Mackiewicz, 1993)

Images are particularly helpful when:

- information on the basis of which people have to make decisions is complex, conflicting and/or incomplete
- information is either insufficient or too wide-ranging to be able to judge
- people have a degree of involvement that is too low to be able to go through an extensive information-processing process
- there are certain conditions in the environment that obstruct the decision-making process, such as time constraints. (Poiesz, 1988)

this is the growing interest in studies of corporate image. The research agency Research and Marketing (R + M) confirms that image studies are being commissioned both by individual companies and by an increasing number of sectors within Dutch society, including the construction industry, education, farming and the health sector (Cramwinckel and Nelissen, 1990). The importance of image research thus extends across a wide field.

The image is extremely important both to the source of the image (the image object), and to the receiver (the subject). The source (the organization) considers that the transmission of a positive image is an essential precondition for establishing a commercial relationship with target groups. It is the best way to enter the 'evoked set' of the target group. For the subject, the image constitutes a way of summarizing the 'truth' about the object in terms of a set of simplifications (good-bad, usable-unusable, and so forth). There is a relationship between the importance of the corporate image to the source and its importance to the recipient. The greater the reliance that the subject places on the (corporate) image when making decisions, the more important it is for the company to build up a sound reputation. Box 3.1 contains a number of arguments often used to emphasize the importance of images.

Poiesz (1988) believes that without the help of images, consumers have difficulty in deciding which products to buy. Consumers are steadily losing their ability to act rationally. They are not familiar with all the alternatives on the market. They are not aware of all the features of a particular product. They are not able to judge all those features in the correct way. They cannot make use of all their previous experience, because their memories are not perfect. Furthermore, they are not always able to process and store new experiences. This inability to act rationally leads consumers to seek other grounds on which to make their decisions. They are inclined to base decisions on earlier, imperfect consumption experiences; feelings; incomplete information; simple guidelines; symbolic information; and unconscious processes (Poiesz, 1988).

Poiesz lists a number of different functions performed for the consumer by the image. These are the knowledge function, the expectation function and the consistency function. By performing these functions, the image simplifies information processing (Lilli, 1983). Images are useful in the search process: attention is directed towards objects with a positive image. The image can also serve as a simple rule for making decisions: if the degree of involvement is low, buy the product with the most favourable image. The level of involvement, and its influence on consumer information processing, will be discussed further in section 3.4.2.

The position of Pruyn (1990) is broadly similar to that of Poiesz. When considering the relevance of an image, he places greater emphasis on the viewpoint of the source. He, too, perceives an increasing uniformity among products and brands (and companies: Cees van Riel). This leads to increasing difficulty in making distinctions on the basis of price and intrinsic functional characteristics of the product. For this reason, according to Pruyn, people look for ways of making value distinctions based on subjective, non-observable features of the product. This mainly involves symbolic aspects which the subject ascribes to the object by associative processes (Pruyn, 1990).

As will be explained in section 3.4.2, there are various ways in which the concept of (corporate) image may be approached. Consequently, definitions vary. Box 3.2 contains a number of definitions of (corporate) image which occur in the literature.

A definition of image which was mentioned earlier in this book, and which,

Box 3.2 Definitions of (corporate) image

Image is subjective knowledge. (Boulding, 1956)

Image is the sum of functional qualities and psychological attributes in the mind of the consumer. (Martineau, 1958)

Image is the result of the way in which the individual assesses the object in the following terms: tangibility, personal relevance and degree of correspondence with the self-image. (Enis, 1967)

Image is used to refer to a memory code or associative mediator that provides spatially parallel information that can mediate overt responses without necessarily being consciously experienced as a visual image. (Paivio, 1971)

Image is the profile of the object, meaning the sum of impressions and expectations as gathered in the memory of an individual. (Topalian, 1984)

Image is a combination of product aspects that are distinct from the physical product characteristics but are nevertheless identified with the product. Examples are the brand-name, symbols used in advertising, endorsement by a well-known figure, and country of origin. (Erickson, Johannsen and Chao, 1984)

Image is a hierarchical meaning structure consisting of means-end (/value) chains. (Reynolds & Gutman, 1984)

Image is the sum of experiences that someone has with the institution. (Ford, 1987)

Image is a subjective and multi-dimensional form of representation or imprint of reality in the human brain, as a consequence of which this reality is presented in a reduced, coloured and thus often transformed manner. (Fauconnier, 1988)

 Image refers to a holistic and vivid impression held by a particular group towards a corporation, partly as a result of information processing (sensemaking) carried out by the group's members and partly by the aggregated communication of the corporation in questions concerning its nature, i.e. the fabricated and projected picture of itself. (Alvesson, 1990)

in my opinion, is very useful, is that given by Dowling in his article 'Managing Your Corporate Image' (1986). Following the work of Aaker and Myers (1982), he states:

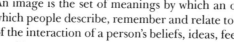 An image is the set of meanings by which an object is known and through which people describe, remember and relate to it. That is, it is the net result of the interaction of a person's beliefs, ideas, feelings and impressions about an object.

For 'object', one may substitute 'brand', 'organization', etc., so as to make the definition appropriate to different levels. It follows from this definition that different people may have a different picture of the same object. It appears also that the image is determined both by the person who perceives the image and by the object. There are, therefore, two ways in which an image can be adjusted. First, the object itself can be changed. Second, one can adjust communication to the target groups, and try to change people's 'beliefs, ideas, feelings and impressions about an object'.

3.4 Trends in the literature

Writers on (corporate) image may be divided into three groups. This division offers a way of classifying the many viewpoints that appear in the literature. The distinction between the three groups is relative. Some writers may even qualify for inclusion in two of the groups, on the evidence of different publications. Nevertheless, I feel that it would be helpful to attempt to categorize the multitude of viewpoints on 'image'.

The first group contains the social critics. These include, for example, Boorstin (1961), Alvesson (1990), and Morgan (1986). They consider images from a social or sociological standpoint. The second group contains writers with an analytic orientation, such as Poiesz (1988), Verhallen (1988), Pruyn (1990), Beijk and van Raaij (1989), Wierenga and van Raaij (1987), and Reynolds and Gutman (1984). Their ~~~~ interest is in the meaning of the term, and in the methods of measu~~~~ ~~~~riving from it. The third group contains writers who are interested ~~~~ity aspect. This group is represented in the academic world by Ker~~~~ (1977), van Raaij (1986) and Dowling (1986), who are concerned with the ~~image~~ formation process. In the applied field, there are Olins (1989), Ind (1990), Blauw (1994), and Bernstein (1986) and Gray and Smeltzer (1985), who are interested in multi-step plans. The first group of utility-oriented writers are interested primarily in the question of how an image is formed. Those in the second group have a primarily practical interest: what must be done to create a favourable image?

3.4.1 Social critics

The writers in this group describe and criticize the role of images in contemporary society. They express a rather different view from that to be found in the marketing and communication literature. However, their view must be taken into account when forming definitions and theories relating to the concept of image. The first writer to apply the concept of image to society was Boorstin in 1961. In his book *The Image, or What Happened to the American Dream*, he criticizes American society, which he says is excessively influenced by pseudo-events. In his view, 'apparent' reality is emphasized, at the expense of 'real' reality. Initially, the image is the representation of reality, but ultimately reality becomes a representation of the image.

A sociological view of images is offered by Alvesson in his article 'Organization: From substance to image?' (1990). In his view, an image consists of the picture that someone has of an organization (the sense image) and the impressions that the organization communicates (the communicated image). An image arises primarily out of information that is transmitted via the mass media and through interpersonal communication, and which is haphazard, infrequent and superficial in nature. It does not arise from own direct experiences with the 'real' organization. At the heart of Alvesson's critique is the belief that Western society is flooded with images. This means that organizations must continually create stronger and perhaps less accurate images, in order to stand out from the mass. This can lead to confusion when the discrepancies between encountered reality (personal experiences) and created images (pictures in the mass media) become too great. A more literary exposition of the view expressed by Alvesson, and, more especially, by Boorstin, may be found in the work of Milan Kundera (1990). He describes the pernicious influence of image-forming in our society. The following quotation is from his section on 'Imageology':

> If the imageologists have decided that all the walls of the gymnasium which Agnes visits are to be covered with huge mirrors, this is not so that people can watch themselves exercising. It is because the lucky number in the imageological roulette fell upon mirrors. If as I write these pages everyone has decided to make Heidegger out to be a scatterbrain and a black sheep, this is not because his thinking has been overtaken by that of other philosophers, but because at that moment he has become the unlucky number in the imageological roulette, the anti-ideal. The imageologists create systems of ideals and anti-ideals, short-lived systems which follow each other in rapid succession, but which influence our behaviour, our political opinions and aesthetic tastes, the colour of carpets and the choice of books, just as strongly as ideological systems used to do.

Another social critic who should be mentioned here is Morgan. Morgan's position is less moralistic than those of Boorstin and Alvesson. In his book *Images of Organization* (1986), he shows how people have standard, learned ways of viewing organizations. The ways in which people view organizations influence their judgements about them. Our ideas about management and organization are based on a few images which we accept as true. We see the organization either as a machine (Taylorism), or as an organism or person. By looking at different 'images', we can think of the organization in different ways, which yields a more complete picture. An organization can be regarded as a brain, capable of self-regulation and learning; as a culture, with shared values and regard for the symbolic meaning of rational events; as a political system, within which different groups develop activities that serve their own interests; as a psychological prison, in which irrationality and concealed aims play an important part; as a stream and a process of transformation, in which changes play a major role; and, finally, as an instrument of oppression, where that which is rational for one party may be catastrophic for another.

3.4.2 Analytic writers

Writers in this group offer opinions as to what constitutes an image, and how it may be measured. The group includes Poiesz (1988), Wierenga and van Raaij (1987), Verhallen (1988), Beijk and van Raaij (1989), Pruyn (1990), and Reynolds and Gutman (1988). In order to understand the positions that they adopt, we must first give brief consideration to theories about how individuals process information.

Information processing in individual image formation

An image is formed as a result of a range of stimuli presented to a subject by an object – directly or indirectly. The interpretation and the evaluation of these stimuli can be influenced by many factors. In order to understand how the evaluation takes place, we must gain some insight into the way in which information is processed by the individual.

According to McGuire (1976), information processing may be divided into five phases. It is clear from Figure 3.1 that the stimuli that are received can only be effectively retained if all the stages of information processing are completed. It is therefore in the interest of the source of the information to pilot these stimuli through all the stages. Even if the source succeeds in making

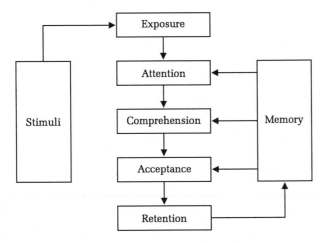

Figure 3.1 Information processing according to Engel *et al.* (1990)

contact and in drawing attention to the message that it wishes to communicate, there may still be a considerable barrier to be overcome, since the comprehension, acceptance and retention phases remain to be completed.

In the comprehension phase, the subject must attach meaning to the stimuli that are offered. This requires categorization of the stimuli by means of concepts stored in the memory. The processes described in Gestalt theory are among those that are relevant here.

The acceptance phase centres on the question of whether the information produces the effect desired by the source. This depends, among other things, on the extent to which the information offered is integrated into the existing conceptual system. An important part is played by 'elaboration', defined by Engel, Blackwell and Miniard as 'the amount of integration between the new information and existing knowledge stored in memory' (1990). The more favourable the reactions to the stimuli in the comprehension phase, the greater the probability of their reaching the retention phase.

The final phase of information processing by the individual centres on possible storage in the long-term memory. The human memory has three components: sensory memory, short-term memory and long-term memory. A stimulus enters the sensory memory via the senses. A sensory impression is formed from information about shape, colour, pitch, etc. At this stage, no meaning is assigned to the stimulus.

Information that is to be analyzed further is transferred to the short-term memory. This may be described as working memory, in which the meaning of the stimulus is determined by combining it with information stored in the long-term memory. The capacity of the short-term memory is limited. To achieve the best possible use of this limited capacity, information from the sensory registers is combined by means of 'chunking' into comprehensible units. The 'chunks' may be compared with images. Like images, chunks are simplifications of reality. Image formation may therefore also be regarded as a kind of 'chunking'. When these chunks appear repeatedly in the short-term memory, they may be transferred to the long-term memory. Long-term memory is regarded as an unlimited, permanent storage capacity in which information is stored in an organized manner. It contains the lasting deposits of our experiences and knowledge. The working of the memory is represented by the diagram in Figure 3.2.

The influence of the information transmitted during the process of communication depends on the extent of the 'elaboration' which occurs during information processing. In their elaboration likelihood model (ELM), Petty and Cacioppo (1986) postulate that if the degree of elaboration is high, the subject is on the central route to conviction (see also Beijk and van Raaij, 1989). The only elements ('signs', or 'cues') that are important during information processing are those that are relevant to the formation of a rational opinion. Opinion formation is influenced by the content and the force of arguments.

If the degree of elaboration is low, the subject is on the 'peripheral route'

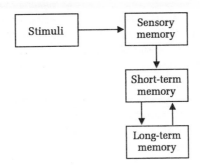

Figure 3.2 How the memory works (Engel *et al.*, 1990)

to conviction. In this situation, elements of the message that are irrelevant to the formation of a rational opinion become important. Peripheral cues, such as the attractiveness of the person conveying the message, or the number of arguments contained in the message, begin to play a part in opinion formation (Wierenga and van Raaij, 1987). Which route is followed is determined in part by the degree to which people are motivated to process the information.

Factors that are important in this respect are involvement, the personal characteristics of the receiver and whether the message is consonant with the experience of the receiver. If, for example, the level of involvement is high, the central route will be followed; if it is low, the peripheral route will be taken.

Table 3.1 Three ways of approaching the image concept (based upon Poiesz, 1988 and others)

Degree of elaboration	Conceptualization	Typology	Measurement implications	Measuring method
High	Image is retained as network of meanings in memory of consumer	Image is structured in complex manner	Qualitative research: dig deeper for associations	Free-format method Structure method – laddering – Kelly Grid
Middle	Image is the sum of conceptions about an object: perceptions about salient attributes × importance of these attributes	Image is an attitude	Explicit methods: identify salient attributes and present them in form of statements	Attitude questionnaire – considerations – appraisals
Low	Image is a general holistic impression of the position of the object in relation to its competitors	Image is a global impression	Implicit methods: relative positioning of the object by means of multidimensional scaling	Multi-dimensional scaling of: – similarities – preferences

If 'need for knowledge' is a characteristic of the subject, there is a greater probability that the level of involvement will be high. The time that is available to the subject also plays a part in determining which route will be followed. When a quick decision must be made, it is likely that the peripheral route will be taken.

When information processing follows the peripheral route, the part played by images is substantial. This means that they are important in situations where the subject lacks the motivation, readiness or knowledge to make a judgement based on a complex reality.

Three image levels, based on degree of elaboration

Images are simplifications of reality; they will only be elaborated further if the object becomes more important to the subject. Based on the degree of elaboration, which is determined by the importance of the object to the subject, three kinds of images may be distinguished. Table 3.1 provides an overview of degrees of elaboration and connected measuring methods.

Selected subjects for corporate image research can have three degrees of elaboration (concerning information about a chosen object): high, middle or low. Roughly speaking, this can be explained by the psychological and physical distance between a subject and an object: the *greater* the *distance* between subject and object, the *lower* the degree of elaboration. Knowledge about the degree of elaboration enables a researcher to choose an applicable method for gathering image data. One has to choose a method that is appealing for survey respondents in the sense that it allows them to show sophisticated knowledge (high degree of elaboration) or to 'hide' a lack of knowledge by answering questions that 'only' force the respondent to make comparisons between objects on general attributes (given a low degree of elaboration). See Table 3.2.

Corporate image research needs to be approached from the perspective of the interaction between a subject and an object. Questions have to be answered, like 'Which subjects are interesting to focus on?', 'Which part of the organization needs to be examined?', etc. (see Box 3.3).

Box 3.3 Questions concerning corporate image research

Subjects
- who
- possibilities for segmentation
- accessibility
- consciousness of external consequences
- costs
- planning (time) schedule

Objects
- which part of the organizations
- possibilities for segmentation
- accessibility
- consciousness of internal consequences
- information needs
- time schedule

Table 3.2 Interaction of subjects and objects

S—O	Short psychological/ physical distance	High degree of elaboration	Necessity to select a measuring method that uncovers deeper associations
S——O	Middle psychological/ physical distance	Middle degree of elaboration	Necessity to select a method that measures considerations and appraisal with respondents
S———O	Long psychological/ physical distance	Low degree of elaboration	Similarities and preference on general attributes

Corporate image research is often carried out among a variety of stake-holders. One may suppose that these groups differ in their degree of elaboration. As a consequence one has to be aware of the fact that using one single method might lead to data that are not reliable, because some target groups may be confronted with questions that they could not be expected to answer. Differentiation in degrees of elaboration within the chosen target groups forces organizations to combine methods to measure image in a proper way.

High degree of elaboration: image is complex/hierarchically structured

When the degree of elaboration is high, the image that the subject has of the object will be retained as a network of meanings in their memory. Objects can represent different values to different people. Besides purely functional values, affective values are also important. Within this framework, one often speaks of a 'ladder of signification structure'. Seen in this light, Reynolds and Gutman (1984) describe an image as hierarchically structured. According to them, the image object has a number of meanings for the subject which can be indicated by means of a hierarchical so called means-end chain. This can be presented schematically with the help of Figure 3.3.

Olsen and O'Neill (1989) have further elaborated the means-end chain into a 'six-level means-end chain' which is presented in Figure 3.4.

To measure an image which is stored in the form of a hierarchy, a structured

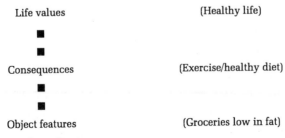

Figure 3.3 Ladder of signification structure

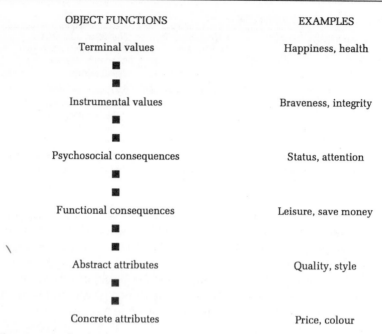

| OBJECT FUNCTIONS | EXAMPLES |

Terminal values   Happiness, health

Instrumental values   Braveness, integrity

Psychosocial consequences   Status, attention

Functional consequences   Leisure, save money

Abstract attributes   Quality, style

Concrete attributes   Price, colour

Figure 3.4 Six-level means-end chain (Olsen and O'Neill, 1989)

method and/or a free-format method may be used. This is a qualitative method based on the assumption that image concepts are stored by means of memory links. The links between the object of the image and attributes, consequences and values can be traced by means of analysis of the structure of meaning, or 'laddering'.

Based on this view of the way in which images are stored in the memory network, Pruyn (1990) suggests the use of associative techniques to investigate the relationships between values assigned to objects. Techniques for analyzing the structure of meaning, e.g. 'laddering' (Reynolds and Gutman, 1988; Pieters, 1989) and Kelly's Repertory Grid are suitable for revealing the hierarchies in which company characteristics, consistencies and values are stored in the memory of the consumer. Pruyn describes the following five stages in the process of tracing the respondent's memory links:

1. In the first stage, the salient features must be identified. There are various methods which may be used for this; the free-format method is one example. The respondents may be given sorting tasks, in which they are required to sort cards into two piles. The cards show different image objects belonging to one object category, e.g. Tesco, Sainsbury's. The respondents are asked to state explicitly the features on which they base their decisions.
2. In the second stage, attributes are selected for use in further analysis.
3. In the third stage, respondents are asked which features of the objects they

prefer. If the respondent states that the size of an object is important, e.g. the floorspace of a shop, they are then asked to indicate whether they prefer a large or a small shop.

4. In the fourth stage, an attempt is made to trace the hierarchy in the subject's memory. He or she is repeatedly asked the question 'Why?' 'Why do you prefer a large shop?', 'Why do you find that important?' and so on. If the respondent has difficulty in finding reasons, or if the topic is becoming too sensitive, the interviewer can help in one of the following ways: by giving a context in which the object is used; by offering a context from which the object is absent; by continuing the interview in the third person; by pausing; or by summarizing briefly the answers given so far, and asking whether this was what the subject meant.

5. In the fifth and final stage, the answers must be statistically processed and interpreted. With the aid of content analysis, the answers can be classified in the means-end chain according to content and level. This can be done either for individual respondents or at an aggregated level.

Intermediate level of elaboration: image as attitude

Where there is an intermediate degree of elaboration, the image may be regarded as an attitude. An attitude may be viewed as the balanced sum of ideas about an image object. Attitudes are used to explain and predict behaviour (Fishbein and Ajzen, 1975). When an attitude, or an image, is positive, the probability of positive behaviour towards the image object is greater.

An attitude can be measured by explicit methods. The researcher can ask the respondent for a total judgement on the image object. More commonly, respondents are presented with a number of statements about the image object. They must then indicate how far they agree with each statement. The attitude is derived by weighting and adding up the statements. The weighting can be done in different ways.

In the Fishbein and Ajzen attitude model, the respondent is asked to give a judgement about the attributes of a given image object, and also to attach a value to each of the attributes. This value is the weight which is assigned to the attribute. In the following formula

$$A = \sum_{i=1}^{n} O_i x W_i$$

A represents attitude, O_i the judgement of attribute i, and W_i the appraisal of attribute i.

The following example will serve as an illustration. Taking Tesco as the image object, the respondent may be asked to give it scores for a number of attributes, such as:

- Tesco sells quality products.
- Tesco staff are friendly.

- Tesco is cheap.
- etc.

These attributes are scored on an x-point scale. One of the most frequently used is a five-point Likert scale, ranging from 'totally agree' to 'totally disagree'. The advantage of a scale with an odd number of points is that it allows the respondent to give a neutral answer. Values are then given to the attributes. Here too, judgements are made on a five-point scale, ranging from 'very important' to 'not important', as shown below:

	very important			quite unimportant
I think that the purchase of quality products is				
I think that friendly personnel is				
I think that buying cheap products is				
etc.				

The score assigned to the object for each attribute is then multiplied by the value assigned to that attribute. The sum of all the values thus obtained is the attitude score.

   Attitudes can also be measured using the semantic differential procedure. The reactions of the respondents are measured on a bipolar scale (good/bad, cheap/expensive, etc.).

   An advantage of the explicit method is that it offers a relatively simple way of gaining insight into the image and its structure. Furthermore, images of different objects can be compared, because they are measured on the same attributes. This makes it possible to obtain a detailed understanding of the strengths and weaknesses of different objects. A disadvantage is that the researcher must be well aware of the different attributes that play a part in determining attitudes. This usually necessitates preliminary research. Another disadvantage is that respondents must often fill in lengthy questionnaires. This may lead to loss of motivation, which will affect the results. The difficulty may be partly overcome by presenting the questions in a different order each time. Another possibility is for the researcher to reduce the number of attributes by means of factor analysis. However, this too requires preliminary research, in which the full set of attributes is presented. A third disadvantage is that the research itself can shape attitudes. When respondents are presented with the attributes of an image object, they start to think about them. Finally, there is the possibility that the attitude is more than the sum of the separate attributes. The semantic differential has an extra disadvantage, namely that respondents cannot indicate for themselves the importance of a given attribute.

Low level of elaboration: image as a general impression

At a low level of elaboration, the image is merely an overall impression in the subject's memory. The subject has received too much information and too many impressions to be able to process them in a structured and rational manner. Images at this level are diffuse, which makes it difficult to identify the concrete attributes that influence the subject's picture of the object.

It is, however, possible to trace the position of the object relative to other objects by means of its image. An implicit method, which measures the degree of perceived similarity between different image objects, is suitable for this. Returning to the example of the chain stores, the respondent could be asked: 'How similar do you think the two chain stores in each pair are to each other?'

	are very similar			are totally dissimilar
Tesco-Sainsbury's				
Sainsbury's-Marks & Spencer				
Tesco-Marks & Spencer				
etc.				

Using multidimensional scaling, information can be obtained about the relative positions of the competing objects. The (dis)similarity judgements are entered in an n-dimensional perceptual chart, in which the distances between the objects indicate as accurately as possible the degree of (dis)similarity. An example of a two-dimensional perceptual chart is given in Figure 3.5.

A great advantage of the implicit method is that no preliminary research is required, since it is not necessary to know what attributes are important to the subject. Another advantage is that a large number of objects can be included in the research. It should be noted, however, that the number of pair comparisons that the respondent has to make increases very steeply. When the task becomes too big, the results can be affected. However, the number of objects to be compared should equally not be too small. A minimum of seven objects should be included in the study to give a good perceptual chart (Pruyn, 1990).

Need for a critical approach to choice of measurement method

Before choosing between the methods of measurement described in this section, one must know the degree of the subject's involvement with the object and the way in which the image object is stored in their memory. These two factors not only determine which method of measurement is appropriate but also the kind of communication policy that will be needed to adjust the image, determined by the level of elaboration. An illustration of the dos and don'ts regarding an (international) image study is shown in Box 3.4.

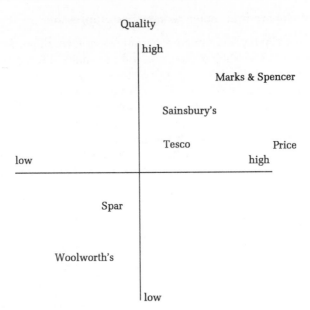

Figure 3.5 A two-dimensional structure of the perception of stores, based on fictitious similarity data

3.4.3 *Writers interested in utility*

Writers who are interested in utility may be placed in two categories. In the first category are academic writers such as van Raaij (1986), Dowling (1986) and Kennedy (1977), whose chief interest is in the process of company image formation. The second category includes, among others, Bernstein (1986), Garbett (1988), Olins (1989) and Blauw (1994), who are less interested in the theory of images than in the use of information about them to create the best possible image among members of target groups. They have designed multi-stage plans for this purpose. These plans emphasize the need for a sound identity if a good image is to be created and maintained. At this point, the interests of the utility-oriented writers coincide with the area of planning corporate identity policy, which will be discussed in detail in Chapter 4. However, some brief remarks should be included in this section about utility-oriented writers.

Formation of the corporate image

The utility-oriented writers who emphasize the formation process of the corporate image focus on the statement that an image arises as a result of a range of impressions. Personal impressions, interpersonal communication and mass media communication combine to produce a mixture of real and parallel impressions, the totality of which forms the image. Garbett (1988) takes a number of elements which together form the corporate image and combines

Box 3.4 Gist Brocades; dos and don'ts in an international image study

General information about the company

Royal Gist Brocades NV is an international group of companies whose core business is biotechnology. Its most important products derive from fermentation processes. The group is one of the largest producers in the world of baker's yeast, penicillin and its derivatives and enzymes.

One of the mainstays of the company is research, which is an integral part of the group's commercial operations. Gist Brocades has production units and/or sales organizations in nine European countries, the United States, Latin America and the Far East.

The company has three divisions:

- The Food Ingredients Division (FID) produces mainly yeast, bakery ingredients, yeast extracts and derivates. Baker's yeast is an important product in the bakery market, although bread improvers and pastry ingredients are playing an increasingly prominent role. In addition, a growing supply of yeast extract, used as a natural savoury ingredient, is finding its way to the international foodstuffs industry.
- The Industrial Pharmaceutical Products Division (IPPD) supplies the pharmaceutical industry with penicillin and intermediates. The IPPD is the world's largest industrial producer of penicillin and has an important position in the market for penicillin derivatives used in the production of antibiotics. Its strong position in the biotechnology sector and the industrial pharmaceutical market constitutes the basis for the development of new products.
- The Bio-Specialities Division (BSD) develops and produces enzymes and related biotechnology products for a range of applications, primarily for the dairy, detergents, drink, textile, starch and animal feed industries.

In 1993 turnover at Gist Brocades amounted to Dfl. 1,703 m. At 31 December 1993, the company had a worksforce of 5,299.

Internal changes: from product orientation towards market orientation

The year 1992 was marked by laying the future foundations for Gist Brocades as a market-driven company with enterprising staff, working together in multidisiplinary teams to achieve the best possible results. Work was carried out on many fronts on the Gist Brocades of the future, e.g. implementing cost leadership programmes such as the corporate 'Advance' project, aimed at creating a result-oriented type of behaviour among middle and senior management.

Business environment

Since 1974, Gist Brocades has been engaged in recombinant DNA techniques and the production of DNA-based products. Although primarily a producer

▶

of raw materials and additives and not of consumer products, Gist Brocades, like all comparable companies, faces criticism for the technology it applies, from pressure groups protesting against biotechnology. It seems that the products or the method of production as such are not the issue. Nor is it their safety, since the processes are virtually identical to those used to develop other, acceptable, products. The opposition stems from people's feelings towards the particular way in which genetic material is used. Gist Brocades continues to do its share in promoting the social acceptance of modern biotechnology products in a large number of Dutch and European industry organizations.

Image study

The majority of the internal stakeholders are convinced that Gist Brocades is developing rapidly from a product-oriented towards a market- and service-driven company. Nevertheless there are serious doubts about the degree to which external stakeholders are familiar with these recent changes in the company.

In order to find out whether or not relevant external stakeholders are aware of recent changes in the company, the board of Gist Brocades wanted to know more about the actual international (corporate) image of the firm. Three key questions were paramount:

1. Are stakeholders familiar with relevant facts and figures about Gist Brocades: do they know the product range, do they know the product names, do they know the company behind the brand?
2. Do stakeholders recognize and appreciate recent changes within the company – more specifically, do they recognize the desired image attributes like flexibility, service orientation, tailor-made delivery as supplier to global giants in e.g. the detergents market, etc.?
3. Does the 'corporate brand' Gist Brocades have added value for business units of the Gist Brocades group?

What should the company do?

In order to be able to give an efficient briefing to an agency to study the image of the company, the following issues were established (see the eight steps in Figure 3.6):

1   What is the desired image and what has the company done in recent years to depict the organization in the desired way? In other words, what kind of cues (through behaviour, communications and symbolism) has it transmitted to convince external and internal target groups?
2.   Are image data already available? In the case of Gist Brocades, as in many such cases, these data may well exist. (See Figure 3.12 on p. 106, showing the familiarity and favourability of the company with general practitioners.) Although these data hardly answer the three questions of Gist Brocades' management, they can be considered as one of the indicators to be used to describe the actual image of the company.

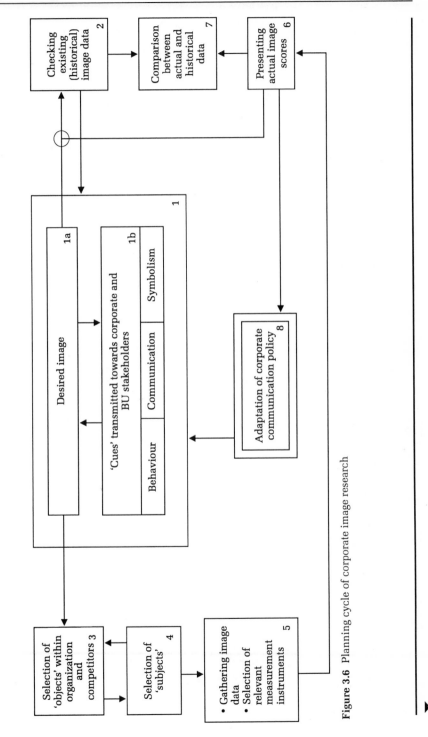

Figure 3.6 Planning cycle of corporate image research

3/4. In the third and fourth steps, in order to prepare an image study one has to decide in general terms *who* (subjects) and *what* (objects) specific parts of the company should be studied. The following scheme can be useful in making a final decision.

5.   In the fifth step data are gathered applying the most relevant measurement instruments.

The final selection for the image study should be made by first selecting vital stakeholders (from a commercial point of view) and, second, stakeholders who indirectly influence the success of the company. In the case of Gist Brocades this meant (a) a selection of business-to-business clients in the most relevant countries and (b) a selection of respondents active in the political environment in order to pick up opinions on biotechnology production methods. Depending on the budget and availability of existing image data, one then has to make a final choice.

6.   In the sixth step the research agency should present the data gathered, explaining how they were gathered, what were the main results and above all the answers to the three questions asked by the company at the beginning of the study.

	Enabling government stockholders commissioners	Normative competition sector suppliers	Functional output own employees	Functional input clients groups	Diffused environmental groups unions
Corporate					
Bakery ingredients Division (BID)					
Business Unit Savoury ingredients					
Industrial Pharmaceutical Product Division (IPPD)					
Bio Specialities Division (BSD)					

7.   In the seventh step, both the research agency and the communication department have to compare the results of the latest image study with previously gathered data and with the desired image as was formulated at the outset.

8. Finally, in step eight the company's communication department should write a short report, to be discussed with (senior) management, summarizing the main results of the study and advising the adaptation of the company's future corporate communication policy in either a fundamental or a minor way (depending on the results of the study).

them into the following formula, which may be regarded as a checklist:

$$\begin{array}{c}\text{Reality}\\\text{of the}\\\text{company}\end{array} + \begin{array}{c}\text{Newsworthiness}\\\text{of company}\\\text{activities}\end{array} + \begin{array}{c}\text{Communications}\\\text{efforts}\end{array} \times \text{Time} - \begin{array}{c}\text{Memory}\\\text{decay}\end{array} = \begin{array}{c}\text{Company}\\\text{image}\end{array}$$

A more elaborate model for the development of the corporate image was developed by Dowling (1986); this model is shown in Figure 3.7. It is clear from the model that a number of factors are important in the formation of the image, namely the internal behaviour of the organization, the picture conveyed via the media to the outside world, and personal experiences and communication.

The policy of the organization is depicted in published materials such as yearly reports, and other information available to outsiders, e.g. details of products, prices, etc. The policy of the organization is influenced by its culture, the nature of which can be deduced from managerial behaviour, reward structures, values held by the company, and company rituals.

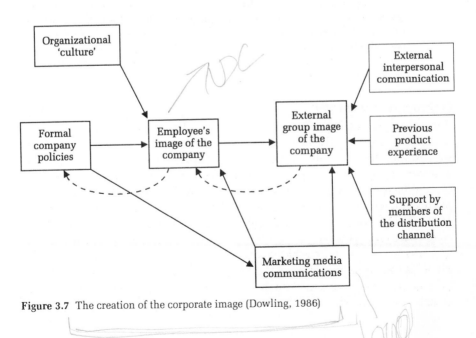

Figure 3.7 The creation of the corporate image (Dowling, 1986)

Groups external to the organization judge it on the basis of factors such as products, prices and quality, service, attitudes of employees, advertising, etc. The most important factors include communication transmitted by the organization via the media, previous experience of the products, interpersonal communication, and the support given by staff in the distribution sector, e.g. product displays, promotions, etc. The media are more effective in creating awareness of an organization and knowledge about it, whereas, according to Dowling, interpersonal communication has a greater effect in the formation of attitudes towards the organization.

Kennedy, in her discussion of the formation of the corporate image (1977), states that the corporate image is based primarily on 'our total experience of the company'. In her view, the experience that people accumulate of a company – especially in the business-to-business sector – is influenced most of all by personal contact with employees of the company. Since employees play a crucial role in determining the external image, Kennedy believes that management policy must guarantee that 'the information, and hence the image they transmit, is compatible with the way in which top management wishes to be seen'. For this reason, her article 'Nurturing Corporate Images' is primarily concerned with image formation among a company's own employees. In Kennedy's view, every employee is in principle a potential 'sales person for the company'. The extent to which an employee is a good 'sales person' depends on their own attitude towards the company.

> In turn this will follow from the policies made by the management of the company, and the way they are communicated to the various company members. Desirable policies which are well communicated and implemented are likely to lead to a well disposed workforce, undesirable policies, or those which are distorted in their communication are apt to have the opposite effect. Accordingly the extent to which a company has a good image among its employees and subsequently among those outside it, rests in the hands of top management. (Kennedy, 1977)

Impression management

'Impression management' is suggested by van Raaij (1986) as a possible way of creating or protecting an image among members of target groups. This suggestion is based partly on the work of Tedeschi (1981). Van Raaij offers the following definition: 'Impression management is the company's policy of presenting itself to target groups in such a way as to evoke in them a favourable picture [image] or to avoid an unfavourable picture.' This definition is based on a theory taken from social psychology, that people – and probably companies too, according to van Raaij – tend to convey to others an identity that is as favourable as possible. In this way, 'social power' (goodwill) is gained, which can be used to influence the behaviour of the groups concerned, and to facilitate transactions with them. Impression management can be assertive or defensive. Assertive impression management is a 'proactive' policy aimed at creating a good image in the target group. It attempts to associate positive events with the organization. Defensive impression management is a reactive policy aimed at protecting the image of an organization. It is a reaction to an (expected) accusation. It attempts to ascribe negative events to causes outside the organization. Tactical impression management operates in the short term and in a specific situation; strategic impression management operates over the longer term, and is not tied to a particular time or situation. When particular tactical manoeuvres are repeated frequently, they become strategic impression management.

Combining the two dimensions of impression management yields four possibilities, as shown in Figure 3.8.

Explaining, apologizing and confessing are examples of tactical defensive impression management. The long-term effects of defensive impression management can be undesirable. When a company adopts a policy of strategic defensive management, it may appear dependent and in need of help; this is a negative situation for most organizations.

An example of tactical assertive impression management would be 'ingratiation', i.e. efforts on the part of the organization to gain the sympathy of target groups by transmitting positive information about itself, doing good deeds, etc. Other instances are example-setting, which means adopting a policy of serving as a good example to other organizations, and 'entitlement', which is claiming responsibility for a positive event. Assertive impression management leads in the long term to a favourable image, thus increasing

	DEFENSIVE	ASSERTIVE
TACTICAL	Explanation Apology Justification Disclaimer Meaning Pro-social behaviour	Ingratiate the organization Self-promotion Exemplification Intimidation Supplication Entitlement Enhancement
STRATEGIC	Dependence Weakness Indigence Helplessness Do not stand out negatively	Attraction Prestige Esteem Status Credibility Specific characteristics

Figure 3.8 Impression management (van Raaij, 1986)

social power and the ability to influence others. Strategic assertive impression management attracts the most attention in the literature. Organizations that practise this form of impression management in the right way see a growth in esteem for the organization, and in its credibility, status and prestige.

There is an important prerequisite for consistent impression management. The relevant communication must not only be directed outwards. Employees must also be motivated through internal impression management to behave according to the picture that the organization wishes to transmit to the outside world (van Raaij, 1986).

Multistep plans

Although different authors stress different aspects, most multistep plans designed by utility-oriented writers are basically the same. Starting with Dowling's five-step model (1986), this section gives an overview of steps to be taken in order to adjust the corporate image (see Figure 3.9).

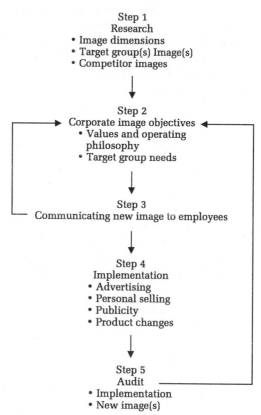

Figure 3.9 Five-step model by Dowling

In the first step, the image dimensions that are important to the company's target groups must be identified. In-depth interviewing may be used for this purpose. The images of competitors should also be taken into account, so that the company's relative position and room for manoeuvre can be determined.

In the second step, the picture that the organization wishes to create among target groups must be compared with the needs of those groups, and with reality, i.e. the organization as it is. The policy to be implemented by the organization is derived from these comparisons. If the principal target group is conservative, the company should not present itself as progressive and modern. Equally, a rigid, bureaucratic company should not present itself as a fast, modern, flexible organization, since the consequences are likely to be unfortunate.

In the third step, the chosen policy should be explained to the employees, so that they may convey it to the public. Acceptance on the part of the employees may be facilitated by means of seminars, brochures, etc.

The fourth step is the implementation of the policy, by means of advertising, public relations, changes in product and product price, visual symbols, and changes in employee attitudes. The nature of the campaign and the choice of media are dictated by the objectives of the corporate image campaign.

Finally, the effectiveness of the campaign should be assessed. Assessment methods include drawing 'perceptual maps', and research into changes in sales patterns, staff turnover, consumer complaints, and so on.

3.5 Measurement methods in practice

3.5.1 Hit lists

'Hit lists' are often used to assess images. The best-known hit list is compiled as a result of research carried out by *Fortune*, an American periodical, into the reputations of the largest American companies. More than 10,000 eminent people in business life are asked to rate the largest companies in their own commercial sector on eight key factors, using a scale of 0 to 10. The eight factors are as follows:

- quality of management
- quality of products or services
- financial soundness
- ability to attract, develop and keep talented people
- use of corporate assets
- value as long-term investment
- innovativeness
- community and environmental responsibility.

A comparable study by *The Financial Times*/Price Waterhouse, asking top managers to name the competitors they most respected on seven factors of business performance and to list the qualities that contributed to 'excellence', resulted in the following Europe-focused list (i.e. in contrast to *Fortune*'s North American 'bias'):

- Automobiles/Auto Trucks and Parts
  1. Bayerische Motoren Werke   Germany
  2. Bosch (Robert)   Germany
  3. Peugeot   France
- Banks and Financial Institutions
  1. Deutsche Bank   Germany
  2. Union Bank of Switzerland   Switzerland
  3. Lloyds Bank   UK
- Beverages and Tobacco
  1. Moet Hennessy Louis Vuitton   France
  2. Heineken   Netherlands
  3. Guinness   UK
- Chemicals, Paper and Packaging
  1. Ciba-Geigy   Switzerland
  2. Air Liquide   France
  3. ICI   UK
- Construction and Building Materials
  1. Holzmann, Philipp   Germany
  2. RMC Group   UK
  3. Pilkington   UK
- Diversified Holding Companies
  1. BTR   UK
  2. Rentokil   UK
  3. Hanson   UK
- Electricity and Water
  1. RWE   Germany
  2. Powergen   UK
  3. Electrabel   Belgium
- Electronics and Electrical Components
  1. Siemens   Germany
  2. Alcatel   France
  3. Nokia   Finland
- Engineering
  1. ABB Asea Brown Boveri   Sweden/Switzerland
  2. Rolls-Royce   UK
  3. Unde   Germany
- Food Processors
  1. Unilever   Netherlands/UK

  2 Nestlé   Switzerland
  3 BSN   France

- Insurance
  1 Munchener Ruckversicherungs
     Gesellschaft   Germany
  2 Fortis   Belgium/Netherlands
  3 Swiss Reinsurance   Switzerland
- Media
  1 Reuters Holdings   UK
  2 Reed Elsevier   UK
  3 Bertelsmann   Germany
- Oil, Gas and Mining
  1 Royal Dutch/Shell   Netherlands/UK
  2 Repsol   Spain
  3 British Gas   UK
- Pharmaceuticals and Healthcare
  1 Roche   Switzerland
  2 Astra   Sweden
  3 Glaxo   UK
- Retail
  1 Marks and Spencer   UK
  2 J Sainsbury   UK
  3 John Lewis   UK
- Telecoms and Communications
  1 British Telecom   UK
  2 PTT Telecom   Netherlands
  3 Vodafone   UK
- Transport
  1 British Airways   UK
  2 BAA   UK
  3 Swire (John) & Sons   UK

(Source: Price Waterhouse, in *The Financial Times*, 27 June 1994)

Fortune's Corporate Reputation Index and comparable 'barometers' such as the British *Financial Times*/Price Waterhouse top list have recently faced a lot of criticism (Maathuis, 1993; Fryxell and Wang, 1994). The value of these surveys is limited in so far as they are based solely on the opinion of 'experts'. It is likely that quite different results would be obtained were the same measurement instrument to be used by a different group. For research purposes the usefulness of, for example, *Fortune* reputation data is limited. The major underlying factor of the *Fortune* database appears to be its predominantly financial orientation. As a consequence 'reputation' scores, as evaluated by the *Fortune* respondents, relate most directly to 'reputation' as a measure of 'an investment' (Fryxell and Wang, 1994).

According to a study of the relationship between corporate performance and corporate image by Fombrun and Shanley (1989), profit has the greatest effect on reputation, followed by risk (negative influence) and the market value of the organization. The visibility of the organization in the media is also important. Other factors that influence reputation are: the extent to which institutional investors hold shares in the organization; the dividend pay-out ratio (a high ratio has a negative influence, because if pay-outs are too high, too little money is being reinvested in the organization); social concern; size of the organization; and the extent of advertising. Maathuis (1993) extended the body of knowledge on this subject by proving the impact of familiarity, branch characteristics and economic climate on appreciation of an organization. Particularly well-known companies appeared to be rated significantly higher than less familiar companies. The rating of *less* well-known companies is strongly influenced by the general economic climate and the sector climate in which they have to operate. Such conditions are not necessarily under the control of all organizations. See Figure 3.10.

Although the position of a company on the hit list is to some extent arbitrary, it nevertheless indicates general trends. It also shows the organization

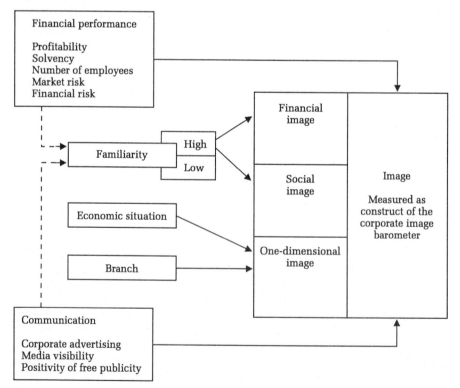

Figure 3.10 Impact of corporate performance and corporate communication on corporate image (Maathuis, 1993)

that it is being watched by people who may be directly or indirectly involved with it. The organization is thereby compelled to realize that the opinion of target groups is important for successful functioning.

In the Netherlands, the best-known hit list is the corporate image barometer, developed by the De Telegraaf/Bonaventura publishing group. The method for constructing the barometer will be described in section 3.5.2.

3.5.2 Research methods: an overview of practice

In the Netherlands, there are many marketing, PR and specialized research agencies that are active in the measurement of corporate images. Most of these agencies publish little about the methods of measurement that they use. The best-known and most extensive research is the development of the corporate image barometer. This research is carried out by Research and Marketing Ltd at Heerlen. In addition to this method, there are at least four others which should be described at this point. A variant of corporate image research inspired by the approach of the UK agency MORI (Market and Opinion Research International) has been developed by the Amsterdam research bureau Motivaction. The CS technique, a variant of the card-sorting method as used by the Institut für Demoskopie at Allensbach, has been developed and used by NSS Market Research, in collaboration with Ahold. The natural grouping method has been developed by Research International. Lastly, mention should be made of the photosort method developed by the BBDO advertising agency. There are, of course, many other methods developed by different research agencies. It is not possible to describe them all in this book.

Corporate image barometer (R + M)

In the Netherlands, a written survey of about two thousand opinion leaders has been carried out at two-year intervals since 1982 for the purpose of constructing the corporate image barometer (CIB). The surveys were conducted by Research and Marketing, Heerlen (R + M). The barometer is an initiative of the publishing company Bonaventura and De Telegraaf (Cramwinckel and Nelissen, 1990).

This particular research concentrates on two central elements. The first is the familiarity of the company (is it well known? do people hear or read much about it?). The second is the appraisal of the company by opinion leaders. This second element is divided into (a) ten general aspects which may be regarded as measuring the evaluative component, and (b) one that measures the behavioural or conative component. The behavioural component is assessed by asking whether the respondents would recommend the company as an investment. The ten general or evaluative aspects are as follows:

- profit/rate of return
- attention to the environment
- raw materials and safety

- the company as an employer
- innovativeness
- degree of market orientation
- importance to the Dutch economy
- expectations for the future
- product quality
- supply of information.

A general report is drawn up on the basis of the information obtained in the survey. Individual companies are scored for familiarity and appraisal within the appropriate business or industrial sector, the sectors being banking, insurance and investment companies; transport; consumer goods; chemical and metal industries; and computers. A graph is then constructed using 'familiarity' and 'appraisal' as axes, and the fifty companies with the highest scores across all the sectors are entered in it. For the ten best-known companies, scores are given for the ten evaluative aspects. Further information is provided, about which companies are regarded as the most attractive investment prospects; what the image of the government departments is; how the different departments are rated on the image aspects; and what are the current problems in trade and industry (*Corporate Image Barometer*, 1990).

In addition to the general report, it is possible for the individual company to obtain an analysis of its performance in the CIB in the preceding years. This is linked to the Decision Makers study for the same year. The result is a clear picture of the company's corporate image within particular Decision-Making Units. It also permits specification of image components according to socioeconomic and sociodemographic data.

The CIPA model of Motivaction

In 1985 Motivaction Amsterdam BV introduced a corporate image study into the Netherlands which was based on a model developed by the British research agency MORI. This quantitative research model was employed to measure the current image of companies among the Dutch public as well as in the business-to-business sector. The research model has been further developed into a corporate image and performance analysis (CIPA) model in which not only the image (awareness and evaluation) but also the performance of the company is measured.

The essence of this research model is that the attitudes of the respondents towards a large number of competitive companies are measured. By placing the perceived attitudes to similar (competitive) companies side by side, the relative position of a company can be determined and strong and weak elements may be viewed in perspective.

The research model encompasses six topics for systematic exploration:

1. A map of the composition of the decision-making unit (DMU) and the evaluation criteria used: against which criteria is company and organizational performance measured?

2. A determination of the attitude towards companies: the degree of aware-ness (spontaneous and prompted) and the degree of appreciation or favourability, divided into various topics and resulting in a company strengths/weakness analysis *vis-à-vis* competitors.

3. The ascertainment of satisfaction with certain aspects of the company; for instance, product quality, assortment, price, service, etc.

4. A determination of the image profile; associations with reliability, dynamics, progressiveness (adapted for each company).

5. A map of the communication channels and the media that are important in the construction of the image.

6. A determination of the opportunities for and threats to the organization, together with trends in the market or sector.

The CIPA study can be carried out by means of face-to-face interviews or by telephone. CIPA is a research method that can map the position of a company as perceived by consumers and also in the business-to-business sector. The set-up of the study is such that the results can be contrasted with the image of the organization that exists *internally*. As a result, internal and external research can be cross-referenced. In Figure 3.11 the four perspectives on image and identity are illustrated to show their interrelationship.

Setting up a CIPA study involves a number of phases. In the first phase the relative degree of awareness of companies involved in the study is determined with the help of a five-point scale. In the next phase, appreciation of or favourability towards the company is indicated on a five-point scale (by those who are familiar with the company): Once these two measurements are known, they can be plotted against each other on a graph. By including the scores of competitors as well, the relative position of the company can be indicated (see Figure 3.12).

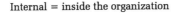

Internal = inside the organization

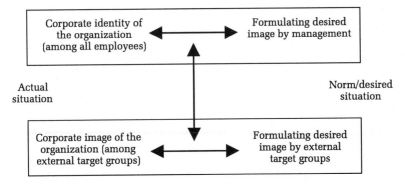

External = outside the organization

Figure 3.11 Internal versus external image/identity

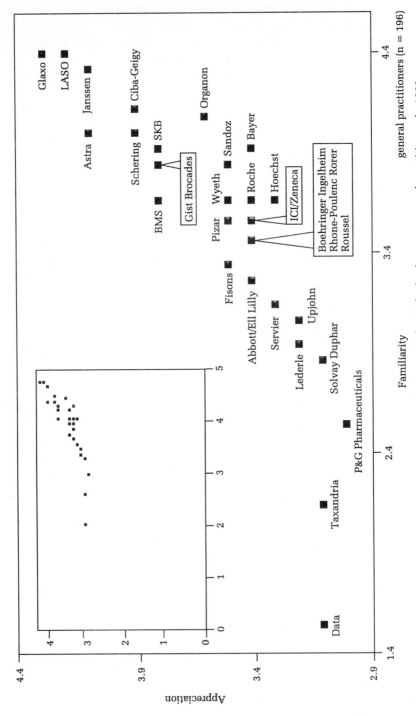

Figure 3.12 Familiarity and favourability of the pharmaceutical industry in the Netherlands among general practitioners in 1993

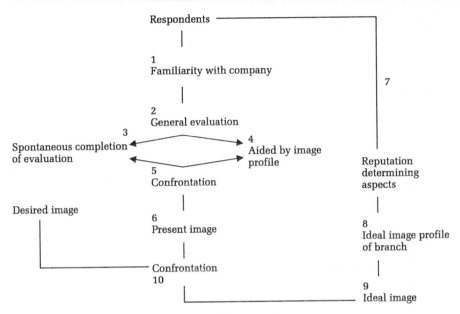

Figure 3.13 Approach of multiclient research Motivaction

In the following phases the causes of the differences in evaluation are further studied in depth; in this way, the strong and weak aspects of the client company and its competitors can be determined and satisfaction with the organization and its goods and/or services systematically mapped. Utilizing the large number of statements drawn up beforehand, the image profile of the client and the main competitors can then be constructed. This profile can be contrasted with the 'ideal image' one has of a company. With the help of regression analyses it is then possible to indicate accurately which image aspects of the profile determine the general appreciation most. This analysis is a useful aid in determining priorities in marketing and communication policies. The research process can be represented schematically as in Figure 3.13.

Depending on the construction of questions put to the client, the CIPA study can be tailored to individual circumstances. If, say, there is primarily a need for information about the image of a company, this part of the study is consequently focused on. Where an evaluation of the product offer or the provision of services is important, then the satisfaction analysis receives more emphasis.

The CS Technique (NSS)

The director of NSS Market Research, van Westendorp, believes that too little attention is paid to the difference between associative reactions and judgements (van Westendorp and van der Herberg, 1984). It is appropriate to use the term 'judgements' when the respondents in a study are reasonably well acquainted with a company and its many characteristics. However, in many cases, and especially in pure image research, it is not concrete judgements that are required, but a kind of associative knowledge which may be more or less remote from reality. These images resemble stereotypes of the kind discussed in social psychology, e.g. 'Germans are industrious'. According to Spiegel (1961), a genuine image (or image feature) only exists if associative impressions of the kind described play a more important part in the significance of the object than knowledge based on reality. Van Westendorp argues that many of the usual methods of measurement, involving rating scales, include a mixture of associative and judgement tasks. The use of rating scales to measure judgements presents no problems; however, it is difficult for respondents to measure associations in terms of a marking system, since they tend to be of an 'all-or-nothing' nature.

The choice of measuring technique must depend, according to van Westendorp, on the kind of target group to be studied. If the respondents have a good and detailed knowledge of the company as a whole, a judgement scale is appropriate.

NSS Market Research has further refined the card-sorting method developed by the German Institut für Demoskopie. The result of this is the CS technique, which is intended in principle for 'genuine' image measurement, i.e. tracing associative reactions.

The CS technique is distinguished by its simplicity and speed of application. The respondents are presented with a series of attributes, which are depicted on cards in personal interviews, or read out in telephone interviews. They are asked to say which ones describe the company 'well'. The attributes are then presented a second time, and the respondents are asked to say which ones describe it 'not at all'. The procedure can be shortened by presenting the attributes only once, and asking the respondents to place them into three categories: 'fits well', 'fits not at all', and 'no choice'.

The speed of this technique gives it a considerable advantage: it saves 25 per cent or more of the time needed for the more usual methods based on rating scales. At the same time, van Westendorp and van der Herberg point out that it is better suited to the 'all-or-nothing' character of genuine images than the usual rating techniques based on intervals or ranking. The procedure does not require the researchers to invent word pairs, which can create difficulties when bipolar-scales are used. There are no difficulties with the interpretation of a 'middle category'.

It should also be noted that the respondent is not obliged to make a choice. 'No choice' is a valid answer, and is used in the interpretation of results. The total number of choices made offers a direct indication of how meaningful the chosen attributes were for the respondents. It is easy to change the order in which attributes are presented to different respondents, thus avoiding sequential effects. Finally, multivariate analysis can be performed on results obtained with the CS technique. Correspondence analysis procedures are the most appropriate. In this way, it is possible to trace the dimensions that underlie the patterns of associations (van Westendorp and van der Herberg, 1984).

In most cases, two characteristics are derived from the CS results, namely, profiling and relative image value. Profiling is based on the total number of choices made. It shows how far the attributes have meaning for the respondents in relation to the company. A high level of profiling indicates the importance of the attribute. Provided that profiling has occurred, relative image value indicates the quality of the image.

Natural grouping (Research International)

At the beginning of section 3.5.2, various methods of measurement were discussed according to the degree of elaboration of the image. Unfortunately, one cannot always know in advance the subject's level of involvement with the object, nor can one know prior to measurement the way in which the image is stored in their memory. For the purposes of the natural grouping method, this is not necessary. The method combines elements of the structural method with elements of the implicit method, and it can be used to measure the total of all associations, features and conceptions evoked by the image object. Different respondents have images at different levels of elaboration, ranging from complex, elaborated meaning structures to overall general impressions.

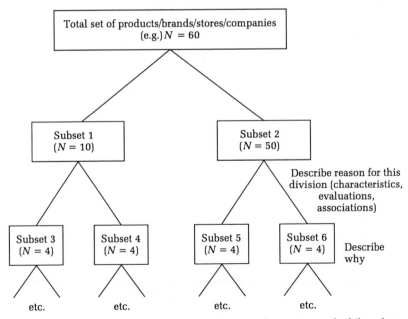

Figure 3.14 Tree structure of image objects for the natural grouping method (based on Verhallen, 1988)

The natural grouping method is described by Verhallen (1988). It involves presenting a large number of objects, up to a maximum of eighty, to the respondents, who are asked to sort them into two subsets. The respondents are also asked to state what criteria they have used in sorting, and to describe their subsets in their own words. The process is repeated until the respondents can make no further subdivisions. The method is illustrated in Figure 3.14 (p. 109).

An *n*-dimensional perceptual chart can be created from the data in the tree diagram by means of correspondence analysis. This chart would be comparable to the graph in Figure 3.5. The greatest advantage of this method is that it does not require prior knowledge of the level at which the image object is stored in the memory of the subject. Another advantage is that detailed information about the image object can be obtained from different target groups in a simple manner, using a computer if desired (Sikkel, 1991), which speeds the procedure. The researcher does not need to give any guidance, because the respondents themselves indicate the salient attributes.

A disadvantage of the method is that the amount of interpretation depends upon the extent to which the particular topics are important to the subjects. The spontaneous answers are sometimes lacking in detail.

The photosort method (FHV/BBDO)

Numerous sorting methods are used in image research. Another good example, in addition to those already discussed, is the photosort method developed by FHV/BBDO. This is a projective research technique for measuring images. It was developed as a result of dissatisfaction with existing methods of measurement. In the opinion of the FHV/BBDO researchers, many of the methods that have been discussed up to this point suffer from the disadvantage that they require the respondent to verbalize images. An image, however, is a non-verbal phenomenon, and it has been argued that it would be better to measure it by non-verbal methods. The photosort technique may offer a way of bringing less conscious, deep feelings and associations, which are difficult to verbalize, to the surface, by the use of photographs. These feelings could then be discussed. If non-verbal methods of measurement are used, respondents do not need to have a highly developed ability to put their feelings into words (Russell and Starkman, 1990). In addition, whole images remain more or less intact, since they are not split into attributes, as in the case of much of the image research which uses verbal techniques. The photosort method, which is a classical method developed further by the FHV/BBDO advertising agency, is a non-verbal method of measuring the affective components in a (corporate) image.

The photosort method uses photographs of human faces. The respondents give a judgement about an image object with the aid of the photographs. The photosort method is an indirect method of image measurement. Its advantage is that respondents are less inhibited in expressing their opinions.

This means that their emotions surface more clearly and visibly. Another advantage is that a face represents a totality of emotions. For each beholder, a face holds a complex whole, or Gestalt of emotions. From their earliest days, people learn to attach a wealth of significance to faces and their expressions.

The photographs used in the method must meet certain requirements. The set of photographs must represent all the emotional dimensions that are important to people when they make judgements about a company or a brand. The meaning of the photographs should be clear, so that the results can be interpreted in a satisfactory and unambiguous fashion. The set of photographs is revised from time to time, so that they do not become dated. As a result of its researches, FHV/BBDO has compiled a set of 130 photographs of different kinds of people. The distinctive characteristics or attributes of the photographs are determined during preliminary research. During the image study, the respondent is given a set of about 35 photographs relevant to the image object. Figure 3.15 shows a photograph with the meanings that it holds for people.

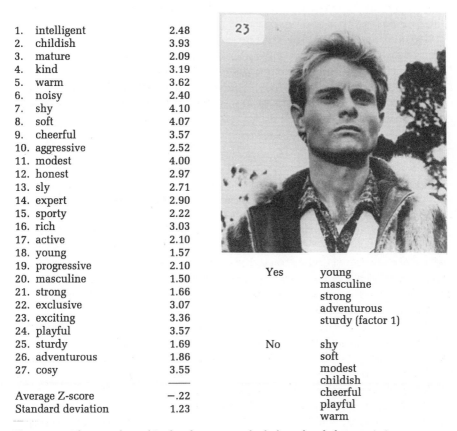

1.	intelligent	2.48
2.	childish	3.93
3.	mature	2.09
4.	kind	3.19
5.	warm	3.62
6.	noisy	2.40
7.	shy	4.10
8.	soft	4.07
9.	cheerful	3.57
10.	aggressive	2.52
11.	modest	4.00
12.	honest	2.97
13.	sly	2.71
14.	expert	2.90
15.	sporty	2.22
16.	rich	3.03
17.	active	2.10
18.	young	1.57
19.	progressive	2.10
20.	masculine	1.50
21.	strong	1.66
22.	exclusive	3.07
23.	exciting	3.36
24.	playful	3.57
25.	sturdy	1.69
26.	adventurous	1.86
27.	cosy	3.55

Average Z-score −.22
Standard deviation 1.23

Yes   young
      masculine
      strong
      adventurous
      sturdy (factor 1)

No   shy
      soft
      modest
      childish
      cheerful
      playful
      warm

Figure 3.15 Photograph used in the photosort method plus related characteristics

If the photosort method is to be used in quantitative image research, a sample of at least seventy-five respondents is desirable. This number must be increased in proportion to the number of target groups to be analyzed. The costs of photosort are otherwise relatively small, since administering the task does not take long. Respondents are observed through a one-way mirror, or recorded on video while they select and label the photographs that they consider appropriate to the image object.

When the photosort method is used in a qualitative study, it is important to know which photographs are associated with which objects. In qualitative studies, the photographs function primarily as 'pacemakers' in talking about things that are difficult to put into words.

According to Russell and Starkman (1990) respondents have no initial difficulty in making associations between objects and photographs. In the discussion that follows, respondents are extremely curious about the reasons behind their associations. When the subjects have chosen a photograph to go with an object, they are asked to give the reasons for their choice. They are also asked to say what, in their opinion, should be taken as illustrative of the image that the user has of the brand or company.

As mentioned above, the method can also be used for the purposes of a quantitative study. For each respondent, an affinity score is calculated: this is a measure of the affinity of the respondent with the person in the photograph. The final outcome of the photosort study is the description of an image object in terms of a set of interrelated attributes which together represent the Gestalt of a brand or a company.

3.6 Conclusions

The number of publications on corporate image has increased considerably in recent years. Initially, the emphasis in articles and other publications was on the importance to organizations of building a good reputation. It seems that the writers of these publications have more than accomplished their objective, since the subject has attracted great interest, not only among communication specialists, but also among senior management. Some have even said that they intend to add the corporate image to the company balance sheet, as a 'corporate asset' (Rock, 1984).

There is surprisingly little hard evidence in the literature to support the assumption that a positive company image is of great importance. However, there is a steady increase in the number of publications containing material that could help to form a basis for this claim. Usually, this material is implicit, although sometimes it is made explicit.

The most explicit material may be found in a publication by Fombrun and Shanley, who have carried out research into the relationship between corporate image and a wide range of demonstrable company achievements. However great the achievements of an organization, there is no guarantee that it will enjoy a good image. Explanations for this appear mainly in the writings of the 'analytic' group. Building on the ELM model developed by Petty and Cacioppo, they consider in greater detail the possible barriers to working through the different phases of individual information processing. The works of the writers discussed in section 3.4.2 contain material that implicitly supports the claim that a positive corporate image is of vital importance to an organization.

It is much to the credit of Poiesz, Verhallen and Pruyn, among others, that they have made further progress in developing both the concept and the operational application of (corporate) image, using the ELM model. The next stage, in my opinion, should be follow-up research aimed at identifying the conditions under which individuals most readily accept stimuli relating to the image object. One may hope that research of this kind will eventually lead to concrete tools for the construction of corporate identity programmes.

Before proceeding to the fourth chapter, which deals with theoretical bases for building successful corporate identity, a final comment may be made about applied image research. In this chapter, various methods which are in frequent use have been discussed. It should be clearly understood that the quality of image research is determined not only by the methods used by a given agency, but also by the quality of the questions formulated by the client company. The degree of detail in the question determines the degree of possible refinement in the answer.

Image research tailored to one company is obviously more expensive. Companies are not always inclined to pay that price. They often prefer to limit themselves to kinds of research in which they can participate free of charge, or at low cost. This often means taking part in research that will yield 'only' an overall impression. This is useful as a first step, but if the company requires further information about its reputation, then it must embark upon research in greater depth. This, of course, is inevitably more expensive.

Chapter 4

An effective corporate identity programme

In the following sections, several reference models will be discussed in turn; they are taken from advertising and from the public relations literature (4.2). This will be followed by a description of several, existing practical models which have been developed in the context of a more holistic corporate communication approach (4.3). After this comes a brief discussion of several corporate identity programme models which are described in the international literature (4.4). My own model will be presented (4.5) and elaborated upon with regard to the five core communication elements of a corporate identity policy programme (4.6).

4.1 Introduction

Corporate communication involves three focal responsibilities (see p. 22). The first of these is developing initiatives aimed at narrowing the gap between the company's desired image and its actual image. Second, common starting points must be established to enable organizations to flesh out a consistent profile of 'the company behind the brand'. The third element is the organization of communication; developing and implementing guidelines for the coordination of all internal and external communication, and to control and regulate communication in practice.

Although these three elements are closely related, they clearly involve many different activities, and it is not possible to devise one single plan which will cover them all. A corporate communication plan is usually related to a corporate image campaign. This means that it is a systematic, long-term approach in which all of the organization's communication activities (in both the broad and the narrow sense) are directed towards achieving a positive starting position (direct and indirect) with the target groups with which the company has a dependency relationship. In practice, there are various checklists, action plans and so forth which can be helpful in making the correct decisions in such situations. In the specialist literature, relevant material may be found primarily within the two basic disciplines of corporate communication, i.e. advertising and public relations. The applied nature of action plans makes it difficult to formulate one model that could be described as 'scientific'. However, the literature does offer models that do more than simply offer a list of possibly helpful points. Examples are the work of Bernstein (1986), Olins (1989) and Ind (1990).

4.2 Reference models

Most handbooks of marketing communication contain an implicit model according to which an 'ideal' framework for advertising and promotion can be constructed. An 'ideal' approach of this kind is described by Ray in his book *Advertising and Communication Management* (1982). The first task is to determine the general features of the item or issue to be communicated. The marketing objectives must then be established, and the total available communication budget divided between the different elements in the promotional mix. Ray's model is shown in Figure 4.1.

The procedure may be summarized as follows:

1. A situation analysis is performed in order to establish the company's strong and weak points, and to identify objectives, products, prices, consumers and business relations.
2. Marketing objectives are then determined.
3. The total communication budget for the campaign is established.
4. Resources are allocated to the different communication activities that will form part of the campaign. The different activities must be coordinated.
5. Specific decisions are taken with respect to putting the communication activities into operation. This involves establishing communication objectives, the positioning of communication, and choosing the message content and the media to be used.
6. The final form of the budgets is determined, and the control procedures for implementation are introduced.

The Dutch literature offers another model. In part 7 of their eight-part series *Het Merk* ('The Brand') (1990), Franzen and Holzhauer describe with the aid of a model how an ideal advertising unit should be developed. Unlike Ray's model, which is based primarily on internal company decisions, the approach adopted by Franzen and Holzhauer is based on the perspective of the external advertising agency. The structure of their model is shown in Figure 4.2.

The model has five main stages. First comes the situation analysis. At this stage, detailed attention must be paid both to the position of competitors and to the nature of the problem which gives rise to the subject matter of the communication. Second, a clear picture must be developed of the potential strengths and weaknesses of the source of the communication: who is the source, what are they offering, what demands are they making, and how has

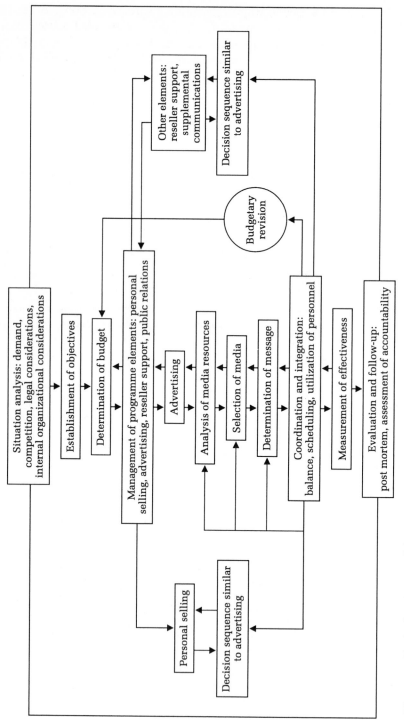

Figure 4.1 Ray's advertising model (1982)

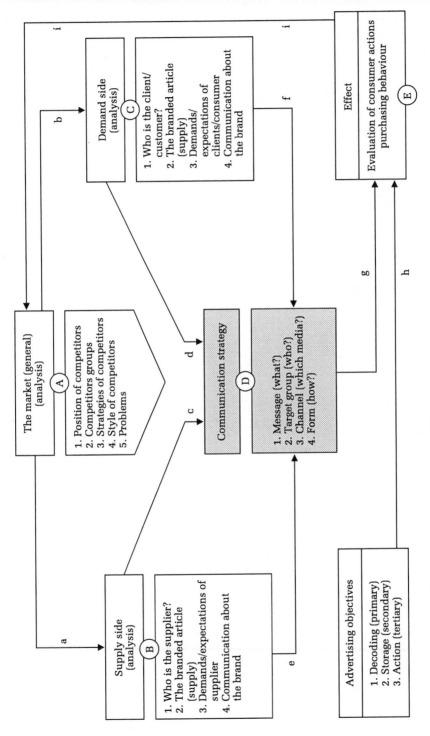

Figure 4.2 Franzen and Holzhauer's advertising model (1990)

communication been carried out up to the present? Third, more information should be gathered about the target group; the same questions should be asked as were used for gathering information about the source. Fourth, the communication strategy must be chosen, i.e. decisions must be made regarding what is to be communicated, to whom, through what medium, and how. Fifth, the effect of the advertising campaign should be assessed.

Models of this kind may also be found in the public relations literature. A good example is the four-step public relations process, developed by Cutlip, Center and Broom (1994). The same basic elements are present in their model (see Figure 4.3).

In good American tradition, the authors have formulated four concise sentences to describe the essential steps in their model. Step 1 is concerned with answering the question 'What's happening now?' This calls into action the 'intelligence' function of the company's PR department, i.e. research must be carried out to determine the nature of the problem which is the subject matter of communication. In step 2, an attempt is made to answer the question 'What should we do and why?' The answer should result in decisions relating to objectives and target groups, proposals for the application of resources, and selection of procedures for putting the whole plan into action. Step 3 is concerned with the implementation of the chosen strategy. It is summarized in

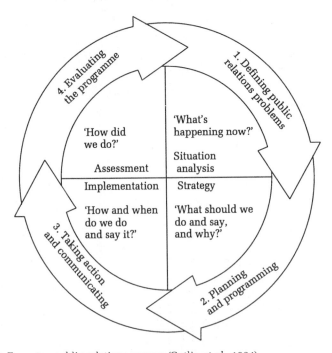

Figure 4.3 Four-step public relations process (Cutlip *et al.*, 1994)

the question 'How and when do we do and say it?' Finally, in step 4, an answer must be given to the evaluative question, 'How did we do?'

The models discussed up to this point may be regarded as representative of the range of models to be found in the literature. They are generally similar, and all of them can be broadly divided into three more or less distinguishable stages: preparation, implementation, and evaluation. It is noticeable that the literature offers most information about the preparation stage, whereas it seems that in practice the most effort and money are devoted to implementation. A similar contradiction exists in relation to the evaluating stage: this too receives a great deal of attention in the literature. In practice, however, little use seems to be made of knowledge that is available. There are pragmatic reasons for this, such as the expense of the research. It is also partly attributable to the 'demands' of science. Van Woerkum (1984) has remarked that too much of the evaluation work continues to be done on paper. While this may be scientifi- cally valuable, it is of little practical use. I will elaborate on these aspects in Chapter 5.

4.3 Practical models

In the past decade, many consultancies have begun to offer their services in the field of corporate communication. Among the first products they tried to sell were their own systems for developing and implementing corporate iden- tity/image campaigns. The larger consultancies have made their approaches available to a wider public by means of lectures and publications, which means that they can be discussed in this book.

The basic essentials of these practical models may be summarized as follows. When setting up a corporate communication programme, all the models involve the use of research data to make a comparison between the compa- ny's actual situation at moment X in respect of both identity and image, and the desired situation at moment Y. This is shown in Table 4.1.

In almost all practical models, this analysis forms the basis for devising the most realistic plan for reducing the gap between the actual situation and the desired situation in respect of identity and image. Almost all the practical models to be discussed here offer no more than a picture of the general approach adopted by the various consultancies. Necessary adjustments are, of course, made according to the problems identified within the organ- ization.

Table 4.1 From actual situation to desired situation

	Identity	*Image*
Moment X	Actual situation (1)	Actual situation (2)
Moment Y	Desired situation (3)	Desired situation (4)

4.3.1 Practical model 1: Thomas and Kleyn

The Thomas and Kleyn model starts with the 'research and analysis phase'. The data collected in this phase form the basis of a multistage plan which indicates what supplementary information needs to be collected about internal and external target groups, so that a communication strategy can be formulated. The following elements are always central to the communication strategy:

(a) What is the actual problem?
(b) What objectives must be realized?
(c) Target groups: these should be divided into competitors and allies on the supply side; the consumers of the company's goods or services (demand side); and the organizations that occupy an intermediate position between the parties on the demand side and those on the supply side.
(d) Message.
(e) Choice of media.
(f) Setting priorities, i.e. choosing the ways in which the target groups will be approached.
(g) Testing the choices at conceptual level by briefing creative specialists (pretesting).
(h) Actual creative phase following pretest.
(i) Carrying out the campaign.
(j) Evaluating the campaign.

4.3.2 Practical model 2: Blauw and Blank

Here too, the research basis of the corporate communication programme is emphasized. The model consists of twelve steps:

1. Inventories and research.
2. Proposition.
3. Identity.
4. Target groups and setting objectives.
5. Mission statement.
6. Positioning.
7. Strategy.
8. Tactics.
9. Budget planning.
10. Scenario.
11. Implementation.
12. Evaluation.

According to Blauw, positioning is the core of the image strategy (1994). An attempt is made by means of balanced positioning to build up an exclusive and distinctive image position in the memories of all members of the company's target groups. In the model developed by Blauw and Blank, considerable emphasis is placed upon the choice of a distinctive element to be included in the corporate communication message. This is less explicit in the other practical models. The emphasis chosen by Blauw and Blank is doubtless connected with the corporate advertising background of the driving forces within this agency.

4.3.3 Who does what?

In both models, a distinction is made between the strategy formulation phase and the implementation phase. The amount of attention paid to implementation varies according to the emphases that are present in the model used by the agency, and therefore in the advice that it offers. According to Blauw, most corporate communication consultants emphasize strategy formulation, whereas advertising agencies, which also work in this area, emphasize implementation. Since implementation claims the largest share of the corporate communication budget, it follows that advertising agencies are responsible for spending that share. It also means that more kinds of advisory agencies could – and perhaps should – be involved in the total corporate communication process.

4.4 International literature

Much space has been devoted in the international literature to the ideal way of setting up an effective corporate identity programme. With a few exceptions (e.g. Lux, 1986; Ind, 1990; Keller, 1990), the authors tend to list the aspects of the models that, in their opinion, are the most important, without explicitly describing a multiphase plan. Bernstein (1986) points out the importance of achieving 'clarity at home' before embarking on an external campaign. The 'company wheel' (Figure 4.4) can then be used as an aid in coordinating all the company's communication activities.

The American author Garbett (1988) advocates using the corporate mission as the starting point for a corporate identity programme. He believes that all communication output should be in line with 'the basic vision of the company'. Ind (1990) adopts a similar position by stressing the inseparability of identity and strategy. He bases his corporate identity model on Porter's five-force model (1985), in order to gain insight into 'the forces that drive competition within an industry'. Next, the 'corporate positioning' must be established. 'A company that has a clear generic strategy is likely to perform well. A company that does not pursue a clear strategy will tend to be stuck in the middle and thus perform poorly.' Ind was one of the first authors to consider the problems of

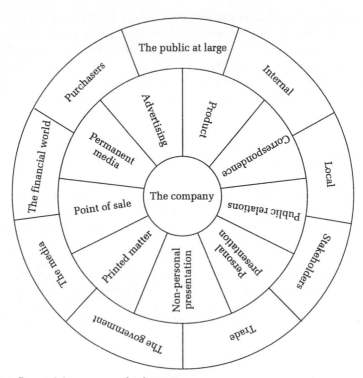

Figure 4.4 Bernstein's company wheel (1986)

implementing a corporate identity programme. He draws attention to the necessity of allowing a long running period for such a programme – 'sometimes it takes literally years to complete' – and the need for a 'work plan' and a 'manual', in which the priorities are stated. Finally, the 'ownership' of particular tasks in the field must be established.

Olins (1989), Napoles (1988) and Carter (1982), three well-known corporate design specialists, lay strong emphasis on the development of the visual aspects of company identity. Olins gives a detailed description of the multiphase plan that he uses to create a new identity for an organization. First, key internal and external figures are interviewed in order to gain a general orientation. These are followed first by a (visual) audit, then by a communication audit and a behavioural audit. When these analyses have been completed, the structure of the identity should be clear, and work can begin on the new visual identity. After testing of the concepts to be developed, implementation can start with a 'launch/introduction'.

In the German literature, multiphase corporate identity plans are offered by Lux (see Birkigt and Stadler, 1986) and Keller (1990). Central to both models are the analysis of the actual situation, and the determination of the desired situation. Keller describes five phases:

1. Preparation and problem definition.
2. Analysis of actual identity.
3. Design for desired identity and management system.
4. Concept production.
5. Implementation and performance assessment.

4.5 Corporate identity policy planning

Almost all the information that is needed to set up a corporate identity programme may be found in broad outline both in the theoretical models that exist within the various special areas of communication, and in the practical models for integrated corporate communication. The only disadvantage of the models is that they may overemphasize communication in the narrow sense. They also pay insufficient attention to the 'managerial' side of a corporate identity programme, in relation to both the strategy and the organization of communication.

I shall now proceed to describe a personal model for a corporate identity programme. This model builds on those described above, and is consistent with my broad conception of corporate identity as described in Chapter 2. In my view, a *corporate identity programme* may be described as *a systematic, long-term approach to an organization's total communication activities (in both the broad and the narrow sense). Its aim is the achievement by the company of a positive starting position (direct and indirect) in relation to the target groups with which the company has dependency relationships by improving familiarity with and appreciation of the organization's intentions.*

The term 'corporate identity policy programme' (CIPP) is used here to denote the framework for a corporate identity programme. The CIPP consists of ten important steps (see Figure 4.5).

4.5.1 Step 1: Problem analysis

In all the models discussed in sections 4.2 to 4.4, a constant theme is the problem that is to be the subject of communication. The emphasis is often placed on a partial problem being experienced by the company, e.g. a point of conflict with an external interested party, or a bottleneck causing a decrease in market share in a particular product/market combination. However, a CI programme requires a more holistic approach, because ways of shaping the identity of the organization must be considered. In concrete terms, this means that the distinctive characteristics of the organization as they appear in its behaviour must be identified. In other words, the 'problem' for a corporate identity programme is to find central characteristics of an organization that

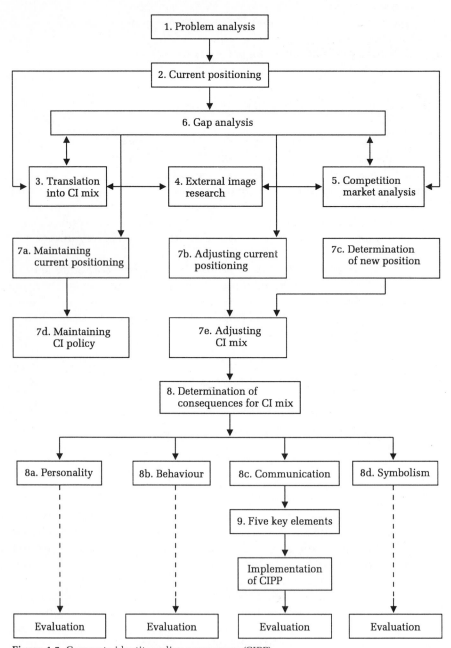

Figure 4.5 Corporate identity policy programme (CIPP)

appear to be the same over time and distinctive compared with other organizations in the branch.

4.5.2 Step 2: Determining the current positioning

Descriptions may be found in the academic literature of various methods that are helpful in identifying the distinguishing characteristics of products, especially of new products. Many of these techniques can also be used at organizational level. Examples are techniques used in image measurement, and other methods based on perception and preference. There are also methods that have been developed specifically for use at organizational level. Descriptions of these techniques are to be found mainly in strategic management publications. They include SWOT analysis (strengths, weaknesses, opportunities and threats), Porter's sector and industry analysis (1985) and other comparable techniques, e.g. that of Daems and Douma (1989). The various kinds of portfolio analysis can also be useful.

Before the decision is taken to embark on a new course, based on a new positioning, it is advisable to consider what course was chosen in the past, why it was chosen, and what are the changes in circumstances that would justify a change in strategy. Every line of strategy is – or should be – the logical consequence of setting priorities for choosing a competitive advantage. The techniques designed to achieve this are usually called 'positioning'. Ray states that 'Positioning is the combination of the appeal and the competitive considerations that can give a brand (company) a distinctive perception or position in the consumer's (target audience's) mind' (Ray, 1982).

Essentially, the task is to locate, with the aid of the various positioning techniques, three interrelated clusters containing information about the strong and weak points in the organization, the nature of the market or target groups, and the weak and strong points of the competition. Van Min (1990) illustrates this by means of a diagram (see Figure 4.6). The necessary information can be obtained from existing reports or by interviewing key figures inside or outside the organization.

The analysis of the target group can be carried out using theories and models taken from the field of consumer behaviour. An example would be the charting of individual and group factors that influence members of the target

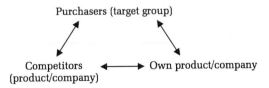

Purchasers (target group)

Competitors (product/company) ⟷ Own product/company

Figure 4.6 Van Min's positioning scheme (1990)

group when they make the final decision to purchase. It should be pointed out that there are differences between the way in which a purchasing decision is made by consumers and the way in which it is made by (industrial) organizations (see Kotler, 1988). In practice, use may be made of databases that are available worldwide, and which contain information about the general characteristics of target groups in relation to their media consumption patterns and their specific perceptions and preferences with respect to particular products.

An analysis of the organization can be carried out using one of the many SWOT variants, or an overall auditing technique, possibly in combination with audits of special functions. Various audits are available for quality management, marketing, finance, production and so forth.

A similarly large assortment of techniques is available for analysis of industry and/or competition (see Daems and Douma, 1989).

4.5.3 Step 3: Testing the translation of the current positioning into the CI mix

Once the (strategic) positioning of an organization has been determined, it is necessary to check whether the previously chosen distinguishing characteristics were translated in a consistent fashion into explicit forms of communication (behaviour) and implicit forms (communication and symbolism). This is important not only at organization level, but also at the level of the operating companies or functional areas. From the communication point of view, close attention should be paid to the way in which strategic positioning is translated into communicative profiling.

4.5.4 Step 4: Determining the image of the organization among the most important target groups

The way in which the company previously wished to present itself should be tested against its image among major stakeholders. This implies firstly that the company has a clear picture of the most important target groups upon which it depends and which it aims to influence, both for direct commercial reasons and because of other, less commercial, considerations. A method that is widely used to chart these groups is the well-known stakeholder analysis. Stakeholders are groups of people who may or may not be represented in organizations, and with which the organization has an interdependent relationship.

Second, it implies familiarity with the images that different elements within target groups have of the organization, and an understanding of these images. Most large organizations have recently had various image studies carried out for them, so the degree of agreement between recent positioning and 'the' image can be broadly assessed with the help of this material. However, there are many cases in which this information is not available, or if there are data to hand, they are not completely applicable to all the company's target groups. In these circumstances, it is still desirable to try to gain insight into the image of the organization among the various relevant target groups. There is little sense in making changes if it is not clear that they are necessary, or what they should be. Appropriate methods are discussed in Chapter 3.

4.5.5 Step 5: Determining CI mix of competitors

When deciding whether an organization should maintain its previous positioning, some thought must be given not only to internal changes and discrepancies between identity and image, but also to changes in the CI mix of competitors. A change of strategy on the part of a competitor will lead in the long term to a change in its approach to communication. A change of this kind should be carefully monitored, and constitutes grounds for a critical reappraisal of one's own CI approach.

When analyzing the CI approach of competitors, one is frequently inclined to reason from the outside in. This means that, initially, attention is directed primarily towards public information, in which indications may be found of changes of direction. Public information includes articles in newspapers or professional magazines, annual reports and other materials produced for financial target groups, advertisements, brochures, etc. If such public sources do not yield enough information, 'indirect' methods may be used, for example interviewing representatives of the company, or introducing an 'unattributable source'. However, people usually limit themselves to public sources.

4.5.6 Step 6: Gap analysis: should the CI mix be retained or renewed?

The current positioning should be determined and considered in relation to three core factors, namely the extent to which the positioning has been translated into the CI mix, the attitude of competitors, and the external image. This permits a balanced decision to be made as to whether the current positioning, and therefore the resultant CI mix, should be changed, and if so, to what extent. The analysis could, of course, lead to the conclusion that there is no reason for change. However, this will not happen often, since it is probable that if there were no reason for change, the exercise would not have been embarked upon in the first place.

The choice between adjusting parts of the positioning and renewing it completely – both of which necessitate changes to the CI mix – may be made according to the nature of the gap between the four factors mentioned above (see Figure 4.7).

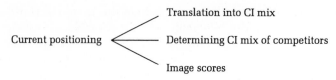

Figure 4.7 Gap analysis

There is no clear criterion for deciding whether the gaps are such that one or more of them must be closed. However, the analysis does show whether gaps exist, and where the particular problems lie. It is then much easier to identify the lines along which a solution should be sought.

4.5.7 Step 7: Outcomes of gap analysis

There are three possible conclusions to which gap analysis may lead. First, it may be that all is well and that no action is needed. Second, it may become apparent that certain parts of the CI mix do not fully answer the needs of the positioning. In this case, it is 'only' necessary to make adjustments in sub-areas. The third possible outcome of the gap analysis, and the one that has the most far-reaching implications, is that the strategic positioning as a whole needs to be adjusted or renewed, which of course sets different requirements for the CI mix.

4.5.8 Step 8: Implications for the CI mix

In the last of the situations just described, the (strategic) positioning must be transformed into (communicative) profiling. Profiling is the communicative translation of the selected (strategic) positioning in concepts that are appealing for the selected target audiences. This applies both to communication in the broad sense (behaviour of the organization) and to communication in the narrow sense (communication and symbolism of the organization). In order to make the communicative profiling broadly applicable to all relevant areas of communication, it is necessary to locate the so-called 'common starting points in communication'. This means identifying at an abstract level the central value or values that could be translated into PR or marketing terms, or carried over into other areas of communication. A hypothetical example may serve to clarify this approach. Let us suppose that a company has chosen a strategic positioning which allows the entrepreneur more freedom of action. This new positioning could be put into practice by introducing leasing and factoring, which would allow the entrepreneurs to rid themselves of certain tasks. This would be a demonstrable change. The central theme of communication within the various market areas can only be presented consistently if there is clear agreement on how the term 'increased freedom of action', which is capable of

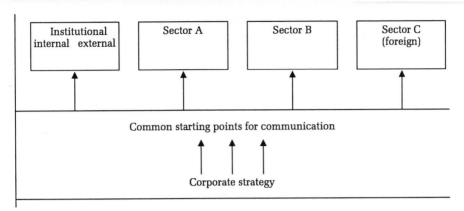

Figure 4.8 Definition of common starting points for all organizational communication

different interpretations, should in fact be translated into the various forms of communication used by the company.

In order to allow some degree of freedom for communication within the various markets, it is useful to specify a certain bandwidth (common starting points for communication) within which communication must operate. This means specifying expectations regarding desired knowledge, attitude (what feelings are to be evoked about it) and the behaviour that one wishes to stimulate. An appropriate story will, of course, be tailored to suit each target group, but in essence all the stories should be the same. Figure 4.8 illustrates this situation for an imaginary organization.

4.5.9 Step 9: Corporate identity policy programme: five communication elements

When the common starting points for all areas of communication have been defined, the corporate identity programme can be constructed. Broadly speaking, the issues that are discussed in the academic literature and those discussed in practical publications are the same. Briefly, there is always an internal and external analysis, following which the strategy is determined; then, in the implementation phase, the message concept is defined, media are chosen, and the general organization of the project is decided upon. In the concluding phase, all writers stress the need for evaluation, i.e. assessment of the extent to which the objectives have been fulfilled.

It is clear from the work of, for example, van Woerkum (1984), that such programmes should be regarded not as traditional multiphase plans, but rather as iterative search processes. Van Woerkum describes what he calls the cognitive path (i.e. gathering knowledge) and the choice path (making choices) in relation to making decisions about programming communication activities. He says that the cognitive path supplies understanding, while the choice path moves us towards decisions; in practice, there is continuous two-way movement, leading to increased understanding and to decisions becoming more concrete (see van Woerkum, 1984).

Van Woerkum's remarks relate in principle to the systematic preparation of a campaign. However, there are at least two essential differences between a corporate identity programme and a multiphase campaign plan. First, a corporate identity programme involves paying attention to communication in both the broad sense and the narrow sense. Second, it is concerned not with one campaign or modality, but with the total communication of an organization as a result of a change in positioning. Once the common starting points for communication have been established, several multiphase plans must be constructed at the same time. This involves internal communication and all forms of external communication used by the organization.

For practical reasons, this fourth chapter does not deal with which points should be considered for each element of the communication mix. Instead, a line of argument will be constructed for each of the five core elements in communication, i.e. objectives, target groups, message, channels, and organization of communication. The general arguments will be valid also for the components of these elements.

The tenth and final step will now be described, following which a more detailed discussion will be presented of the factors that influence the making of decisions about the five core elements of a corporate identity policy programme.

4.5.10 Step 10: Evaluation

It is often difficult to quantify the contribution that communication makes towards realizing the objectives of an organization. One important reason for this is the lack of a standard procedure for automatic measurement. This does not mean that it would be a simple matter to determine whether the objectives have been met, although it is by no means impossible.

Both process and product evaluations can be adapted for measuring a CIPP programme. A process evaluation is the evaluation, by means of theoretically derived standard protocols, of internal processes during the preparation and implementation phases. A product evaluation is aimed at determining whether the communication objectives *vis-à-vis* the target group have been met. This may be analyzed in terms of changes in knowledge, attitude and behavioural intentions. Cutlip, Center and Broom (1994) have summarized evaluation criteria for the three different phases (preparation, implementation and impact) in a diagram which is reproduced in Figure 4.9.

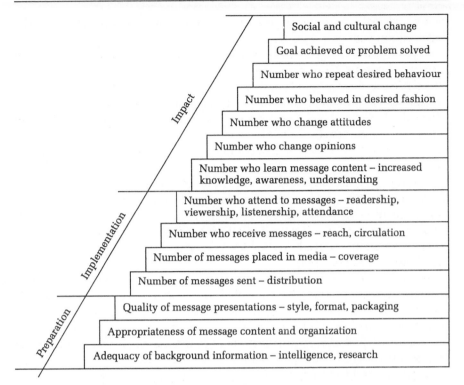

Figure 4.9 Criteria for evaluating corporate identity programmes at different stages (Cutlip *et al.*, 1994)

4.6 Five core communication elements in a corporate identity programme

4.6.1 Determining communication objectives

Everyone who has had experience of administration, even if it was 'only' managing the local sports team, knows how difficult it is to establish objectives. Nevertheless, some clarity must be achieved about the organization's preferences before objectives can be set for communication. If those responsible for communication are involved from the beginning in defining the goals of the organization, they will be able to advise on the feasibility or otherwise of realizing the objectives, as far as communication is concerned. This is the 'mirror function' of communication (see Chapter 1).

Generally speaking, an objective of an organization is relatively abstract, whereas a communication objective must be as concrete as possible. There is a strict hierarchical relationship between the two kinds of objectives. The communication objective is always derived from the objective of the organization (van den Ban, 1982).

Communication objectives are usually divided into cognitive, affective and conative elements. Grunig and Hunt (1984) refer to this as the nature of the effect. Ideally, there would be a domino effect (see Figure 4.10).

This threefold division offers an extremely suitable starting point for setting objectives for a corporate identity programme. In practice, however, the realization of communication objectives is much more complex. Kotler (1988) provides a helpful overview of the various theoretical positions on the hierarchy of effects.

Controversy exists as to whether the traditional stages shown in the domino model accurately represent the stages through which a target group must pass before reaching the final stage. Van Raaij was one of the first to suggest in the academic literature that the traditional order might be changed; he suggests that attitude should precede knowledge as a focus of interest (primary affective reactions) (van Raaij, 1984).

The order in which cognitive, affective and conative phases are placed strongly influences the way in which the communication campaign is constructed. The 'co-orientation model' developed by McLeod and Chaffee (1973) can be helpful in making the final choice of communication objectives (see Figure 4.11). Working from the point of view of the organization, the model can be used to gain an understanding of 'perceptual gaps' between the organization and its target groups.

The model starts with the definition of object K as seen by the organization. This sounds simple, but in practice it can be difficult, because of the many internal perceptions of K. However, once the view of the organization has been established, suppositions must be formulated about the target group's perceptions of K. If this is done behind a desk, the result could be totally inaccurate. To gain more information about reactions within the target group, it is useful

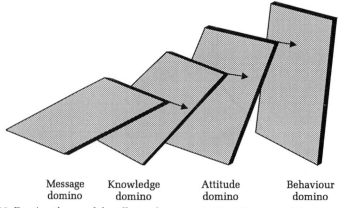

| Message domino | Knowledge domino | Attitude domino | Behaviour domino |

Figure 4.10 Domino theory of the effects of communication (Grunig and Hunt, 1984)

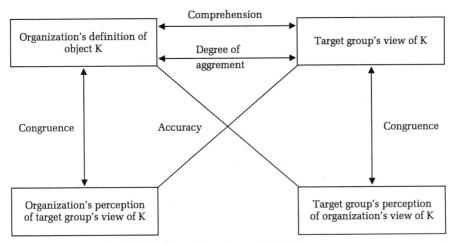

Figure 4.11 McLeod and Chaffee's co-orientation model (1973)

to ask members of the group directly what they think about K, and how they imagine that the organization perceives it. This material yields greater understanding of the various perceptual gaps. McLeod and Chaffee distinguish four possible problems: lack of congruence, lack of accuracy, lack of comprehension, and lack of agreement on how the situation should be defined.

Congruence is the level of agreement on the degree to which one person believes that he or she thinks the same about an object as another person. Accuracy is the degree of precision of the beliefs on both sides. Understanding is the level of agreement between the two perceptions. Agreement is the degree of identity between the evaluations.

Communication objectives can only be established if there is some understanding both of the situation within the organization and of that within the target group. The co-orientation model, for example, may have been used to gain this understanding. If the study indicates that the problem is mainly one of accuracy, then forms of communication aimed at increasing comprehension should be the focus of effort.

> The recipients of the message do not necessarily agree with the message or plan to do anything about it. They simply remember what you said. Targets know the other's beliefs and evaluations. They do not necessarily hold the same beliefs and evaluations, however. (Grunig and Hunt, 1984)

If the problem seems to be one of understanding, then an effort must be made to ensure that the message is accepted: 'The target not only retains the message explaining the other's beliefs, but accepts the message as its beliefs about reality.'

Finally, if the problem is that there is a perceptual gap between evaluations on each side (agreement), a change in attitude is required.

4.6.2 Selection of target groups

A target group can be simply described as a group in relation to which an organization wishes to realize an objective. In other words, one must know what the objective is before deciding on the target group. It often happens in practice that an organization has to adapt its objective according to the communication problems presented by the target group. This means in effect that there is interaction between the choice of objectives and the choice of target groups.

When target groups are being chosen for communication, two tasks must be carried out. First, a distinction should be made between more important and less important target groups. Second, those characteristics of the selected target groups that are important for communication purposes should be studied. Greater understanding of the target group can be gained by researching the socioeconomic characteristics of its members, their motivation, their perception of the most important features of the organization, their knowledge of the company and their attitude towards it, and some general factors such as lifestyle and media consumption patterns.

Segmentation based on dependency relationships

Target groups can be classified as primary or secondary according to the strength of the organization's dependency relationships with similar groups. Grunig and Hunt (1984) have taken this as the starting point for their 'linkage model'. The model (target group classification) is based on the resource dependency perspective model developed by Pfeffer and Salancik (1978). Groups are classified according to the degree to which the organization has a dependency relationship (linkage) with them in respect of access to crucial resources. This is represented in the diagram in Figure 4.12.

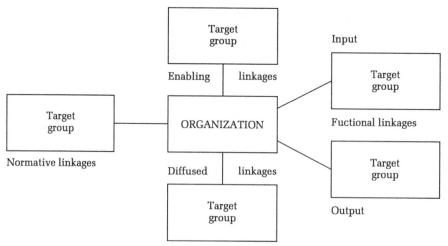

Figure 4.12 Linkage model (Grunig and Hunt, 1984)

Enabling linkages are linkages with target groups which create necessary conditions for the company to operate, e.g. shareholders, financial backers, institutions which generate knowledge. Functional linkages are linkages with groups which deal with the input and output of the organization's primary process. They should be divided into input target groups (employees) and output target groups (purchasers). The term 'normative linkages' is used by Grunig and Hunt to mean organizations of competitors or allies. These may be competitors within the same branch, or allies sharing the same interest. Finally, there are diffused linkages, which are 'linkages that cannot clearly be identified by membership in formal organizations' (Grunig and Hunt, 1984).

The five main target groups identified in this way must be analyzed for the degree to which they are involved with the objectives of the organization, and are therefore inclined to permit access to their 'safeguarded' resources, which are of vital importance to the organization. Four out of the five target groups identified by Grunig and Hunt are not of direct interest to the organization from this point of view. One category of target groups is of direct commercial interest, namely the functional output linkage groups. These are often referred to in the literature as the marketing target group. Much has been written on the subject, especially in the marketing literature, under the heading 'market segmentation'. For the purposes of corporate communication, it must be clearly understood that if relevant background data are to be gathered for all five kinds of target group, different kinds of information must be collected, so that an adequate response may be made to the needs of each target group. According to van Raaij and Verhallen (1994), three kinds of characteristics of marketing target groups must be studied: general, domain-specific and brand-specific (see Table 4.2).

As for the four other categories of target groups, which are better described as public relations target groups, information is needed about three factors:

Table 4.2 Division of marketing target groups (van Raaij and Verhallen, 1994)

	Objective	Subjective
A. *Brand-specific* (use of brand)	Brand loyalty (behaviour) Frequency of use Actions	Brand loyalty (attitude) Preference Evaluation Purchasing intentions
B. *Domain-specific* (use of product class)	Frequency of use Substitution Complementing Behaviour	Interests, opinions Perception Attitude Domain-specific value
C. *General* (behaviour patterns; personality characteristics)	Income Age Education Place of residence Behaviour patterns	Lifestyle Personality General values

problem recognition, constraint recognition and level of involvement (Grunig and Hunt, 1984).

Segmentation of functional output linkages

From a marketing point of view, the characteristics of target groups can be classified into three categories. First there are the brand-specific characteristics of the group: these relate to the way in which the target group uses the brand. An example would be brand loyalty to a particular malt beer, and frequency of consumption. Second, there are the product-class-specific characteristics. These self-evidently relate to the use of goods in a certain product class, e.g. the consumption of alcohol-free beer. Finally, there are the general characteristics of the target group, e.g. education, marital status, lifestyle.

The segmentation process usually starts at the product-class-specific level. Van Raaij advocates taking an initial look at product-class-related personal characteristics in relation to specific behaviours related to that product class. This information should then be compared with the general characteristics of the target group (socioeconomic variables), the main product-class-specific categories, and the brand-specific characteristics. This is shown in the diagram in Table 4.2.

Van Raaij's analysis should form the basis for segmentation of the target group. In addition, some practical points made by Kotler (1988), among others, should be borne in mind. Kotler mentions four important factors: measurability, substantiality, accessibility and actionability (Kotler, 1988).

Segmentation of the four remaining linkages

The method described by van Raaij and Verhallen may indeed be applied if there is a direct interest at stake and if one wishes to establish interaction with a target group. However, the approach is much less useful if the interest is indirect, and if the linkage is long term rather than short term. For the non-functional output linkages, therefore, Grunig and Hunt emphasize the importance of dividing the target groups according to their degree of involvement with the organization or with the specific object about which the organization wishes to communicate. They also stress the need to pay attention to 'problem recognition' and 'constraint recognition'. If a simple bipolar division is made according to high or low involvement, the result is a matrix containing eight kinds of target group (Table 4.3).

4.6.3 Message formulation

'If the message is outstanding, other parts of the marketing communication will be multiplied in their effects' (Ray, 1982). This probably holds good not only for marketing communication, but also for all other areas of communication. In the final choice of a 'concept' for the message, two closely related

Table 4.3 Classification of target groups (Grunig and Hunt, 1984)

	High involvement (HI)		Low involvement (LI)	
	Behaviour type	Type of public	Behaviour type	Type of public
Problem-facing behaviour (PF): High problem recognition, low constraint recognition	HIPF	Active	LIPF	Aware/active
Constrained behaviour (CE): High problem recognition, high constraint recognition	HICB	Aware/active	LICB	Latent/aware
Routine behaviour (RB): Low problem recognition, low constraint recognition	HIRB	Active (reinforcing)	LIRB	None/latent
Fatalistic behaviour (FB): Low problem recognition, high constraint recognition	HIFB	Latent	LIFB	None

questions are always involved. The first is 'What should be said?' (promise, proposition, evidence). The second is, 'How should it be said?' (style of writing, form, tone, etc.). The most important information needed for filling in the PPT formula (promise, prove, tone) is to be found in the choices that were made when objectives were being set and target groups chosen. The transformation of this information into an appealing and distinctive message depends on the skills and artistic talents of the creative members of the communication team. In the words of Geursen (1990):

> Conceptualisation is a process in which many things happen at the same time. The inert words of the proposition are brought to life and intensified. Abstract language is made concrete. Ratios are given an emotional wrapping. Last but not least, an idea is added to the brand or product. The message gains a third dimension.

The following five points should be kept in mind during the briefing of the creative communication specialists, in a 'copy platform':

1. Market information (condensed into main points).
2. Essential information on competitors, relating both to general strategy and to communication strategy.
3. A short description of the central promises to be used in the campaign, and the evidence to be used, preferably linked to the main current of the creative strategy to be chosen.
4. Information on the tone to be used: should the message be emotional or rational? (See Rossiter and Percy, 1987.) Should a competitive tone be used, or would it be out of place? What limits are there on formulating a firm message and making a credible impression?
5. An initial set of priorities for choice of format.

Table 4.4 Ray's creative strategy (Ray, 1982)

Briefing	Decision what	Choice how	Test expression
Target market	Promise	Style	• Fits strategy
			• Fits target segment
Appeal	Evidence	Tone	• Appropriate for communication mix
Competition		Shape	• Leverage
			• Simplicity
Tone of voice		Humour	• Specificity
Rationale			• Mass communication potential
			• Resistance to counter attack
			• Durability

Ray (1982) suggests that once a message concept has been developed, it should be tested by applying the following questions (see Table 4.4):

- Is it consonant with the corporate strategy?
- Does it suit the nature of the target group?
- Does it fit into the total communication policy?
- Does the idea have a 'leverage effect' ('multiplier effect')?
- Is the concept too complicated?
- Is the concept distinctive enough?
- Could the concept be used in the different forms of mass communication?
- Is there a danger of being ridiculed by competitors?
- Will it last long enough?

4.6.4 Media selection and planning

The choices made with respect to objective, target group, message concept and ultimate means of distribution, or media, are inextricably interlinked.

The choice of media is at least as important as the setting of priorities in the other areas of the CI programme. McLuhan's slogan 'The medium is the message' may be out of date, but it remains a splendid exaggeration of a problem that is often underestimated, namely the choice of the most suitable media mix. An indication of the importance of the media strategy is the fact that about 90 per cent of the total communication budget (with the exception of personal sales figures) is devoted to the use of all kinds of media.

A crucial factor in the choice of media is the fact that 'the medium or media selected must be able to convey the creative content of the campaign in a way that meets the communication objectives' (Rossiter and Percy, 1987). Depending on which phase the product (or the organization, or organizational design) has currently reached, something may be learned from the product lifecycle approach, as promoted in the communication field in the 1970s by Rogers and Shoemaker. In broad outline, this means that, initially, a mass media campaign should be used to create 'awareness'. Subsequently, it should be refined into all kinds of interpersonal communication, with different emphases for different adoption categories. The aim is to convince, i.e. to bring about changes in attitude and/or behaviour.

In general, media are chosen according to four criteria: budget, range, frequency of exposure, and continuity. Rossiter and Percy (1987) have illustrated this by means of their 'media balloon' (Figure 4.13).

> If the balloon is tied off (representing a fixed media budget), the manager cannot make one sphere larger without squeezing at least one of the other two. However, if the manager is allowed to inflate the balloon to any necessary size (representing an open media budget) then all three spheres will enlarge and a more comprehensive media plan will result. (Rossiter and Percy, 1987)

Increasing use can be made of computer models in the development of

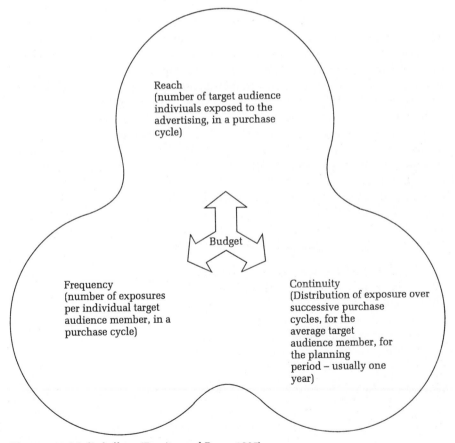

Figure 4.13 Media balloon (Rossiter and Percy, 1987)

media strategy. Examples are MEDICA (Little and Lodish, 1966), and ADMOD (Lancaster and Katz, 1989). The disadvantage of these models is that they were designed primarily for advertising, and are therefore more easily adapted to the needs of that sector. They are particularly suited to the making of mass media decisions in an advertising campaign.

Minekus (1989) has addressed another problem which arises in connection with the choice of the best communication media:

> The most difficult task is to establish what combination of media will give the largest synergetic return in a particular case: when does $1 + 1 + 1$ equal 2.7, and when does it equal 3.3? When is the best solution advertising + PR + direct marketing communication, and when is it direct marketing + sponsoring + product placement? We may be able at present to answer this question intuitively, but we certainly cannot answer it scientifically. There is, quite simply, very little systematic knowledge about the effects of communication, even of the effects of a single objective in a single medium, let alone the synergetic effect of media amongst themselves.

Rinnooy Kan and Knaap (1988) have suggested in their publication *Marketing Communication* that this problem might be solved by assessing the available media on a number of features, and then deciding to what extent their weak and strong points can complement or compensate each other to give a synergetic mix. This evaluation should, of course, be performed on a continuous basis, with reference to the target group and the objectives.

Minekus offers the following list of twelve criteria for assessing media in particular cases. They include, as one would expect, the core concepts of classic media planning. In addition, the topical term *Umfeld* ('surrounding field' or media environment) is included: this refers to all editorial articles, programmes or other forms of expression that can be perceived at virtually the same time as a given communication expression (Knecht and Stoelinga, 1988). This list is probably not exhaustive, and every criterion may not be suited to each problem. It has proved useful in practice to make the evaluations using a five-point scale (e.g. 'very suitable' to 'very unsuitable').

1. Capacity for emotional communication.
2. Capacity for cognitive communication.
3. Conative activity.
4. Bilaterality.
5. Coerciveness/probability of confrontation.
6. Controllability of time/place/frequency.
7. Range/selectivity.
8. *Umfeld*/media environment.
9. Degree of control.
10. Surprise factor.
11. Internal/external pacing.
12. Open/closed.

4.6.5 *Organizing communication*

As stated in section 4.1, the organization of communication consists in the establishment of starting points for coordinating all internal and external communication output and for controlling and managing operations in the field of communication.

These matters will be discussed further in Chapter 5.

4.7 Conclusions

In this chapter, an attempt has been made to clarify the issues that are important for the formulation of an effective corporate identity policy programme. It appears from the literature that disciplines that until recently, focused on developments within their own boundaries, in fact exhibit considerable similarities of approach, and produce similar normative protocols. It is to the credit of corporate communication experts that they have bridged the traditional gaps between, for example, public relations and marketing communication. Working from the position that the total communication effort must serve the corporate strategy, the importance of which is paramount, they found it natural to link the two disciplines. This does not mean, however, that it is a simple matter to put such an ideal approach into practice.

I would contend that the following problems lie behind the gap between the models for corporate identity policy plans and the day-to-day reality of corporate communication practice. First, there are not enough practical tools for aligning the activities of the various internal and external communication specialists. The 'planning models' which have now been available for some time (van Woerkum, 1984; van Riel, 1986) should be extended to provide 'integral communication planning systems' (van Riel and van Dijk, 1991).

Second, methods are lacking for the alignment of communication in the narrow sense (expressions produced within communication modalities) and communication in the broad sense (the behaviour of the company).

A third problem is the fragmented state of knowledge about the steps involved in changing the 'personality' and 'behaviour' elements in the CI mix. The corporate communication specialist reaches a 'no-man's land' between their original area of expertise in communication and the broad field of strategic management, organization and marketing. Much effort will have to be devoted in the near future to linking up the content of these last three disciplines, and to developing the combined expertise from all elements of the communications mix into a consistent whole. The growing acceptance of corporate communication as a discipline and the increasing enthusiasm for the holistic approach to corporate identity lead one to anticipate progress in this field.

Chapter 5

Organizing corporate communication

This chapter deals with four interrelated themes central to the organization of corporate communication. The first is the location of the communication function (tasks, communication departments, hierarchical position within the organization, etc.). The second is the organization of the communication process (planning of all forms of communication, integrating communication in the commercial cycle, etc.). The third is the coordination of both the functions of and the procedures relating to all communication activities. Finally the chapter examines the establishment of critical success factors for producing effective and efficient organization of communication.

5.1 Introduction

Most definitions of corporate communication start with the pursuit of synergy as the most important issue affecting the way in which organizations deploy communication as a management tool. Blauw speaks of the 'integrated approach to all expressions' (Blauw, 1994); my own description of corporate communication emphasizes the need for 'harmonization of all forms of internal and external communication' (van Riel, 1990).

In this context, it is clear that there is a growing need for knowledge about how to give form to the pursuit of coordination and integration in communication. This means gaining insight into efficient and effective decision-making procedures and related organizational structures, in order to make successful linkages between the organization' s strategy and the structure and implementation of the overall communication strategy.

Until now, 'organization of communication' as a subject has received little attention in the literature. The few publications dedicated to the topic deal mainly with the organization of communication campaigns. Examples are the many planning models, operational plans, checklists and so forth which were discussed in Chapter 4. Compared with theoretical developments in the fields of corporate image and corporate identity, academic knowledge in this area is relatively limited, with some exceptions (Grunig, 1989; Adema, van Riel and Wierenga, 1993; and van Riel, 1994).

142

Results of these studies and discussions with practising specialists have resulted in a deeper understanding of the specific problems presented by the organization of communication, and of possible lines along which solutions might be sought.

The organization of communication has affinities with theory formation in strategic management (van den Bosch, 1989), and in organizational science. In the strategic management literature, an initial link may be made with the literature on planning; also with 'implementation theory' (see e.g. Cozijnsen and Vrakking, 1986) in the field of organizational science.

In practice, a number of interesting developments are taking place which could at least serve as examples to other companies. They could also be a source of inspiration for scientific research in the coming years. The coordination techniques applied by several companies are described later in this chapter. Other practical developments which are also of great interest include the familiar house style manuals and the more recent use of databases for issuing press information. These databases contain an outline of the position of the organization on a number of topical questions, plus data on whom has been given this information and in what detail, and what (external) publications have resulted from this.

As a subject, the organization of communication consists of four interrelated themes. The first is the location of the communication function within organizations, i.e. what are the tasks that properly belong to communication and what organizational structures or departments should be created to implement them? The second is the organization of the communication process, i.e. the planning of all forms of internal and external communication used by the organization. The third is the coordination of both the function and the process of all communication activities in a company. The fourth is the establishment of critical success factors for effective and efficient organization of both the communication function and the communication process.

5.2 Organization of the communication function

Everyone in an organization engages in communication. For pragmatic reasons, a decision is usually taken early in the life of an organization to engage *professionals* who will specialize in a particular communication task. As we saw in Chapter 1, there are, roughly speaking, three main kinds of communication: management communication, the various forms of organizational communication (usually operating under the 'flag' of public relations), and marketing communication. The many forms of organizational communication can be placed on the organizational chart in different ways. Figure 1.1 (p. 4) shows how this might look. However, in most organizations, a dominant position is still reserved – and rightly so – for public relations. This chapter will therefore initially address the situation in which the communication function is performed by a centrally operating PR department.

This will be followed by discussion of the other 'traditional' communication function, namely marketing communication. The subsequent section is concerned with 'new' forms of communication, and how they could be incorporated into other (non-marketing) functional management areas within the structure of the organization.

5.2.1 PR and marketing communication: the organization chart

Public relations can be built into the organizational scheme in different ways. The positioning of this department within the organization depends, of course, on the weight of the tasks assigned to it. De Roode (1986) identifies five main tasks:

1. Determining the position of the organization in society.
2. Formulating and establishing PR policy.
3. Selecting and developing PR strategy.
4. Constructing and implementing an internal and external PR programme (external presentation of the organization, establishing and monitoring media channels, personal representation, sponsorship, etc.).
5. Evaluation of PR activities (monitoring etc.).

In practice, public relations encompasses a great variety of tasks, and therefore of organizational forms. However, it seems to be generally accepted that pubic relations is a staff function. In the management literature, a staff function is a function where the manager has no direct executive power over the primary process or responsibility for it, but fulfils an advisory role, based on specific expertise, to all departments within the organization.

Rigidly speaking the distinction between line and staff managers is 'giving orders versus giving advice'. More positively expressed, this means that the job of a PR staff officer is to advise staff managers and to support and assist line managers. This implies a loyal, service-oriented attitude on the part of PR managers, but it also means that the PR manager should have a privileged position with respect to the flow of information: they must have access to all communication channels which connect the organization as a system with external and internal subsystems.

In organizations in which public relations is seen as communication output only, the function becomes routine and highly structured. Practitioners work primarily as communications technicians in these settings, dealing with 'programmed decisions', such as issuing weekly news briefings and publishing the monthly employee newsletter. When public relations operates in the realm of programmed decisions, it is seen as part of organizational routine and overheads. On the other hand, when it participates in 'non-programmed' decisions, it will be an important player in achieving organizational goals and contributing to the bottom line (Cutlip, Center and Broom, 1994).

Marketing communication is an integral part of the functional management area of marketing. Unlike public relations, it is usually a typical line function. The main difference here from a staff function is that line managers are considered completely responsible for their role in carrying out the primary process. As with public relations, the ideal position in the organizational scheme depends on the nature and scale of the tasks that the department is expected to perform. In addition to formulating and fixing the policy for marketing communication, and developing and implementing the marketing communication strategy, the department must evaluate the effects of marketing communication. According to Kotler (1988), the communications manager deals with mass media communication and promotion, and specializes in 'the development of messages, media and publicity'.

There is no ideal way of organizing the marketing (communication) function. According to Verhage and Cunningham (1989), there are only four types of marketing organizations. Within these four types, marketing communication appears either as a separate specialization or as an integrated part of the total set of tasks of the marketing manager. The four organizational forms of the marketing function may be described as follows:

1. *The functional organization* This is the simplest structure, often used by young companies. Within the department there are functional specialists who are responsible for product planning, advertising, sales, etc. Since nobody has exclusive responsibility for a product or market, this structure does not promote coordination.
2. *The market-oriented organization* The company groups its marketing department around the markets in which it is active, or around industrial purchasers who account for a large proportion of sales. The marketing manager, who must serve the specific needs of purchasers, is supported by specialists in subdisciplines.
3. *The product-oriented organization* In this structure, one employee is responsible for all activities connected with the marketing strategy for a particular product. While this product manager carries the responsibility for the success of the product, they lack the line authority needed to make the decisions basic to this success.
4. *The matrix organization* This is in fact a combination of the three organizational forms just described. In this case, the company first divides its marketing department according to the specific markets that it wishes to serve. Each market has its own manager, whose task is to plan and coordinate marketing activities for their own market segment. Using this division as a basis, the company then proceeds to apply the traditional system of product management. As a result, the functional specialist reports not

only to the manager responsible for that market, but also to a brand manager or marketing manager. The advantage of a matrix organization is that equal attention can be paid to products and to market segments. The disadvantage is the high cost of the structure; this is a result of the large number of specialists needed. It means also that there are many links in the decision-making chain.

5.2.2 Communication in other functional management areas

Communication is no longer restricted to PR and/or marketing communication. Other functional management areas are becoming increasingly aware of the importance of communication. In human resource management, communication is used as one of the management tools for recruiting and retaining valuable personnel. In addition to labour market communication, the HRM manager is also concerned with internal motivation programmes, aimed at raising the quality of the primary work process. Financial management deals with communication directed towards obtaining, retaining and sometimes disposing of funds which are vital to the survival of the company. In addition to external investor relations, the financial manager also uses communication for internal objectives, such as encouraging (prompt) input of correct data for internal control purposes, or promoting financial self-control. The production management field uses communication for improving contacts with suppliers, and for 'bench working' with co-producers. Within their own organization, production managers are also involved in quality programmes and, more recently, environmental communication.

The broad acceptance of the value of communication as an instrument within all functional management areas implies that the financial manager, the HRM manager and others must accept full responsibility for the communication function. It does not, however, imply complete decentralization of the communication function to the various parts of the company. There is almost always a PR department at organizational level, which can support other communication units operating within line functions.

In addition, such a view of the role of communication has three implications. First, it implies a conscious inclusion of the professional use of communication among the tools of line managers in the functional management areas. The line manager does not have to be a communication specialist, but he does need to know enough about communication as a tool to be able to direct and advise those affected by its use, whether inside or outside the company. Second, a corporate or overall communication policy needs to be carried out at a central level, i.e. at the level of company management, so that the communication activities of the different parts of the company can be coordinated. The third factor is related: it concerns awareness of the consequences of one's 'individual' communication input for the 'overall' communication policy.

5.3 Organizing the communication process

5.3.1 The ITO model

The organization of the communication process can be described as the planning of all forms of internal and external communication used by the organization. In systems terminology, the communication process can be divided into three sequential phases: the input phase, the throughput phase, and the output phase. The input phase is concerned with the preparation of communication activities (analysis and strategy); the throughput phase is concerned with the execution of the plans adopted (decision-making and implementation); the output phase deals with the final expressions of all the forms of communication, and their effects on the target group.

This process may be represented by the ITO model (input, throughput and output) (see Figure 5.1).

For practical purposes, the distinction drawn here is only between organizational and marketing communication.

Each phase in the ITO model is characterized by controllable and uncontrollable factors. This balance varies considerably between phases. In general, the activities in the phase of analysis and strategy formation tend to be controllable, but the level of control decreases in the subsequent phases. This results from internal contradictions within the company and intervening external factors.

Organizations appear to be heavily dependent on the quality of the work of their suppliers (advertisers/consultants), although of course their major dependency is on the 'obstinate' public (Bauer's *The Obstinate Audience*, 1964), which is by no means as easy to influence.

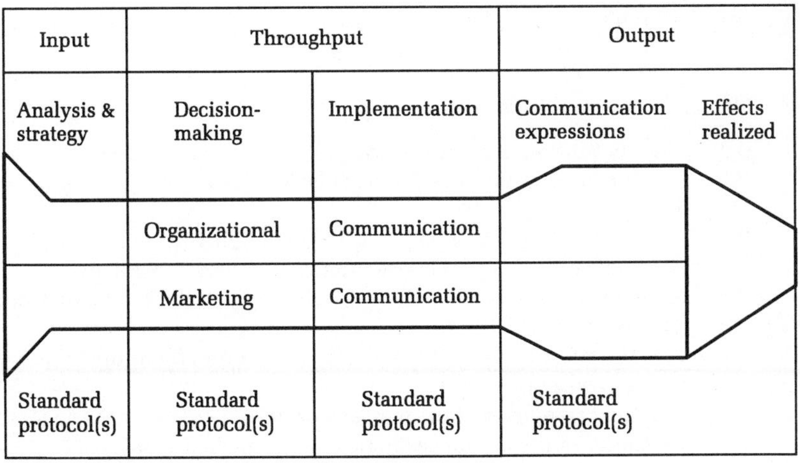

Input	Throughput		Output	
Analysis & strategy	Decision-making	Implementation	Communication expressions	Effects realized
	Organizational	Communication		
	Marketing	Communication		
Standard protocol(s)	Standard protocol(s)	Standard protocol(s)	Standard protocol(s)	

Figure 5.1 ITO model

The communication process could become much more controllable if there were an unambiguous demand for an 'ideal' approach for each phase of the ITO model. Many such 'normative protocols', indicating the best way of working to achieve an optimal result, are available for the input phase of the ITO model, for example the many variants on multiphase plans for formulating company communication strategy. Protocols for the output phase are mainly implicit (see Chapter 4). Traditionally, three approaches are distinguished in measuring the effects of communication. In most cases, effective communication is identified with success in changing the knowledge, attitudes and behavioural intentions of the target group. In other cases, communication is only considered effective if it is demonstrably related to an increase in sales. Finally, success (not effectiveness) is sometimes judged according to creative criteria (professional awards).

Unlike the input and output phases, the throughput phase is almost without normative protocols. This phase consists of complex activities. It is concerned with an 'ideal outcome' approach to implementing the communication strategy devised in the input phase. This includes execution of the creative strategy, the choice of message and medium, the level of integration of the means of

---

Box 5.1 Protocol input phase: ITO model

A   *Defining the problem*

   A.1   The problem is written down in a formal document.
   A.2   The problem is analyzed within the context of current competitive activity.
   A.3   The definition of the problem is discussed with the external agency (strategy and creative director).
   A.4   All internal and external participants familiarize themselves with the definition of the problem.

B   *Designing communication strategy*

   B.1   Clear definition of priorities for goals; what, who and when?
   B.2   Is it clear how to achieve these goals; tone of voice, media, format, etc.?
   B.3   Selection of target groups based on availability of resources?
   B.4   Is the message a logical consequence of corporate strategy?
   B.5   Is the message unique and does it distinguish the company from its competitors?
   B.6   Will the message be applicable for long-term communication (at least five years)?
   B.7   Has the formulation of the message been influenced by the specific 'demands' of the audiences to be communicated with?

Box 5.2 Protocol throughput phase: ITO model

C   *Implementation*

C.1   All internal and external communication managers support the chosen goals, target groups, message concept, etc.

C.2   Top management is involved.

C.3   Business unit management is involved.

C.4   Use common starting points as the baseline for the communication campaign.

C.5   Decide on key issues through a corporate campaign coordinating committee.

C.6   Quality of decision-making in coordinating committee.

C.7   Quality of concept development process: problem definition has been written down in a briefing document, the creative debriefing has been checked by the company's communication department before it was executed, creative director had to work within the framework of strict rules formulated by the company.

Box 5.3 Protocol output phase: ITO model

D   *Evaluating*

D.1   Measure the effectiveness of the programme's preparation.

D.2   Measure the effectiveness of the programme's implementation by evaluating changes in knowledge, attitude and behaviour among selected target groups.

---

communication being used and, last but not least, the decision-making process in which all those involved address the coordination of communication policy across all its manifestations. Adema, van Riel and Wierenga (1993) recently presented a study in which a protocol may be identified for each of the central focus points in the three ITO phases delineated above (see Boxes 5.1, 5.2, 5.3).

5.3.2 From campaign planning to overall planning

For some time, interest has been focused on the long-term coordination of PR and marketing communication campaigns (projects), for example on annual reconciliations of all activities that can be forecast. A standard operating procedure has gradually evolved, at campaign level in particular. Its general outline is that of van Gent's basic model for information supply (1973). This model is derived from planned change theory (see e.g. Bennis, Benne, Chin and Corey, 1976), and shows the ideal order in which the different phases of an information supply process should occur. For each phase, van Gent has formulated a number of criteria that the process should meet (van Gent, 1973). These are diagnosis, formulation of objectives, strategy formulation, implementation and evaluation. Following the publication of van Gent's work, a number of authors, both in the academic world and in the field, have expanded upon the basic premises of this model.

In addition to models concerning information supply, there are others to be found in the fields of PR and marketing communication. It was pointed out in the previous chapter that all the models are based on roughly the same approach. In the literature to date, there has been a one-sided emphasis on the planning of a campaign. Interest is seldom shown in ways in which several campaigns could be planned simultaneously, let alone simultaneous planning of all the communication activities of the organization.

An attempt to approach effectively the planning of the total of communication activities in a company is shown in Figure 5.2.

Figure 5.2 shows the ideal route followed by a planning procedure through the various communication processes in the company. The model starts with the collection of information from the external environment, and sorting it for relevance. An environmental scan (1) results in a report which forms one of the bases for the strategic business plan in which the organizational communication strategy is formulated. The strategic business plan (organizational strategy (2)) is also determined by the input of the strategic plans (3) from the five functional management fields (marketing, production, human resource management, finance, and organization and information). Each of these fields makes demands on the communication strategy. The strategic business plan is translated on the one hand into plans for the five functional management fields, while on the other it forms the basis for the organizational communication plan (4).

The (operational) plans in the five functional management fields also have certain consequences for communication, which are laid down in individual communication plans (5). To avoid producing a fragmented and even contradictory picture of the organization as a result of the overall communication plan (4) and the individual communication plans of the functional management fields (5), the plans must be internally coordinated, i.e. within the functional management fields and within the department responsible for organizational communication. This can be achieved with the aid of the CSPs, or common starting points, in communication (6). CSPs may be used to indicate which central values can be used as a basis for clear and consistent translation into all forms of communication used by the company. The CSPs are,

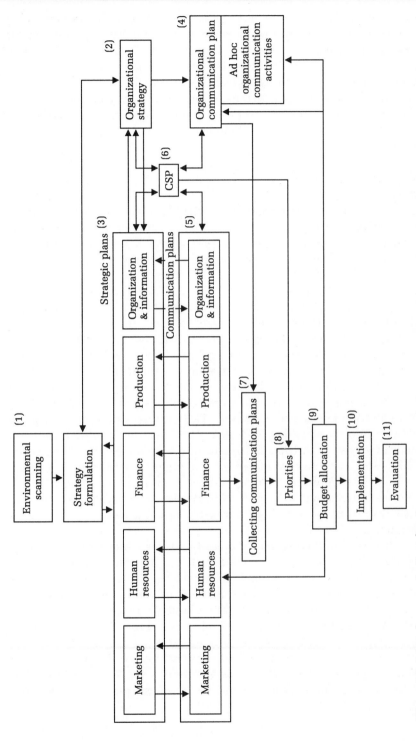

Figure 5.2 Integral communication planning

of course, derived directly from the organizational communication strategy and the strategies of the five functional management fields. When proposed plans have been put on paper and tested against the CSPs (voluntarily or not) by all the functional management fields and by those responsible for organizational communication, a coordinating body should collate them all (7). On the basis of the organizational strategy (2), the CSPs (6), and the available budget, priorities (8) should be set for the proposed communication plans. In the final budget allocation (9), resources should be allocated on the basis of three activities:

1. Communication arising from the plans of the functional management areas.
2. Communication arising from the organizational communication strategy, i.e. involving the total organization with respect to the corporate strategy.
3. Communication, particularly at corporate level, that cannot be predicted but which does require action. This is 'ad hoc communication'.

As soon as the budgets have been allocated, action can proceed. At the implementation stage (10), careful attention should be paid to the guidelines arising out of the CSP. Finally, it is advisable to carry out an evaluation (11) of the activities as they proceed. Coordination of all forms of internal and external communications according to the procedures described above will be much easier to implement if the company introduces a system of logging (which may or may not be computerized) the most important communication decisions. Such a system makes it possible to gain a complete picture of the organization's total communications activities. This picture can form a basis for integrating and coordinating all forms of internal and external communication (van Riel and van Dijk, 1991). A further advantage of a common operational system recorded by means of a logging or registration system is that it forces communication managers to meet certain minimum quality standards, thus 'quantifying' their professional role. As a consequence, they will be taken more seriously both in their own departments as well as in other departments.

It is clear that budgeting plays a crucial part within the system of integral communication planning, since it has a key role in setting priorities for the separately presented proposals, supported by individual financial arguments. In the literature, various methods are discussed on how to arrive at 'well-considered decisions' on the allocation of the communication budget. Most writers distinguish six methods. From a study of twenty companies quoted on the Stock Exchange (van Riel and van den Broek, 1992), it would seem that a seventh method needs adding to the list. This is the 'historic extrapolation' method (see Box 5.4), which seems to be used frequently by organizational communication managers. The seven methods are described in Box 5.4.

Box 5.4 Budgeting

Random allocation

Resources are allocated on the basis of non-economic and non-psychological factors without any kind of research. The available means are divided among the communication activities without regard for any objective, not even profit, and often according to the personal preference of the person responsible.

This preference can vary from the choice of media to the actual content of the communication. It is clear that this method can lead to inefficient use of available funds.

Percentage of sales (previous year's or forecast sales)

The amount to be spent on promotion is set at a given percentage of company sales. The percentage usually remains constant over the years, at 2 per cent for example. This method gives the management an illusion of clarity and it is quite safe financially because the amount can always be found.

Competitive warfare is also less likely if all participants base their budgets on their market shares. The error inherent in this method is that communication is regarded as a result of sales and not as a cause of sales. The use of this method makes the budget easy to justify to management and shareholders.

Return on investment

Communication has to compete for funds with other possible investments. In this competition, attention is paid to the expected return of each investment over a given period. The expected future returns are added to the net present value. However, the prediction of the net value of a communication budget is very difficult, since one cannot be certain about range and distribution during the return period. Furthermore, it is not clear what part of the return is due to communication.

Competitive parity

The communication budget is set to equal that of competitors in the same branch. The advantage of this method is that it minimizes the likelihood of aggressive market warfare. The disadvantages are that no objectives are set, and the consumer is not taken into account. Moreover, equal spending does not necessarily mean equally effective spending.

All you can afford

Management spends as much as possible without endangering the company's financial liquidity. All funds remaining after a proportion has been set aside as profit, are spent on promotional communication. This usually leads to under- or over-spending.

▶

▷

Objective and task

This method requires the formulation of very detailed objectives, followed by calculation of the cost of realizing them. Some kind of research or analysis is often needed before the objectives can be clearly formulated. One difficulty is that management often has no idea how much it will cost to realize the objectives, or whether it is worth it. The results must be monitored continuously, so that one can learn from them.

The objective and task method constitutes the closest approach to the marginal analysis method. The use of quantitative models does not exclude human judgement; on the contrary, it stimulates it.

Historic extrapolation

The budget is based on that of the previous year. The board of directors will approve a budget that is about the same as last year's much more readily than one that is much higher. A disadvantage is that there is no formulation of new objectives, or calculation of the cost of realizing them. Over a period, this can result in over-spending.

5.3.3 Linking communication to the policy or commercial cycle

It only makes sense to coordinate all forms of communication if communication is also integrated logically with the process of forming corporate policy taking place within the organization. A description of how communication can be integrated into the policy formation processes of government organizations has been provided by Winsemius (1985).

The process of policy formation has a life cycle which can be divided into four phases. The first two phases, namely problem signalling and problem recognition, are concerned with recognizing the problem that will form the subject matter of the policy. The last two phases are concerned with solving the problem and the management and control of the chosen solution. Public attention for a problem follows a curve resembling normal distribution, as shown in Figure 5.3.

The traditional role of communication managers working in government was limited to explaining and illustrating the approved policy (i.e. stating the chosen solution, which is the best approach to the problem in the opinion of the minister or the secretary of state). Thus the communication function was used only to a limited extent by 'advisers' (a term frequently used by government staff to describe communication managers working in the public sector). In the lecture mentioned earlier, Winsemius explained what further role the supply of information could play in achieving optimal integration of the policy formation process.

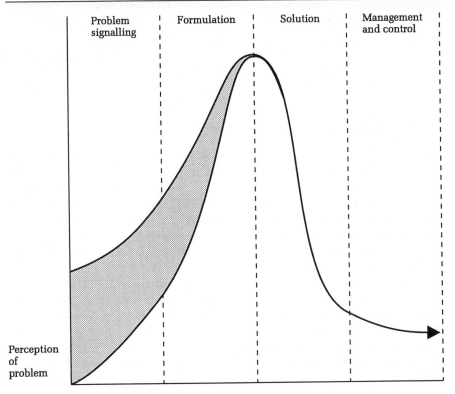

Figure 5.3 Life cycle of policy formation

Information supply can have an 'eyes and ears' role in policy formation: signals from society, politicians and researchers of interest groups can be passed on to the relevant authorities within the same or another department. There must be agreement about the way in which this is approached. This is another way in which information supply can be important. According to Winsemius, it is more important when solving a problem to know what others (i.e. the target groups of the policy) are thinking and doing, than to know what you yourself know and can do. This means that the government needs to study the background to the actions of target groups. Suppliers of information can contribute to this by collecting information about target groups independently, or by consulting representatives of these target groups.

Implementation of the policy is concerned with the actual solving of the problem in question. The function of information supply is, of course, less internally orientated. The concern in this phase is to make a contribution to the realization of the policy: 'helping to promote readiness for action and changes in behaviour and attitude in the target groups, as set down in the policy as formulated, or which can be derived from it' (Winsemius, 1985).

Table 5.1 The process of strategic planning, implementation and control (Kotler, 1988)

Analysis	Planning	Implementing	Controlling
	Corporate planning	Organizing	Measuring results
	Business planning	Implementing	Taking corrective action
	Product planning		

Links with the commercial cycle

In every organization it is possible to identify a more or less definite process through which the most important policy decisions are made. In government organizations, this is the policy life cycle discussed above. In commercial organizations, it follows the so-called commercial life cycle. As a result of the decision-making procedures used by a particular company, commercial policy is developed, approved and carried out. The specific content is naturally different for each company but there is a general uniformity of outline. The four-phase process described by Kotler gives a good general idea of this. The four phases, as shown in Table 5.1, are analysis, planning, implementation and control.

Communication has various functions in the different phases of the decision-making process just described. In the analysis and planning phases, the role of communication consists mainly in charting relevant trends and evaluating ways in which communication can (and, more particularly, cannot) contribute to the realization of the chosen objectives. When drawing up policy plans at different levels the communication manager should formulate communication strategies according to the system described in Chapter 4. During implementation of the plans the communication manager should steer those involved, whether internally or externally, by means of the budgeting mechanism, according to agreements made previously. The primary role of the communication manager during implementation is to engage suitable external agencies to produce the creative executions and identify channels of communication, and to convey them to the target groups. Before the first elements of a communication strategy even reach the audience, an evaluation of the eventual results of that strategy should have started. The results of such investigations must be incorporated into any future activities of a similar nature.

5.3.4 Working with external agents

Introduction

The leading role in the organization of the communication process is played by people inside the company who are involved in communication and corporate policy. However, no company exclusively handles all its communications internally. At the very least, companies use 'suppliers' for the production of promotional materials. Usually, however, the involvement of suppliers goes well beyond this. For example, external consultants may be used to give advice on communication strategy.

Mergers or acquisition, corporate restructuring, down-sizing and re-engineering have reshaped the communication function dramatically during the last decade in both commercial and not-for-profit organizations. Many organizations shifted part of the workload to outside agencies. As a consequence, internal communication departments decreased in size and – although to a comparatively lesser extent – in budget. Communication departments have begun increasingly to specialize in offering strategic advice on communication issues and 'buying' in from outside suppliers elements such as creative concepts and promotional materials (advertisements, brochures, internal magazines, etc.). The shift from 'making' to 'buying' has resulted in a tremendous increase in the turnover of the PR and advertising agencies.

Cooperation with external agencies

Various communication activities are increasingly handed over to external specialists. From a financial point of view, it is neither possible nor desirable to employ all necessary communication expertise within one's own company. Most companies and government organizations do not carry out their own research, development of creative concepts, production of promotional materials, or media planning. This implies, however, that communication managers can concentrate on their 'core business', which is drawing up the general communication strategy, and proceeding to implement and evaluate it.

It was stated in Chapter 1 that the communication function in both PR and marketing communication is being progressively further divided into subspecialisms. The consequence of this is the appearance of progressively more specialized consulting agencies which have contact with the various subspecialisms. In other words, supplying services to communication departments is no longer only the province of advertising and/or PR agencies, but extends across a whole range of external advisers, for example agencies that specialize in labour market communication, environmental communication, investor relations, or producing audio-visual materials.

The purchase of services

The purchase of services in the field of communication is subject to the same principles as in any other field. It is often especially important to be well informed about developments relating to price and quality in the markets in which the various suppliers operate. Other aspects are important when it comes to more vital issues, e.g. strategic or creative matters. The more important and risky the decision, the higher the level in the hierarchy at which it should be taken (Mitchell, 1988; see Mulder, 1991). This applies, for example, to the selection of an advertising agency.

It is apparent in practice that the choice of an external agency is not a

Table 5.2 Factors in relationship between company and external agency (Mulder, 1991)

On the basis of which criteria do advertisers choose agencies?	*What is important in existing relations?*	*What makes it go wrong?*
- Specific knowledge of agencies' previous work	*Quality* - Quality of creative work - Experience of agency's employees - Strength of agency's management	*Re-evaluation/dissatisfaction with agency performance* - Standard of agency creative work - Standard of agency account management - Standard of agency marketing advice
- Seeing some of their work generally - Personal knowledge of a person in agency	*Transaction cost* - Agency meets deadlines - Agency does not abandon the agreed advertising strategy	- Relative sales weakness of campaigns - Relative image weakness of campaigns - Disagreement over advertising objectives - Standard of agency media buying
- Specific knowledge of an individual's work	- Agency does not exceed budget limits - Contacts/meetings with agency are effective - Price level of the agency is acceptable	- Standard of agency sales promotion/public relations - Need for 'full service' agency - Increase in advertising budget
- Direct agency approach - Video showreels - Trade press comments	- Agency is not bureaucratic, which means that there are not too many levels involved - Agency reacts adequately to external changes in, e.g. market, media	- Client/agency personality conflict - Changes in client product management personnel - Changes in agency account management personnel
- Mailing from an agency - Agency advertising in trade press	- People at agency can easily be contacted when necessary *Research* - Quality marketing research - Quality advertising research	*Failed marketing strategies/Changes in client policy* - Decrease in advertising budget - Transfer to below-the-line - Changes in client marketing organization structure - Introduction/development of product management system - Standard of creative work (negative weight) - Relative image weakness of campaigns (negative lading)
	Personal relations - Good personal relations with creative staff - Good personal relations with account staff - Agency has limited staff mobility *Clear task division* - Division of functions and responsibilities are clear	Negative weight, which means there is a relationship between scoring 'important' on other aspects of the factor and 'unimportant' on this aspect. In the case of a high score on this factor, the quality of the creative work was no problem at all.

Full service
- Agency offers varied assortment of advertising and related services, such as PR, marketing research, etc.
- Quality of PR department
- Quality of media planning department

Changes in agency personnel
- In agency creative personnel
- In agency account management personnel
- In agency organization structure
- In agency top management personnel
- Decrease in advertising budget

Other
- Movement to 'in-house'
- Introduction of 'in-house' system
- 'Time for a change'
- Routine re-evaluations of 'short-listed' agencies
- Rationalization of agencies within client group
- Changes in agency creative personnel (negative lading)
- Rationalization of account by agency
- Need for the services of a specialist agency
- Agency involved in merger/acquisition
- Need for a 'full-service' agency
- Increase in advertising budget

Source: E. Santry: Weighty names and ad games, Campaign, Feb. 3, 1989, p. 55.
W. Verbeke: Developing an advertising agency/client relationship in the Netherlands, JAR, December 1988, p. 19.
P. Michell: Auditing of agency-client relations, JAR, December 1986, p. 29.

permanent state of affairs. In the case of advertising agencies, the relationship lasts on average four years. Generally speaking, four phases can be distinguished (as shown in Figure 5.4):

1. *honeymoon trip* (strong emphasis on output: strategic reports, creative concepts, media planning proposals, etc.);
2. *development of relationship* (increasing mutual understanding);
3. *dissatisfaction* (increasing mutual irritations); and finally
4. *termination* (ending the commercial relation).

Mulder has drawn up some possible explanations for the ending of such relationships (see Table 5.2).

In addition to these factors, I believe that there are other issues which are also important. These are the problems described by van Ingen (1991) in connection with the way in which those involved – both internally and externally – see their role in the transformation of strategy into creative communication. According to van Ingen, five parties are involved in the transformation of strategy into the creative concept. These parties (a) often underestimate the value of the part played by the other party, and (b) often take insufficient account of the consequences for the other parties of their own contribution to the creative process. The five parties distinguished by van Ingen are the following:

1. The client.
2. The account manager and strategists in the agency.
3. The creative team.
4. The media planner.
5. The researcher.

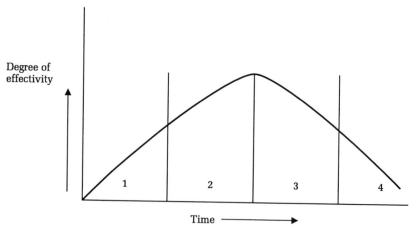

Figure 5.4 Life-cycle of commercial relationship between company and external agency (Klaassen and Mutsaerts, 1993)

Van Ingen suggests that the problems in the process described above could be largely solved if two conditions were met. First, the five parties should be aware that their individual contribution is essential, but that it is only part of the total process. Second, they should be ready to acknowledge and respect the individual contributions of the specialists to the creative process. Van Ingen distinguishes a primary and a secondary responsibility for the five parties. The primary responsibility is to their own specialism. The secondary responsibility is to link up their work with that of other participants in the creative process, or to produce work that is capable of being so linked.

5.4 Coordination of all forms of communication

5.4.1 Introduction

The variety of specialisms in communication and the diversity of hierarchical and geographical responsibilities in communication in general require organizations to develop a clear policy with respect to the degree of freedom that communication managers are allowed to exercise. Organizations can use several methods to stimulate 'cooperation' between all relevant communication specialists: introducing a uniform house style, working with common starting points in communication, guiding decision-making by strict budgeting rules, negotiating about vital communication decisions in coordinating bodies and, last but not least, defining the baseline of corporate communication by choosing one of the three factors central to corporate identity (uniformity, variety or endorsement) as the 'mainstream' corporate identity policy for the organization.

5.4.2 Defining the baseline in corporate communication policy: choosing a 'mainstream' corporate identity policy

A company can choose among three theoretical options for corporate identity policy: the uniformity model (corresponding to corporate profile, BU, and product level), the variety model (all three factors different) and the endorsement model (compromise) (see Chapter 2). The final choice in favour of a particular type of corporate identity policy can be derived from the so called SIDEC model.

SIDEC stands for Strategy, Internal organization, internal Driving forces, Environment and Communication policy. The SIDEC model is represented in Figure 5.5. The presupposition of the SIDEC model is that the final choice of a particular type of *communication policy* is determined by consideration of the interrelationships among: the nature of the *corporate strategy*, the

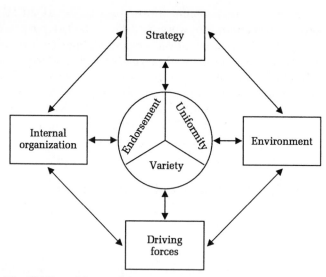

Figure 5.5 The SIDEC model (van Riel, 1994)

homogeneity or heterogeneity of the *driving forces* at a group and BU level, the way in which the *internal organization* operates (in particular as regards 'planning and control' from the head office with respect to the BUs) and the nature of the *environments* in which the organization operates (see van Riel, 1994).

To arrive at a final choice of mainstream in corporate identity policy, the management of a company has to formalize three key issues in corporate communication policy:

1. Definition of common starting points.
2. Establishment of quality standards for a 'common operating system'.
3. Coordination of decision-making in communication (e.g. working with coordinating bodies).

Common starting points for all communication

The impression used to be widespread that corporate communication transformed the total communication activities of a company into a uniform package. If company strategy is aimed at the creation of a purely monolithic image, it follows logically that all internal and external communication should be uniform. However, such strategies are seldom, if ever, found in practice. Total company communication will therefore contain a much richer variety of elements. In order to introduce some consistency, common conditions can be established for communication. This means that there should be a concrete statement from which central values can be translated clearly and consistently into all the forms of communication deployed by the company (see Chapters 1 and 4).

Common operational systems

It would be much easier to coordinate all forms of internal and external communication across a company if all communication managers used the same operational system. It is accepted practice to introduce a uniform operational system in other management fields. This is particularly true of techniques for financial reporting and, to a lesser extent, of the application of planning techniques within other functional management areas.

In fact, there are already many areas of current communication practice in which a common operational system is used. One example is the more or less generally accepted approach to setting up campaigns (the familiar multiphase plans; see Chapter 4). Usually, uniformity is introduced into operational systems in an implicit manner. One way to make it explicit is to introduce a 'logging or registration system' (computerized decision support systems) for vital communication decisions. These systems are already available in marketing (marketing decision support systems) and in marketing communication. We recently developed an integral communication planning system based on the theoretical framework of the model presented in Figure 5.2, the so-called ICPS method.

Coordination of decision-making in communication

Various methods of coordination are being tried in practice. A study by van Riel and Nedela (1989) showed that large American and European financial institutions were using several different forms of coordination to try to orchestrate their total communication output.

In practice several types of coordinating bodies appear to exist:

1. Coordination by one person, solely in charge of all communication departments. This type of coordination will occur especially in small organizations with a limited number of communication departments.
2. Coordination by a steering committee in which representation of all communication departments participate, sometimes extended with representatives of managers with a commercial line function. Coordination is based on the guidelines of a common communication policy.
3. Coordination by *ad hoc* meetings. Meetings are only organized situations where problems arise that need to be solved collectively.
4. Coordination by grouping several communications managers together in one location, so they will be 'forced' to interact frequently, both privately and professionally.
5. Combination of 1, 2, 3 and 4.

5.4.3   Coordination of communication in practice

A number of Dutch companies have recently designed a special decision-making process for steering their total communication. A description follows of the procedures adopted by Rabobank (a large Dutch bank), the ANWB (the Dutch association for tourism), the Hoogovens Group (Dutch steel producers) and the Nederlandse Spoorwegen (Dutch railways).

Rabobank

In 1990, Rabobank introduced radical changes in its communication policy. This will be described in greater detail in Chapter 6.

Before the communication policy was changed, the different product-market combinations within Rabobank could independently evolve their communication policies. The result was a great variety of communication aimed at different target groups. The private investor market was targeted with the slogan 'more bank for your money'; communication directed at the business market consisted of campaign activities using the line 'Take it on with Rabobank'; and the bank presented itself in the foreign market through the artistic efforts of the 'Style group' (including works by Mondriaan). In addition to this diversity in marketing approach, which was also partly the result of working with two advertising agencies, communication was further fragmented by organizational communication units (PR) operating more or less independently from the marketing communication units. Another important factor in the fragmentation was the 'do-it-yourself' approach of several affiliated banks.

Following the decision to adopt a monolithic identity, this autonomy could not continue, especially with the introduction of the new strapline 'Unity in diversity'. This means in practice that uniformity is sought not for its own sake, but purely to promote consistency in the external image. The new policy means that clear internal agreement must be established about the essential basis of communication. Furthermore, all those involved must accept that in the context of a monolithic identity policy, employees previously responsible for communication policy will have to give up the autonomy of their positions in favour of a working model based on consensus.

An attempt has been made within Rabobank to coordinate the work of employees responsible for communication by making clear task-related agreements on the dos and don'ts of communication. The bank has also appointed one advertising agency rather than two. In addition, a special body has been instituted for the coordination of communication. This is to provide a formal channel through which specialists in organizational communication and marketing communication can cooperate to formulate and control the outlines of Rabobank's communication policy. Finally, line staff, especially senior management and the general managers of 'business and private markets', have become more involved in communication policy. Thus the discipline of

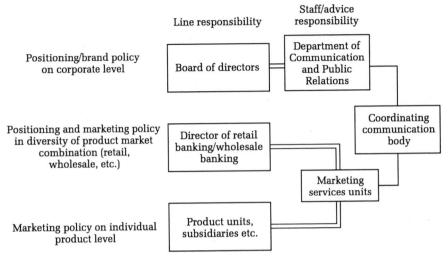

Figure 5.6 Organization of communication at Rabobank

Table 5.3 Organization of communication in Rabobank campaigns

	Briefing				Judgement		
	Formulation report	*Advice*	*Approval*	*Coaching agency*	*Contents*	*Advice*	*Concept format*
Corporate/Rabo brand	CPR	MM	CBD	CPR	CPR	MM	CBD
Brand/PMC brand/product	MS/HPU	CPR	MM	MS	HPU	CPR	MM
Product	MS/HPU	–	MM	MS	HPU	–	MM

Key: CPR = Department of Communication and Public Relations
      MS = Marketing services
      MM = Marketing manager
      CBD = Chair, board of directors
      HPU = Head product unit

communication, in its full breadth, has grown into a mature management tool which is being used in an integrated fashion to realize objectives in the fields of identity, image and marketing.

Rabobank has organized its communication according to the principles outlined in Figure 5.6. In the case of nationwide campaigns, decision-making is organized according to the principles outlined in Table 5.3.

ANWB

The ANWB has chosen to integrate all communication departments which, until recently, operated more or less autonomously. All existing communication departments have been amalgamated into a main department of Internal and External Communication (IEC). IEC now covers internal relations, press services, advertising, presentation and information/public relations, plus the Complaints Department and Internal Quality Control. All strategic BUs (e.g. travel and legal services, media, road services and the 'technocentre') present their communication plans to IEC. IEC provides specialist comment from the communication angle, and advises on the necessary communication budget. The BU then deposits this budget with IEC in a special account. The central communication department will then implement the communication plans. Thus the head of IEC acts as a director of communication.

In addition to coordinating and implementing the plans of the different BUs, IEC is responsible for the presentation of the ANWB as a whole. The strategic business units (SBUs) are responsible for the profiles of their own areas. These are all combined in a yearly communication plan, which sets out the policy for the whole of the ANWB.

Hoogovens Group

Like ANWB, the Hoogovens Group has combined all its communication disciplines into one Department of External Affairs (which in fact deals with both internal and external communication). External Affairs covers two main areas of activity: first, international affairs and government relations; and second, public relations. The department of public relations has five main functions: internal communication, marketing communication, design, events, and policy and projects.

The department responsible for policy and projects prepares the input for the PR policy meeting at organization level. At this meeting, policy proposals are discussed with organizational-level managers of the Hoogovens Group. The board of directors and the various divisional management boards take part in the meeting, as well as a number of managers of staff departments, e.g. external relations, finance and personnel.

The Department of Marketing Communication is responsible for coordinating communication directed towards markets and clients. In collaboration with the marketing staff responsible for each product market combination (PMC), it formulates the marketing communication plans. These are based on marketing plans for the different products. The role of the staff in this department is mainly to coordinate, and many activities are subcontracted. The functional link between the Marketing Communication department and the Department of External Relations is the promotion of consistent policy within the Hoogovens Group.

The Nederlandse Spoorwegen (Dutch railways)

The total communication of the Nederlandse Spoorwegen (NS) is controlled by three departments. The first is marketing communication, or MRCD, which stands for marketing, communication and design. This department deals with commercial communication. The second is the Department of Internal and External Relations (I&E), responsible for public relations and publicity ('free' communication, i.e. free of charge). The third is the secretariat of the board of directors, which deals with public affairs. A deliberate division is made between MRCD and I&E, since the NS does not wish to mix its commercial communication with its 'free' communication. Although it still wishes to maintain this principal division, the NS has been looking for a way to align its total communication efforts in a more effective manner. There was an impression of too little coherence and synergy in overall communication, and in external communication in particular. It has tried to find a solution for such problems by installing a 'core-image group'. Following this development, an organizational identity and organizational image have been developed, coordinated and evaluated by the group. The group has the following structure: internal and external relations manager, sales manager, administration manager and HRM manager.

Increasing coordination in steering groups

In practice, there appear to be a number of ways of coordinating organizational communication and marketing communication. The current preference of most companies seems to be the introduction of a coordinating body, consisting of the managers of the various communication departments, to be responsible for coordinating the various communication projects (Troy, 1993; Smythe, Dorward and Lambert, 1991; Blauw and Maathuis, 1994). Until now, the main task of a body of this kind has been to oversee communication projects, and not to set priorities. It can only only perform its planning task successfully against a background of regular consultation with commercial and policy managers. This keeps communication problems permanently on the agenda of senior management, and the members of the coordinating body are kept informed of current policy decisions within the company.

5.4.4 *Coordination of communication: applying the 'carousel' principle*

One way to achieve cooperation among the various participating communication departments is to adopt the so-called 'carousel' principle. This principle may be explained as follows.

The starting point is that all relevant internal communication staff should be prepared jointly to make decisions on two basic issues: first, about the profile of the 'company behind the BU and the brand', in other words about brand management in a wider corporate context; second, (and vitally), to jointly assess and establish the 'wavelength' in which communication is to operate (see remarks about CSPs in previous chapters).

Both issues concern decision-making in areas involving the company's wider interests. This decision-making process can be effectively streamlined if the following steps are taken. First, a coordinating body (often called 'steering committee', image group, etc.) needs to be established, made up of representatives of the most important communication departments (frequently someone from organizational communication and someone from marketing communication), together with a senior management representative. The latter is not only relevant from a status point of view, but also with respect to senior management's responsibility for communication.

A coordinating body composed in this way might be seen as a kind of rotating carousel at a funfair, i.e. you have to make an effort to stay on it. It is not enough merely to remain passive, only participating to ensure that, say, certain actions do not deviate from the set policy of a certain BU or a specialized area of organizational communication (eg. investor relations). On the contrary, one needs to join in actively to avoid being taken off the ride.

Achievement of active participation in decision-making about collective subjects will naturally be far easier when the senior management representative really feels the need to exercise some sort of influence (implicit and explicit) in this process.

The desirable, if not essential constitution of such a coordinating body (CB) will be even more simplified if the following two procedures are adopted. First, the CB should convene on a daily basis, at which a maximum of three people participate; a chairperson, a company secretary and a member of the committee. Outside this 'core', a wide variety of communication specialists could take part as regular participants in the CB's deliberations. Naturally, only those people who play a major role in communication could become full members. The chairperson needs to be somebody who could form a link in terms of authority and power between the board of directors and the CB.

The second technique is to link the CB to the routine operation of the different communication departments and especially with decision-making procedures applied by senior company management. Let's assume that in a certain company one needs to establish cooperation between organizational communication, the advertising department and those responsible for sponsorship. In each case, the management team has to have a seat on the CB, to maintain the link between the CB and their own department. As the chairperson of the CB is by definition the link with the board of directors, a tighter bond (albeit indirect) will be created between the individual communication function(s) and the company management.

The value of the contributors to the CB has to be 'proved' by presenting short but concise views on the steps needed to be taken in the implementation of the corporate communication policy. Subsequently, the CB has a vital role to play in initiating and 'controlling' the quality of the contribution of each communication department the body represents in negotiation with senior management.

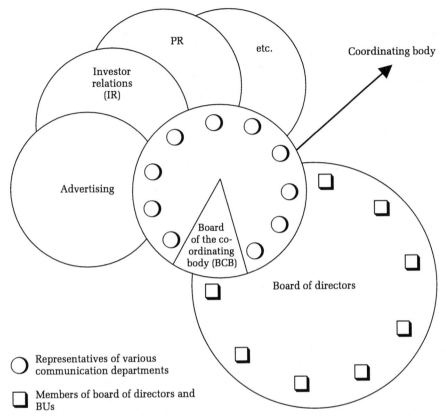

Figure 5.7 Carousel principle

The CB can fulfil the following tasks:

1. Defining and adapting the common starting points for new internal or external development.
2. Defining and controlling quality standards for communication.
3. Stimulating long-term interest in 'communication' as a management tool at board level.

The proposed working method of the CB can be illustrated by Figure 5.7.

5.5 Critical success factors in organizing corporate communication

5.5.1 Introduction

In the previous paragraphs the reader will have found information regarding the 'ideal' framework for the organization of the communication function, the communication process and the coordination of all forms of communication. The key question to be answered is whether the adoption and implementation of such an approach actually makes a difference to the success of corporate communication.

Empirical research in this subject is rather limited and tends to be restricted to only one aspect among all communication activities, i.e. the impact of 'good' communication management on the success of corporate campaigns (Adema, van Riel and Wierenga, 1993). The main conclusions of this study will be presented in the final section of Chapter 5.

5.5.2 The impact of 'good' management by communication managers on 'successful' corporate campaigns

In order to study the impact on 'success' of this 'ideal' approach to the organization of the communication function and the communication process, thirty corporate campaigns were analyzed using the preliminary model in Figure 5.8 as a theoretical framework.

'Good' management is divided in two main clusters of variables describing the ideal approach that should be followed in order to achieve success in communication. The first cluster is characterized as *structural characteristics of corporate communication policy* and contains items such as 'common starting points in corporate communication policy', 'establishment of quality standards for a common operating system' and 'integration of all communication by a coordinating body'.

The second cluster is labelled *campaign-specific characteristics*, containing items

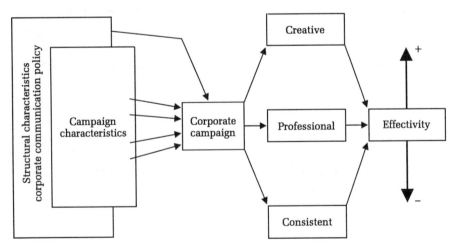

Figure 5.8 Preliminary model: critical success factors in management of corporate communication

related to problem analysis, developing communication strategy, implementing plans and assessing the effectiveness of the corporate communication programme. A detailed description of the items 'behind' these four main characteristics of campaign planning activities can be found in Boxes 5.1, 5.2 and 5.3 on pp. 148–9.

Success of corporate campaigns is not only measured through (perceived) changes in knowledge, attitude and behaviour among the organization's main target audiences, but also through three intervenient clusters of variables that can be seen as proxi (indicators 'forecasting' changes in effectiveness of the campaign) of the ultimate success (effectiveness) of the campaign. These intervenient variables are based on qualitative interviews with communication experts, resulting in eighteen frequently mentioned associations as additional indicators (additional to changes in knowledge, attitude and behaviour) for success in communication campaigns.

The first cluster is labelled *professional*, summarizing items such as 'appealing to target audiences', 'clear promise', 'applicable to company', 'appealing for own employees', 'credible', 'topicality', 'related to present image' and 'recognizable'. The second cluster is labelled *consistent*, summarizing items such as 'consequent', 'cohesive' and 'using one basic concept'. The third cluster is labelled *creative*, summarizing items such as 'distinguishing', 'surprising', 'creative', 'original', 'unique', 'humoristic' and 'striking'.

5.5.3 Impact of structural characteristics on success

All three of the above-mentioned structural characteristics of corporate communication policy appear to influence the success of communication. 'Quality standards' for 'common operating systems' (implying aspects such as defining a clear, long-term corporate communication plan focusing on desired identity and image, quality standards in respect of communication materials, decision-making in communication) all appear to have a significant (perceived) effect on success. More specifically, they have a high impact on consistency, professionalism, (lower) on creativity and ultimately on success in the context of changes in knowledge, attitude and behaviour (summarized as 'effectiveness'). See Table 5.4.

The same can be said of 'integration of decision-making by coordinating bodies' and 'clarifying common starting points to all relevant internal and external stakeholders' (see Table 5.5).

Involvement of the board of directors in the CB positively influences the perceived consistency and (perceived) creativity of the campaign. Involvement implies 'active participation of members of the board of directors in decision-making in corporate communication'. This means contributing to communication policy by clarifying corporate strategy, stimulating middle management to take initiatives in order to 'professionalize' communication and supporting

Table 5.4 Corporate communication policy

Critical success factors	Creative	Professional	Consistent	Changes knowledge	Changes attitude	Changes behaviour	Success
Corporate communication policy	+	+	++	+	+	+	++

Key: ++ strong positive significant relation p < =0.001
      +   positive significant relation 0,001 > p < =0.1
      o   no significant relation
      -   negative significant relation 0,001 > p < =0.1
      –   strong negative significant relation p < =0.001

Table 5.5 Clarity of CSPs

Critical success factors	Creative	Professional	Consistent	Changes knowledge	Changes attitude	Changes behaviour	Success
Coordinating body	o	+	++	o	o	+	+
CSPs are clear to all stakeholders	o	+	+	o	+	+	+

Key: ++ strong positive significant relation p < =0.001
      +   positive significant relation 0,001 > p < =0.1
      o   no significant relation
      -   negative significant relation 0,001 > p < =0.1
      –   strong negative significant relation p < =0.001

the corporate common starting points by setting a personal example in leadership behaviour (i.e. by holding *them* up as examples).

5.5.4 Impact of campaign characteristics on success

Preparing and implementing a corporate campaign involves participation of several internal (both communication and general management) and external stakeholders. Adema, van Riel and Wierenga's (1993) study shows a broad acceptance of the ideal approach to a corporate campaign (see Boxes 5.1, 5.2 and 5.3). Following the protocols of the four campaign phases ('defining the problem', 'designing communication strategy', 'implementing strategy' and 'evaluating the achievements of the campaign') resulted in the perception of a successful campaign by the respondents of this Dutch survey,

The key success factor, however, appears to be striving for consensus omnium'; organizing communication decision-making in such a way that all internal and external stakeholders feel involved. The more stakeholders feel that the information they are given is an attempt by other organizational members to involve them in decision-making in order to reach mutual understanding (especially consensus about *what* needs to be communicated and *how*), the greater will be the level of communication success. See Table 5.6.

In addition to the 'consensus omnium rule', it is vital to inform employees before any external message in a new corporate campaign is publicly announced.

Table 5.6 Consensus omnium

Critical success factors	Creative	Professional	Consistent	Changes knowledge	Changes attitude	Changes behaviour	Success
Degree of consensus	o	+	+	o	+	+	+
Agreement on what should be said	+	+	++	+	++	++	++
Agreement on how it should be said	+	++	++	+	++	++	++
Own colleagues have been informed extensively before external target groups are approached	o	o	++	o	++	+	+

Key: ++ strong positive significant relation p < =0.001
+ positive significant relation 0,001 > p < =0.1
o no significant relation
- negative significant relation 0,001 > p < =0.1
– strong negative significant relation p < =0.001

The results of the study summarized above on the impact of 'good' management on success is 'only' an explorative study and of course limited to the situation in the Netherlands. Nevertheless, it may be considered as one of the first attempts (in the tradition of the important contribution of Fombrun and Shanley) to analyze the 'real' value of how and what to manage in communication programmes. Until now, this has been too often based solely on personal opinion/experiences of individuals.

5.6 Conclusions

In this chapter, the final pieces have been added to the theoretical framework of corporate communication presented in this book. The first four chapters were developed largely on the basis of the work of various specialists in corporate identity, corporate image and corporate identity programmes. Writers on the organization of communication are, unfortunately, few in number, and most of them are concerned primarily with practice. Nevertheless, this chapter was intended to show that there is already a considerable amount of basic knowledge in the area. The theoretical framework presented here may form a basis for new studies of the organization of communication. These may in turn throw light upon the remaining theoretical and practical issues.

The practical examples given in this chapter show that companies at the beginning of the 1990s are experimenting energetically with possible organizational solutions to the problem of fragmentation in company communication.

It is hoped that the solution suggested in this chapter (see Figure 5.2) may offer an integrated approach to the planning and implementation of communication. It does not guarantee success, but it may assist in the search for a workable practical solution.

Chapter 6

Case histories

In previous chapters I have tried to clarify the gradual development of corporate communication into a mature field of study with its own definitions and theoretical framework. There is also a great deal happening in practice. Not every company is willing to publicize its current activities, let alone what it has accomplished. Most likely this stems from the fact that the introduction of the 'corporate communication approach' is not always without its problems. Until recently, experience in this field was limited and the possibility of errors in the process was more than likely. Not only do few organizations wish to publicly admit to their mistakes but they also exhibit a natural tendency to keep information about successful implementation of corporate communication strategy to themselves for competitive reasons.

Fortunately, there are companies and organizations willing to share their experiences in this field. Examples are frequently given at conferences on the subject. A number of practical illustrations can be found in several publications (Birkigt and Stadler, 1986; Olins, 1989; van Riel and Nijhof, 1990). This book contains several case studies involving the following organizations: Rabobank, Akzo Nobel, Canon Europe and Fortis.

6.1 Rabobank: unity in diversity

6.1.1 Introduction

'Rabobank? You know it? Well ... yes and no.' Using this as their opening gambit, Rabobank began advertising in the national press on 20 September 1991. The advertisements were strikingly large (double-page spreads). This marked the end of a silence on the part of the company which had lasted about two and a half years.

Within the organization, this campaign was referred to as a 'catch-up campaign'. It was the first indication of a total reorientation of the bank's communication policy. The reorientation was a logical consequence of the profound changes that had taken place in the strategy of this cooperative financial institution since the mid-1980s.

175

6.1.2   Strategic reorientation

Over the past decade, Rabobank has carried out a thorough review of its identity. The topic under constant discussion was how to achieve a modern identity for a credit-based financial institution.

The bank wished to return to its roots, i.e. to emphasize its core activities as a cooperative credit institution for members/entrepreneurs. Rabobank has always been a traditional lending and savings bank. From this strong base, it is in a position to offer a full range of financial services, primarily to businesses, but also to private customers.

This decision to move back to the core business had important implications for Rabobank Nederland. The cooperative principle had to be put in modern guise, ideally that of a market-oriented organization with clear responsibilities and authority. Local banks remain the pivotal point of the organization.

6.1.3   Rabobank's mission

> Rabobank is a cooperative bank whose aim is to supply finance to its business clients (i.e. members) at competitive rates of interest and on favourable conditions. Rabobank would rather have good and lasting relationships with companies than occasional dealings. This means, for example, that Rabobank will stand behind its clients in difficult times. Operating from a basis of favourable lending terms and reliability, Rabobank seeks to gain economic advantages for companies and clients.

This objective can be realized through the bank's network of independent local banks which offer a wide range of services to companies and private customers. Rabobank Nederland was founded to support the activities of local banks. The aim of Rabobank Nederland is to operate above local level to support the interests of the affiliated banks.

6.1.4   Facts and figures

Rabobank is a cooperative financial organization which supplies financial services. It has more than 800 affiliated banks, which are independent. This means, for instance, that they make their own decisions about relationships with clients and interest rate levels. They can also implement their own marketing and communication policies if they wish to do so. In practice, they usually follow the advice of Rabobank Nederland in these matters.

The cooperative nature of the bank is expressed most clearly in its objectives and structure. Profit is not the primary objective; it is rather a means of achieving the goals of the cooperative.

The organization has a total balance sheet of about 210 thousand million

Dutch guilders, and a credit supply to the private sector of 135 thousand million. Rabobank employs about 35,000 people. In size, it is one of the top three in the Netherlands, even after 'mega mergers'. It is one of the top twenty in Europe, and one of the top fifty banks in the world. It is also one of the few banks in the world with a 'triple-A status'. This creates an impression of financial security.

6.1.5 The historical development of Rabobank's communication strategy

Originally the emphasis in Rabobank's positioning was laid on a specific institutional feature, namely its existence as a cooperative credit institution for members of the local community, such as farmers, market gardeners and small and medium-sized companies. Gradually, the scope of operations (of the then Raiffeisenbank and Boerenleenbank) was extended until they offered the full product range of established banks. The merger in 1973 made it one of the larger banks in the Netherlands. One of the consequences was that Rabobank moved steadily towards being 'a bank for everyone'.

In the 1970s, Rabobank did in fact try to be active in all areas; or, at least, there was no area that was especially singled out in its communication. This may or may not have been deliberate. Much attention was devoted in the communication of the time to the role of the private customer. As a result of the approach made to this target audience via the mass media, the impression was created of Rabobank being primarily a bank for the private market. This was far removed from its original objective as a credit cooperative.

The local banks and the specialized departments within Rabobank began to experience the need to develop specific profiles within their own areas of the market. The differences between the local banks in terms of area of operation and type of client made it impossible to impose a positioning from the centre. Partial positionings developed more or less spontaneously, without clear decisions being made at any level in the organization. Consequently, several different images of Rabobank appeared in the market. The different communications approaches to overlapping target groups created an inconsistent picture of the organization, which was increasingly less likely to convince the audience of the power, effectiveness and quality of Rabobank and its products.

With all this in mind, Rabobank decided to review its communication policy for the 1990s.

6.1.6 Changing Rabobank's communication policy

Rabobank did not change its communication policy overnight. First, its corporate identity and its image among external target audiences were thoroughly analyzed.

An external consultancy carried out a study of Rabobank's identity, based on the Birkigt and Stadler model. It emerged that the communication policy had not been aligned with recent strategic decisions; the bank was still working with clearly distinguishable subpositionings. These subpositionings were related to the different markets in which Rabobank is active, but also reflected the relationships between the affiliated banks and Rabobank Nederland. The subpositionings were communicated too independently of each other, and local and national efforts were not always coordinated. An additional problem was that the various adjustments in concepts and communication strategies made over the years had resulted in an inconsistent image.

The study of the external consultancy firm confirmed a suspicion that already existed within the organization, namely that banks are too much alike in the eyes of the public, and that Rabobank was producing too much product-oriented communication which lacked coherence. The conclusion of the study was that the bank should show more consistency in its communication. An unambiguous positioning should be developed, on the basis of a monolithic identity, to serve as a common basis for all 'Rabo-communication'.

The choice of a monolithic identity was in fact agreed upon by the relevant bodies. Work then began on the development of a new communication policy.

The implementation of the communication policy consists of three closely related activities. This division into three components corresponds exactly to the three core elements (the ABC) of corporate communication as discussed in Chapter 1. In the case of Rabobank, closing the gap between identity and image (A) was a matter of intensifying internal communication, and producing more coherent external communication, aimed both at marketing target groups and organizational target groups. As a basis for producing more coherent communication, a 'set' of common starting points was chosen (B) for the whole of Rabobank. Finally, a new approach has been introduced to streamline the organization of communication (C), using the bank's new monolithic identity.

6.1.7 *Common starting points for communication*

The starting points for all Rabobank communication should, of course, be in line with the mission described above, and with underlying organizational policy. Bearing in mind the results of the Rabobank image and identity study, the consultancy suggested the '3 × 2' formula as a basis for the common starting points. This formula characterizes the essential nature of Rabobank in terms of the following three pairs of concepts:

1. combination of small and large;
2. combination of entrepreneurial and entrepreneur;
3. combination of 'group-driven' nature and basic commercial attitude.

Notes:

Re point 1:   One of the unique strengths of Rabobank is that its affiliated banks are rooted in local communities. The local bank with its local functions stands in the middle of the community. On the other hand, it should not be seen as a 'village bank', in the negative sense; the local bank is always part of a larger organization, which enjoys high status, and is able to supply up-to-date products and services on competitive terms.

Re point 2:   Rabobank is an entrepreneurial bank. Many small and medium-sized companies, and many farmers, have dealings with Rabobank. It is a bank of entrepreneurs, run for their benefit; this is underlined by the independence of the local Rabobank. The manager is an entrepreneur himself, so he is well aware of the needs of his 'fellow entrepreneurs'.

Re point 3:   A modern interpretation is needed for the term 'cooperative'. Its primary objective is to serve the interests of the group and its members. However, it is not a charity. If it is to fulfil its objectives, a modern credit cooperative must operate commercially, and in a correct and businesslike manner.

The following arguments supported this choice:

1. It is consistent with the chosen strategy, since the formula permits positioning of the Rabobank organization as a credit cooperative for clients/members and businesses, with a dominant presence in the private market.

2. The power of the name 'Rabobank'. Research indicates that people associate the name with reliability, professionalism and involvement. These things are of great importance in the world of financial services, because they are 'human values'.

3. The controlling power which results from a monolithic identity is a mainly organizational argument, but equally important. Rabobank has a policy of permitting considerable freedom, although everyone also recognizes the great importance of a coherent image. This means that a generally accepted policy framework is needed, which offers starting points that should be regarded as criteria. If a monolithic identity is adopted, such criteria are relatively easy to formulate, coordinate and control.

4. The importance of unity in the corporate culture. Although Rabobank is active in many areas, there is a strong attachment to a 'uniform' corporate culture. There are certain norms and values which are shared by all Rabobank employees, regardless of their position or specialization. Such norms and values play a central role in market operations. Important features are respect, continuity in the relationship (not too many short-term transaction relationships) and involvement.

5. Efficiency considerations. In times of steadily increasing competition, the

level of costs within the organization should be kept under constant review. The choice of a monolithic identity limits the reasons for hiring consultancies and developing concepts at decentralized levels.

Following internal discussions, the '3 × 2' formula was finally condensed into a communication positioning which can be described in terms of two elements: 'Rabobank is the most involved, leading-edge bank'. 'Most involved' derives from 'small and group-driven'. The term 'leading-edge' refers to large, entrepreneurial, professional, etc.

6.1.8 External identity campaign

Since the autumn of 1991, Rabobank has been implementing an ambitious internal and external communication policy in an attempt to gain acceptance for its new positioning among its most important target groups. The key words in the strategy are 'consistency' and 'coherence'. If these ambitions are to be realized, the long-term communication policy must be characterized by the following:

1. A high level of coherence among all items of the bank's communication output. This should be based on a clear positioning, agreed upon by all concerned, and on a uniform creative concept and a consistent application of the house style.
2. Advertising in the national media, aimed primarily at filling gaps in the knowledge of relevant target groups, and giving shape to the brand name 'Rabobank' (see Figures 6.1 and 6.2).
3. A distinctive and self-confident tone was chosen for communication. It is personal, clear, honest and modern. Extravagant promises are avoided. It is communication without frills, but still striking.
4. A clear division of duties has been introduced between Rabobank Nederland and the affiliated banks regarding allocation of resources. Rabobank Nederland focuses on promoting the brand name 'Rabobank' in the national media, while the affiliated banks take responsibility for communication aimed at supporting sales.
5. There should be strong links between external and internal communication, in terms of timing, theme and tone.

The 'catch-up' campaign

To initiate the implementation of the new communication policy, the bank used the creative concept 'Rabobank. Highly appreciated', developed by Saatchi & Saatchi. On the one hand, this is aimed at reintroducing Rabobank to important market segments, and making up for deficiencies in knowledge and image. On the other, 'Highly appreciated' could be used in the long term as the basis

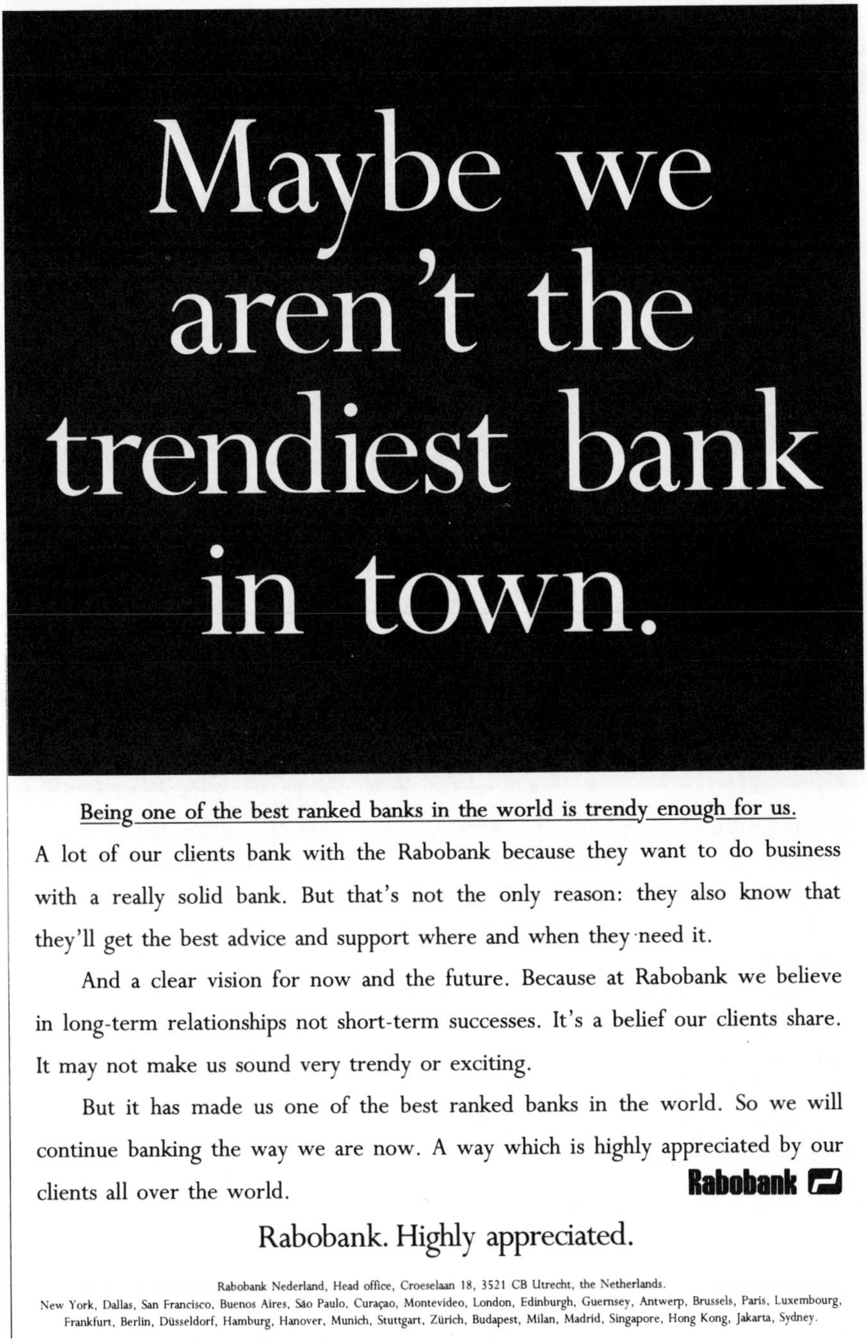

Maybe we aren't the trendiest bank in town.

Being one of the best ranked banks in the world is trendy enough for us.

A lot of our clients bank with the Rabobank because they want to do business with a really solid bank. But that's not the only reason: they also know that they'll get the best advice and support where and when they need it.

And a clear vision for now and the future. Because at Rabobank we believe in long-term relationships not short-term successes. It's a belief our clients share. It may not make us sound very trendy or exciting.

But it has made us one of the best ranked banks in the world. So we will continue banking the way we are now. A way which is highly appreciated by our clients all over the world.   **Rabobank**

Rabobank. Highly appreciated.

Rabobank Nederland, Head office, Croeselaan 18, 3521 CB Utrecht, the Netherlands.
New York, Dallas, San Francisco, Buenos Aires, São Paulo, Curaçao, Montevideo, London, Edinburgh, Guernsey, Antwerp, Brussels, Paris, Luxembourg, Frankfurt, Berlin, Düsseldorf, Hamburg, Hanover, Munich, Stuttgart, Zürich, Budapest, Milan, Madrid, Singapore, Hong Kong, Jakarta, Sydney.

Figure 6.1 Advertisement for Rabobank

Maybe our down-to-earth approach seems a bit dull.

But it has made us one of the world's leading banks in food and agribusiness.
When you bank with the Rabobank you are dealing with a bank that's not particularly trendy.
But, as you know, trends come and go. So we prefer to invest in long-term relationships
rather than short-term successes. Our down-to-earth approach has grown out of our century-
long history in Dutch agribusiness. Today, ninety per cent of it banks with us.

And when our clients started exporting, making Holland the third largest agri-exporter
in the world (with a little help from us), we expanded with them, sharing their success.
Now Rabobank has offices in the world's most important food and agri-ports. And we are
also a respected financier of the agri-commodities trade.

In fact, we are one of the leading banks in the food and agribusiness. Because we know
the roots of your business. Being one of the best ranked banks in the world proves that our
down-to-earth approach is highly appreciated.

Rabobank 🏦

Rabobank. Highly appreciated.

Rabobank Nederland, Head office, Croeselaan 18, 3521 CB Utrecht, the Netherlands.
New York, Dallas, San Francisco, Buenos Aires, São Paulo, Curaçao, Montevideo, London, Edinburgh, Guernsey, Antwerp, Brussels, Paris, Luxembourg,
Frankfurt, Berlin, Düsseldorf, Hamburg, Hanover, Munich, Stuttgart, Zürich, Budapest, Milan, Madrid, Singapore, Hong Kong, Jakarta, Sydney.

Figure 6.2 Advertisement for Rabobank

of a brand image, leading to a perception of Rabobank as the most involved, leading, and therefore the most pleasant, bank. In future campaigns, other characteristics mentioned above, such as expertise, involvement, customer orientation, size and personal approach, should be linked to this concept.

6.1.9 External promises are internal obligations

The external communication objectives can only be accomplished if Rabobank employees cooperate fully in keeping the promises made on their behalf with regard to customer involvement and leadership in the field of the services offered. In addition to the bank's human resources policy, which is aimed at professionalism and improvement in quality, better use should be made of internal communication.

In order to improve internal communication, the number of 'sector magazines' has been increased to five. In addition to magazines for the business sector, the private sector and the line-management sector, there are also magazines for the people who manage the organization (management board and board of control), and for the management of affiliated banks. This means that each employee receives his or her 'own' professional magazine, as well as a general magazine which gives information of interest to everyone. The total amount of written material is being reduced by issuing information through electronic systems that can be consulted whenever the need arises.

As well as issuing information in written and electronic form, Rabobank also makes extensive use of audio-visual communication. A live television programme was broadcast daily over a trial period of two months. The programmes, produced in Eindhoven, were broadcast via satellite and could be seen daily at forty local banks.

Whether this experiment will be turned into a definite policy depends both on financial considerations and on the reactions of the local Rabobanks. Autonomy is a very important factor in Rabobank culture. In the spring of 1992, there was an organization-wide discussion on whether the impact of daily live television would overwhelm local autonomy. The general expectation is that the local banks will allow the advantages of the medium, especially its speed, to prevail. The decision also depends on government broadcasting policy. The government is about to grant a broadcasting licence covering a number of years which will allow the use of the normal channels for sending coded programmes. A decoder is then needed to transform the signal into picture and sound. With this system, the programme can be received throughout the Netherlands by means of cable television or a standard television aerial, i.e. satellites and satellite dishes are not needed. As a result of this development, the expense of satellite broadcasts can be re-examined.

Interpersonal communication

Internal communication takes place not only through various parallel media, but also – and perhaps most of all – through interpersonal communication. Because of its cooperative basis, Rabobank has by definition an intensive pattern of interpersonal communication. Intensive discussion takes place on a continuous basis within the various levels of the bank (management board, directors of affiliated banks, employees, etc.). There are many meetings, and many unwritten agreements are made. Because of the independence of the local banks, matters cannot be arranged by instructions sent down from 'on high'. New policy can only be implemented as a result of conviction and rational argument.

In addition to formal communication through official channels, various improvements in internal communication are in preparation. In a large company such as Rabobank, (physical) distances can be great, so the likelihood of 'miscommunication' is increased.

6.1.10 Conclusion

Rabobank is, in my opinion, particularly interesting in that it was one of the first companies in the Netherlands to put a corporate communication philosophy into practice in a consistent manner. Other companies wishing to change their own approach to corporate communication might be inspired by Rabobank's systematic translation of common starting points for communication (involvement and leadership) into all kinds of external communication, i.e. organizational communication in its many forms, and marketing communication in the different product-market combinations.

6.2 The Canon story: *kyosei* as common starting points

Canon produces many of the world's finest business machines, cameras and optical products (photo cameras, video cameras, colour and black-and-white copiers, fax machines, computer printers, document and information management systems, home office products and industrial products). Canon is a rapidly growing, worldwide organization with Japanese roots, dedicated to the sale of user-friendly, innovative products and technologies which improve (visual) communication between people and provide tangible documents for present and future reference.

Backed by more than half a century of experience and with its name a registered trademark in more than 140 countries, the Canon Group employs more than 64,000 dedicated people. In 1988, a year after its fiftieth anniversary, the company announced its new corporate philosophy of *kyosei*, or 'mutually rewarding coexistence'. Five years later, Canon implemented its global corporation plan in order to create a corporation fully able to realize *kyosei* in its global business expansion in Asia, North America and Europe.

6.2.1 Kyosei, *the corporate philosophy*

kyo   *sei*

Kyosei in written form is composed of two characters: *kyo*, meaning common, shared, together, total; and *sei*, meaning existence, life, to give birth to, grow, livelihood.

The entire concept of *kyosei* is best described as 'mutually rewarding coexistence'. With the *kyosei* concept Canon does not solely want to achieve its business goals, but also wants to contribute to the prosperity of its environment.

Recently, perception has grown of many global imbalances in terms of environmental pollution, trade friction, etc. which have affected Canon as much as anyone. In response, Canon has developed a new philosophy, expressing its corporate responsibility and anticipating external political and ecological criticism.

Canon believes that by creating a symbiotic relationship between humans, technology and the natural environment, society can eliminate these imbalances and ensure itself a prosperous future. It is Canon's aim to promote activities that will contribute to the well-being of people on an international scale. This is being done by eliminating various imbalances that exist in the world, such as trade friction, the uneven distribution of wealth, the depletion of the earth's natural resources, and the damage being inflicted upon the environment.

6.2.2 Research and development based on the kyosei philosophy

Clearly, research and development are very important for a company – as important as they are in contributing to society's well-being. The guidelines for R&D based on the *kyosei* strategy imply five principal rules:

1. Canon rejects R&D programmes for military purposes.
2. Canon does not conduct R&D that is not desirable from an ecological point of view.
3. Canon creates previously unexplored technologies and product categories.

4. Canon respects original technologies and/or product categories created by others.
5. Canon conducts R&D on a global scale and creates new business activities in the country or territory of its finding.

6.2.3 *Corporate excellence based on the* kyosei *philosophy*

To strive for corporate excellence, it is no longer enough for Canon to set goals that can only be measured in terms of higher performance figures. In the spirit of the *kyosei* philosophy, the corporation should judge itself by other rules such as the following:

*   Global rules: rules that ensure the implementation of the *kyosei* philosophy according to the demands of the planet and the natural environment.
*   International rules: rules that ensure the implementation of the *kyosei* philosophy according to the demands of other countries and regions.
*   Social rules: rules that ensure the implementation of the *kyosei* philosophy according to the demands of society and inhabitants of the planet.

6.2.4 *Canon Europe*

Canon Europe NV is an offspring of Canon Inc. Japan. It acts as strategic headquarters for marketing and sales of all Canon products for Europe, Africa and the Middle East.

Canon has gone through profound changes since its arrival in Europe. From a small product distribution centre to independent distributors in the early 1970s, it has grown into a strategic headquarters, employing more than 350 people, of which 110 are Japanese. Its turnover has grown by 45,000 per cent since its establishment in Amsterdam.

The changing European economic climate, manifested in increasing competition, unstable European currencies and the slow pace of the European integration, forced Canon Europe to take a fresh look at, among other things, their communication structure and organization.

6.2.5 *Canon Europe's communication background*

Canon products are the same all over Europe. Basic marketing rules dictate a segmented approach in every country at the absolute minimum. This might be true for consumer products, but appears hardly to be necessary with regard to typical business-to-business products and Canon's target groups. There is a European buyer profile, without significant variances across national borders.

Nevertheless there was no uniform Canon marketing and communication approach in European countries. Campaigns produced by Canon Europe and campaigns produced by national sales companies (United Kingdom, France, etc.) look very different (styles and propositions), but are run side by side in each country. This might be confusing for (internationally oriented) customers, it does not create synergy in communications and ultimately it implies high communication costs. Each sales company develops its own communication plan, which leads to individual (national) expenses for concept development and media buying. As a consequence Canon's European communication could be more effective (less fragmented) and more efficient (less expensive).

At the same time the gross margins of Canon products are under heavy pressure. This pressure is caused by important factors such as high yen appreciation, unstable European currencies, increasing price competition, parallel imports and worldwide overproduction. Under these conditions, it becomes a challenge to maintain and increase Canon's market share. Good communication can make this challenge even more salient. Consequently all distributors should do their utmost to maximize the price/value ratio of their communication investments.

An aspect of Canon's communication behaviour is the fact that there is a tendency by product managers to place strong emphasis on each new product launch. This reinforces Canon's positive brand attributes of innovatism and dynamism. But it also means that relative media presence is always limited. To remedy this, product managers should not allocate a mass media budget for each product launch. Rather, they should invest more in mass media for strategic new products which support the brand.

6.2.6 Canon's European communication guidelines: reactions from the national sales organizations

In 1993, as a first reaction to the problems stemming from lack of efficiency and effectiveness, Canon Europe set out 'European communication guidelines' to be followed by the national sales companies. In order to do so, the company chose to do the following:

1. To develop the 'corporate' Canon brand (company behind the brand):
    (a) develop synergy between local and international campaigns.
2. To shift the emphasis on pure product communication to brand communication:
    (a) become more specific and unified in brand values (based on *kyosei* philosophy);
    (b) create better synergy between product groups.

The national sales companies reactions to these proposals were mixed.

The development of a concrete brand communication policy was generally welcomed. The corporate philosophy *kyosei* as a common starting point was also well received, although differences exist between the respective countries as to the degree of internal acceptance. Some European countries find it 'too Japanese' and 'too philosophical'. Canon organizations in Europe are first and foremost marketing organizations whose success is determined by the sales of products with truly unique selling points. Others think it is desirable that the 'company behind the brand' should be presented, but that the actual corporate advertising was too friendly and generic, and yet others said that it is not Canon-specific or does not directly contribute to local sales.

Intensive information exchange, discussing the pros and cons of the proposed communication guidelines, took place in order to reach mutual understanding. Gradually, consensus was achieved, especially since one argument appeared to be vital in convincing the internal stakeholders to accept the guidelines: synergy creates financial benefits (cost reducing by company-wide concept development and media purchase).

6.2.7 Profiling the company behind the brand

The corporate brand 'Canon' can have added value for the national sales companies when it clearly expresses appealing values for business-to-business customers. In addition to the generally accepted technological values (innovative technologies, user-friendly equipment) that are typical for Japanese companies and especially for Canon, the *kyosei* philosophy is applied as the set of emotional values. Both sets of values can be used as an appealing proposition in a European corporate campaign. The campaign will be primarily directed at the business community (senior management and decision-makers) and other Canon target audiences such as local government, Canon employees, dealers and mass merchandisers.

The key promise in the new corporate campaign will be: Canon applies innovative technology to create user-friendly business machines, which enhance the human capacity to communicate and cooperate, within a context of harmony between humans, machines and nature (according to the *kyosei* philosophy). The (corporate) brand personality has to express characteristics such as: innovator, dynamic, involved partner, leader, trustworthy, authority and concerned with the environment. The tone of voice has to be factual (not dull), self-assured (not arrogant), competent, with an intelligent smile and expressing warmth.

A true – common – European image of Canon will be easier to achieve if the company starts using one clear and distinguishing 'strapline' (see competitors' straplines in Table 6.1), instead of all the different straplines that are used now in the several European countries (see Table 6.2).

Table 6.1 Canon's competitors' straplines

Rank Xerox	•	The document company
Honeywell	•	Helping you to control your world
OKI	•	People-to-people technology
NEC	•	For human potential
Samsung	•	Technology that works for life
Apple	•	The power to be the best
Unisys	•	We make it happen
Panasonic	•	The way ahead
Hewlett Packard	•	The possibility made reality
Sharp	•	The ideas company
Lexmark	•	Make your mark

Table 6.2 Canon straplines used in various different countries

Country	Local	English
Sweden	Kan nön kan ... Canon	If anyone can, Canon can
Denmark	(none)	(none)
Norway	God service er vanskelig a kopiere Blir du ikke sett, blir du heller ikke lest	Good service is difficult to copy If you are not visible, you are not likely to be read
Spain	Es Canon es facil!	It's easy to work with Canon
Finland	Mahdollisuuksia viestiä paremmin	For better communication
Austria	Canon kann's	Canon can do it
Italy	(none)	(none)
Germany	Man versteht sich besser	People will understand each other better
France	Votre business force	Your business power
Belgium	Altijd net iets beter	Always just a bit better
Netherlands	The next step forward	The next step forward
UK	If anyone can, canon can	If anyone can, Canon can
Canon Europe		Colour within reach Performing at your best Image of precision Giving shape to new ideas Canon makes it work

A new strapline for Canon should: be simple, be multilingually adaptable, fit the (corporate) brand personality, fit the positioning, fit *kyosei*, fit the products, and be specific and stand alone. After intensive discussions, three favourites emerged:

- 'Canon, a pleasure to work with';
- 'Canon, tools for better understanding'; and
- 'Canon makes your ideas come to life'.

The final decision was:

Canon

A PLEASURE TO WORK WITH

The new key promise and strapline were translated into a corporate advertising campaign, which was then tested. The results of the testing procedure led to adaptations of advertisements tested, in respect of their contribution to the desired image. Eventually, Canon arrived at the advertisements in Figures 6.3 and 6.4.

6.2.8 Showing the brand in product advertising

Advertisements for Canon's sales companies used to place strong emphasis on each new product launch. As explained earlier, in doing so, Canon's relative media presence was thus always limited. Product advertisements should now support the Canon brand clearly and unmistakably by expressing the same characteristics (innovator, involved partner, leader, concerned with the

Figure 6.3 Advertisement for Canon

Figure 6.4 Advertisement for Canon

environment, etc.) and the same tone of voice (factual, self-assured, competent, etc.).

The key characteristics of the *kyosei* philosophy are applied to product advertisements, through which the products gain added (Canon) brand value. In order to achieve synergy between brand and company communication, Canon developed a procedure to guarantee a common approach to be used for product advertisements. Each product advertisement has to be developed according to the following steps:

1. What is the major issue?
2. What insights does this generate?
3. What emerges as the user benefit?
4. What are the product specifics?

For example, see the concept rationale for the NP 6030 in Figure 6.5.

6.2.9 Canon's communication structure: an overview

Canon's communication structure has to fulfil two important functions: profiling the company behind the brand and showing the brand in product advertisements. This means that the function of communicating the brand is twofold. First, the brand name has to explain the *kyosei* philosophy to corporate

Figure 6.5 Concept rationale and advertisement for Canon's NP 6030 copier

stakeholders such as key accounts, dealers, employees, etc. Second, the brand name has to strengthen the product in terms of quality, safety, environmental care, etc. – factors through which existing and potential customers will decide to buy a Canon product.

Figure 6.6 depicts Canon's communication structure.

6.2.10 The Canon story: conclusions

What is it that makes the Canon story special? Above all, the pan-European approach of the Canon communication policy is one from which a lot of companies can learn. The strategy was based on two goals: efficiency and effectiveness. Canon Europe has managed to implement this dual strategy successfully.

The result is an excellent creative corporate and product campaign, based on the company philosophy *kyosei*. Both product advertisements and corporate advertisements portray the same company, with the same characteristics in the same tone of voice.

Canon has used synergies between product groups and between local and international campaigns. By uniting its resources in this way, Canon has achieved a better image with reduced financial input.

Figure 6.6 Canon's communication structure

6.3 Akzo Nobel: creating the right chemistry

6.3.1 Introduction

Akzo Nobel is an internationally active group of industrial companies. Its headquarters are in Arnhem. Akzo Nobel employs about 73,000 people, spread across sites in over 50 countries. The product range consists of salt and chemical products, paints and coatings, health-care products and fibres. Akzo Nobel consists of four core activities: chemicals, coatings, pharmaceuticals and fibres. Within these core activities there are several business units, all of which have a great deal of devolved authority, enabling them to react swiftly to market developments.

Akzo originated in 1969 as a result of the merger between an international producer of artificial fibres for household and industrial use (AKU) and a supplier of salt, basic chemicals and pharmaceutical products (KZO). AKU worked primarily on a cyclical basis, whereas KZO was a relatively 'continuous process' company. Both cultures were different in character: the first was a tightly run, technically oriented organization and the second had a flexible hierarchy where authority was delegated. The merger between the companies became extremely difficult. Neither of them had fully recovered from previous brushes with mergers. The artificial-fibre company, although highly profitable in the 1960s, went through difficult times in the 1970s owing to enormous overcapacity in the textile industry. The 1980s were marked by a rearrangement in the product range offered by Akzo.

In 1993 Akzo merged with Nobel, a Swedish concern with an emphasis on chemicals and coatings. The company has been called Akzo Nobel since then. Nobel is a chemicals producer which operates in identical markets to those of Akzo. Following the merger an organization emerged which holds leading positions in the market, particularly in Europe and in chemical products, coatings, pharmaceutical products and fibres (see Figure 6.7). It is felt that a synergistic effect was unleashed, which should be fully measurable by 1995. In 1993 both companies reached a turnover of more than 20 billion Dutch guilders and an operating profit of 1.4 billion Dutch guilders.

The challenge to Akzo Nobel consists in ensuring continuity and growth through its strengths and expertise. Initially, it attempted to do so by strengthening the core activities which form the financial and industrial basis for the company. In addition, measures are to be undertaken to combine current marketing and technological knowledge. The product range needs to be balanced so that in the event of an economic recession Akzo Nobel as a whole is less vulnerable. This can be achieved by using elements of synergy and introducing cost control programmes. Akzo Nobel primarily aims at markets where it can become a market leader. See Figures 6.8 and 6.9.

Equally, greater attention is being paid to environmental concerns: products

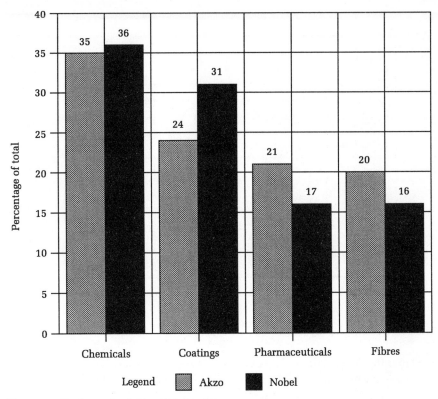

Figure 6.7 Product mix of Akzo Nobel, 1993

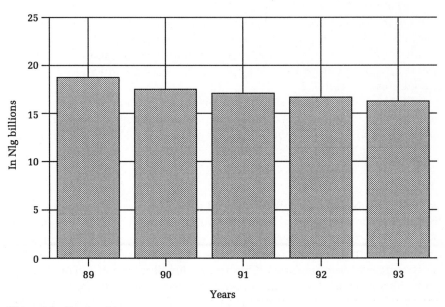

Figure 6.8 Akzo's net turnover

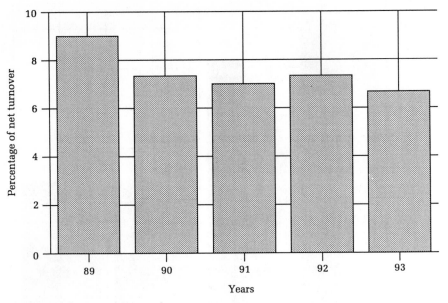

Figure 6.9 Akzo's company results

need to inflict less harm on the environment and non-disposable products need to be reused wherever possible. In 1991 the Internal Environment Care System was introduced. This programme served as the starting point for continual reduction of waste outlets and emissions and monitoring progress according to an established set of priorities.

From the outset Europe has been very important to Akzo Nobel, hence the reason for trying to maintain its position in the European market in all sectors of operation. At the same time, much current growth comes from North America, with expansion also taking place in the Far East and South East Asia. See Figures 6.10 and 6.11.

With a turnover of more than 20 billion Dutch guilders Akzo Nobel ranks ninth in the world ranking of chemical corporations. There are several notable competitors, including Dupont, BASF, Hoechst, Bayer, ICI, Dow, Ciba Geigy, Solvay and the Dutch company DSM.

Structure

In 1993 Akzo Nobel officially introduced a BU structure. Prior to this Akzo had a divisional structure with extended communication links. By introducing BUs, shorter communication links were created between the BUs and the corporate holding company. The BUs have their own responsibilities and they are considered as profit centres. They report directly to the Board of Management. This structure creates an organization that is more efficient and effective. In this way, it is possible to respond faster to new market developments;

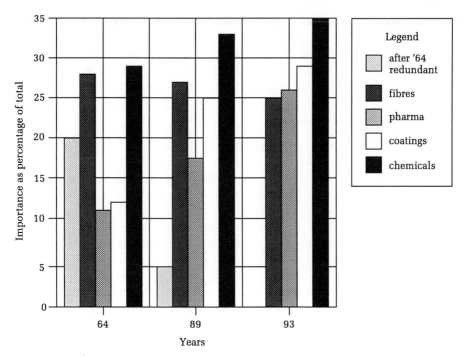

Figure 6.10 Akzo: segmentation of activities

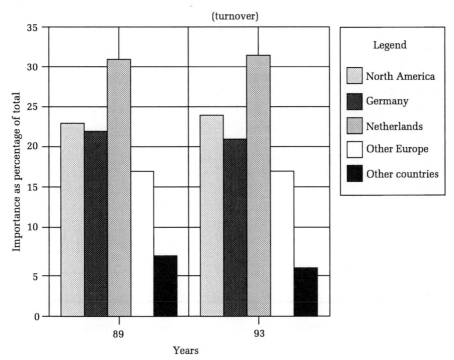

Figure 6.11 Akzo: segmentation to countries

the organization could, however, be even more vigilant. Various functions within Akzo Nobel are executed at a corporate level (e.g. R&D, finance and strategic planning), which means that both synergy and cost reduction occur. The specific BUs could make more use of these services.

Research and development

In chemical corporations R&D forms the basis for the business's secure future. At Akzo Nobel approximately 5.6 per cent of turnover is spent on R&D annually. At Akzo Nobel's health-care department this figure actually amounts to 12 per cent of turnover. Product improvement is not always the primary outcome of such expenditure. Sometimes R&D aims at staying competitive by developing cleaner and more efficient production processes, thereby reducing the impact on the environment. R&D is vitally important for the survival of Akzo Nobel as an entity. Innovations appear to occur at an accelerated rate and are not always self-evident – particularly to the end user. This occurs especially when a new technological breakthrough means that a product will be more expensive through its improved quality. However, the customer is not always aware of the reason for the accompanying price increase. It is therefore highly necessary to aim for clear communication.

Product-market combinations

Akzo Nobel's products are present in many (fast moving) consumer goods. However, the name 'Akzo Nobel' is not always recognized as such. For instance, Akzo Nobel is one of the world's largest salt producers, and one of the largest producers of industrial fibres, car repair finishes and trade paints. Akzo Nobel products are used equally in the manufacture of seatbelts, airbags and car tyres. 'Identifiable' Akzo Nobel end products which do reach the consumer directly are pharmaceutical and diagnostic products for people and animals, and do-it-yourself paint.

Akzo Nobel has recently had to contend with difficult economic conditions. Last year improved results were reported in the United States, but not enough to compensate for European results. Two-thirds of manufactured turnover originates in Europe, of which 32 per cent is from the Netherlands (see Figure 6.11). Growth takes place in sales to the United States at the expense of sales in Europe.

Enterprise strategy

The current strategy is aimed at concentrating on those areas and products (geomix and product mix) in which the company is strong or could achieve a strong position. Various activities have been discontinued completely or are continued elsewhere through alliances. The merger with Nobel should be seen in this context.

The salt and basic chemistry sectors and the traditional segment of the fibre sector are a constant market with no potential for growth. They are nonetheless an important source of revenue. The challenge here is to find ways that lead to further reduction of production costs and achieve increased efficiency in the revenue flow.

In markets that are stable or where growth has decreased, technology needs be to improved, but only if there are still possibilities of enlarging market share by outperforming the competition. In dynamic, mature markets the key to success lies in improved technology, improved marketing and/or geographical expansion. This applies in the case of coatings, chemical products, fibres for industrial applications and certain health-care products.

In the up-and-coming, rapidly growing areas (biotechnology, advanced composites, high-performance fibres, electronic materials), Akzo Nobel must necessarily expand its knowledge and conduct optimal research into all possible permutations for such products.

6.3.2 Corporate communication programme

Changing symbolism

The new identity was derived from the 1985 strategy aiming to take the company into the 1990s. In 1988 Akzo undertook a corporate identity review programme. The reasons that lay behind this were that Akzo was hardly known to the outside world and that there was a lack of unity within the corporation. By the same token, a company that portrays a diffuse image will never be able to attract young scientists to its ranks. This programme pointed to the fact that Akzo needed a more coherent strategy in its internal and external communication. It was also clear that many Akzo divisions successfully undertook their own communication worldwide. It thus became necessary to develop communication concepts at central and local levels and to consider the consequences of this in terms of organization and allocation of tasks. The most striking part of the identity change was the logo created by Wolff Olins. In adopting this logo an attempt was made to find a unifying element for all employees and also to create an impression of clarity to all external target groups. The new symbol was created to suit the multiplicity of purposes – the individual and enterprising aspects of Akzo, together with its interactive cooperation. Emphasis is placed on employees' contribution forming part of Akzo's success (see Figure 6.12).

According to Olins the main problem was that the organization had grown up from a large number of smaller companies which operated as a federation rather than as a single entity. Akzo evolved without a commonly recognized identity, the communal set of values of a shared vision. Therefore the need was felt to introduce something more 'lasting'.

By introducing the new logo, a different way of writing the name and clear

Before 1988   After 1988   After 1994

Figure 6.12 Akzo's logos

company colours, the Board of Management wished to show the outside world that considerable changes had taken place at Akzo; not just cosmetic, but fundamental changes in the company's way of thinking.

Akzo presents itself as a decentralized, flexible, innovative, alert, responsible and enterprising corporation in which the individual is considered the key to success.

Campaigns in 1988

Following the launch of the new corporate identity in 1988, Akzo developed an advertising campaign with the phrase 'leaders in chemicals and pharmaceuticals'. The aim was to establish familiarity with the name and Akzo's image as an innovative and successful company which contributes considerably to the quality of life. This aim was addressed by the line 'we don't always make the headlines, but we're always in the picture'. In the advertisements, products made by Akzo were shown. There followed similar campaigns with headlines such as the following:

- Sometimes we're stronger than cruel nature
- A fatal poison taught us to use a lighter anaesthetic
- The colour samples we used for Turin's revival
- Without our salt you could be in for quite a shock
- Giving credit where credit is due

The visuals were designed to evoke the following reactions: international, quality, innovative, environmentally friendly, diversity of products, financial status, service and care for humankind's well-being (see Figures 6.13 and 6.14). The target groups for the campaign were trade and industry, the financial world, opinion leaders, clients/suppliers and Akzo's (potential) employees.

6.3.3 Akzo and its competitors

Awareness of Akzo and its competitors

Table 6.3 reflects Akzo's performance in relation to that of its competitors. To facilitate comparison, each target group is indicated by country. The figures show the position in 1988.

Figure 6.13 Advertisement for Akzo

Figure 6.14 Advertisement for Akzo

Table 6.3 Familiarity with Akzo's name in relation to its competitors

	Netherlands		USA		Germany	
	Spontaneous	Aided	Spontaneous	Aided	Spontaneous	Aided
Akzo	62	100	1	17	4	30
BASF	14	98	8	66	79	100
Hoechst	19	95	6	40	83	99
ICI	25	87	10	47	22	53
Dow	21	88	31	98	10	75
DSM	48	98	–	11	1	83

Development of corporate advertising by chemicals companies 1988–91

In 1988 a great deal of corporate advertising was initiated by chemical companies. Only three companies (BASF, Dow, DSM) have launched further campaigns since then. This does not imply, however, that during this period there have been no changes to the campaigns.

The most important development is probably increasing environmental awareness. Each company focuses on the environment, some more than others, but it remains a constant theme. This development is particularly noticeable in the case of ICI. Since 1990 ICI has changed its approach and uses the environment as the key theme for its advertisements.

Almost all companies highlight their achievements to underpin their images (see Table 6.4). At the outset, achievements were useful shorthand through which to create awareness among target groups about the enterprise and its activities. The achievements clearly indicated the capabilities and working methods of a company. As time went by, however, nearly every company exploited (the same) achievements. Thus differentiation faded as images presented became indistinguishable.

For example, 'humankind's well-being' is promoted by each company. Each company creates a pleasant and safe environment in which to live, thus each company caters for the needs of humans and the environment (see Table 6.5).

Table 6.4 Review subjects and image aspects of relevant campaigns

	Subjects	Image aspects
Akzo	Achievements	Innovation Caring for human well-being
BASF	Achievements	Diversity and product assortment
Bayer	Achievements	Feeling of responsibility Expertise
Dow	Chemaware programme	Good service
DSM	Achievements	Innovation
Hoechst	Achievements	Feeling of responsibility of environment
ICI	Achievements	Innovation Caring for human well-being

Table 6.5 Straplines used by chemical companies

Akzo	'Creating the right chemistry'
BASF	'Wir tun mehr für Sie'
	'We do more for you'
	'Pour vous, nous faissons encore plus'
	'Menschen mit Verantwortung'
	1993
	'We don't make a lot of products you buy. We make a lot of products you buy better'
	'We don't make the product. We help you make it better'
	'Creative chemistry for creative chemists'
Bayer	'Bayer: Kompetenz und Verantwortung'
	'Bayer: Expertise and responsibility'
	'Bayer: Etre compétent c'est aussi être responsable'
	'Bayer: Expertise met verantwoording'
Dow	'CHEMAWARE: It pays to be safe'
DSM	'We put fantasy to work'
Hoechst	'Hoechst High Chem'
	'Hoechst in Holland. 't is opmerkelijk wat ze daar allemaal doen'
ICI	'ICI World Class'
	'ICI. Fortschritt durch Vernunft'
	'Contribuer à une atmosphère plus pure, c'est notre façon de voir l'innovation'
	'Contribuer au respect des équilibres naturels, c'est notre façon de voir l'innovation'

Budgets for Akzo's corporate identity campaigns and those of selected competitors

Akzo is one of the few chemical companies to have abstained from corporate advertising in its home country. This happened in 1991 and 1992. In 1993 Akzo started to advertise again. In Germany the opposite was the case: corporate advertising was carried out in 1991 and 1992, but in 1993 there was a strong budgetary decrease. Throughout the rest of Europe Akzo is active in the field of corporate advertising, having 'peaked' in 1992. In the United States Akzo is active but expenditure tends to fluctuate.

Hoechst's corporate advertising budget for the Netherlands increased up until 1991, after which a decrease took place. In Germany, Hoechst's expenditure up to 1992 can also be seen to have increased after which a slight decrease appears. Hoechst also invested in corporate advertising in the rest of Europe, but expenditure is relatively low in comparison with the advertising budget in Germany. An upward trend is noticeable in advertising expenditure in the United States.

At ICI, corporate advertising expenditure in the Netherlands to 1990 shows an upward shift after which it declines. In 1993 no corporate advertising was conducted. ICI expenditure in Germany fluctuates; the 1992 and 1993 budgets are very low. In 1991 and 1992 ICI also advertised in other European countries, but with a small budget. In the United States expenditure increased up until 1991, following which there was a strong downward move.

Compared to the other companies, DSM's corporate advertising expenditure in the Netherlands increased up until 1991, but in 1992 a strong decline occurred and in 1993 no corporate advertising was conducted at all. After a break in advertising in Germany, DSM started to advertise there again in 1993. After 1991 there was a decline in corporate advertising in Europe. DSM is not at all active in the United States.

In Germany, BASF corporate advertising expenditure showed an upward move until 1991, and thereafter a slight decrease. This trend is also noticeable in its corporate advertising expenditure in the rest of Europe. After 1991 the decrease mirrors the rise prior to 1991. The expenditure of BASF in the United States fluctuates a little, but after 1991 a downward trend is apparent.

Dow, with its home market in the United States, spends most of its corporate advertising budget in that market. In 1991 and 1992 Dow started advertising in Europe, but minimally in comparison with expenditure in the United States. Its budgets fluctuate markedly.

See Tables 6.6, 6.7, 6.8 and 6.9.

Table 6.6 Corporate advertising budgets in the Netherlands (in thousands of dollars)

	1989	1990	1991	1992	1993
Hoechst	393	518	589	185	282
ICI	455	525	444	205	0
Akzo	267	270	0	0	3
DSM	168	406	456	111	0

Table 6.7 Corporate advertising budgets in Germany (in thousands of dollars)

	1989	1990	1991	1992	1993
BASF	3,300	3,400	4,100	2,000	2,440
Hoechst	3,700	3,900	4,200	4,200	3,000
ICI	1,000	0	2,200	85	3
Akzo	1,600	1,500	870	1,600	420
DSM	0	130	500	0	3

Table 6.8 Corporate advertising budgets in the rest of Europe (in thousands of dollars)

	1989	1990	1991	1992	1993
BASF	38	982	1872	20	5
Hoechst	178	37	54	24	89
ICI	0	0	6	15	0
Akzo	389	342	124	1155	470
Dow	0	0	53	254	0
DSM	1364	287	820	31	0

Table 6.9 Corporate advertising budgets in the USA (in thousands of dollars)

	1989	1990	1991	1992	1993
BASF	15000	11000	13000	10000	9100
Hoechst	1000	800	1600	2000	2300
ICI	9000	11000	12000	10000	5000
Akzo	3000	5000	25000	4000	2900
Dow	110000	105000	91000	137000	92000

Characteristics of the campaigns

Many of Akzo Nobel's competitors use advertising campaigns in newspapers, magazines and specialist chemistry-related magazines such as *Chemical Week*. It is noticeable that all of the advertisements contain something about the environment. Some are more specific than others. Below, the specific characteristics of these campaigns will be discussed.

Dow Chemicals emphasizes safety in its campaigns. Safety and good service to its customers is part of the 'Chemaware' programme, providing extra service to the client by, for example, the supply of information on the effective usage of its products. This programme has been set up internally and is strongly related to Responsible Care, an environmental performance and awareness campaign initiated by the chemical sector. Dow Chemicals shows clearly that it is always ready to assist its customers and is willing to provide information about its products. For this campaign Dow uses television commercials, particularly in the United States.

The German company BASF portrays a large variety of products in its campaigns. From the lines 'We don't make a lot of the products you buy. We make a lot of the products you buy better' and 'We don't make the product. We help you make it better' it appears that the company aims to focus on the quality of its products and their continuous improvement. The advertisements have a 'down-to-earth' theme.

ICI has three types of advertisements, aimed at three different target groups. ICI World Class is aimed at opinion leaders in Germany and France, the industrial and financial world and potential clients. ICI Solutions is aimed at clients and suppliers. ICI Worldproblems is aimed at opinion leaders. ICI focuses its campaigns on innovation and the changes taking place in society, such as environmental concern and the ever-increasing demand for greater product quality and healthy lifestyles.

Responsibility and innovation play an important role in Hoechst's campaigns. These aspects are explained in the form of product examples. The advertisements appear very untidy. In each one a different aspect of the image is emphasized, leading to an incoherent image of the organization as a whole. (See Figure 6.15.)

DSM uses the line 'We put fantasy to work' in its campaigns. The advertisements are no different from those of the competition. DSM uses visuals and

Complex tasks sometimes require thinking in simple terms.

'Hoechst High Chem
C H E M I C A L S

Modern detergent builders are expected to meet a wide range of requirements. In particular, they must soften the water and protect the washing machine and the laundry from lime deposits.

Builder substances should also provide the necessary alkalinity for the washing process and stabilize the pH. In addition, good antideposition capability is important for ensuring that the detached soil is not redeposited onto the fabric. And they should give bleaching agents a long shelf life. All this must be achieved in conjunction with the best possible environmental friendliness.

It's hard to tackle that complex task in all respects. That's why today's detergents contain a mixture of different builder materials providing the total builder effect. One of these substances, sodium silicate, or water glass as it is commonly called, has been used for over one hundred years in detergents. It's a source of alkalinity and helps to protect the washing machine from corrosion.

After intensive development work, Hoechst researchers have succeeded in giving sodium silicate a specific layered structure. The resulting δ-disilicate, which they've named SKS-6, turned out to have multi-functional builder properties: it softens the water well, gives the wash liquor a stable alkalinity, adsorbs the dissolved dirt and can be readily used with bleaching agents, including percarbonate. Moreover, other builders are only needed in smaller quantities, or in some cases not at all (which reduces costs). And that leads to even more compact, environmentally friendly detergents.

To do this complex task, we looked at a traditional chemical, gave it a new structure and thereby turned it into a multi-functional builder. It's a fairly simple step, but one with great implications. That's Hoechst High Chem.

Hoechst AG
Marketing Chemikalien
65926 Frankfurt am Main
Germany

Hoechst

Figure 6.15 Advertisement for Hoechst

copy to explain its activities, concluding with the sentence 'If you're working on tomorrow, please write to DSM. We can shape the future together'. This is intended to indicate DSM's innovation and to focus on both the future and the client. (See Figure 6.16.)

6.3.4 New strapline: 'Creating the right chemistry'

In 1990 Akzo's campaign was inaugurated with the line 'Creating the right chemistry'. In each advertisement one of Akzo's managers appears, mirroring the outline form in the logo, with specific copy below. Following the merger, Akzo Nobel continued this campaign, the only difference being that Nobel has been added to the logo. It is evident that 'people' are the central theme in this campaign. (See Figure 6.17.)

The idea of using actual managers in the campaign has been used before by Akzo and seems to work with its target audiences. Thus it was decided to continue the campaign after the merger. BASF notably tried to imitate Akzo Nobel's line by using 'Creative chemistry for creative chemists' (see Figure 6.18).

Figure 6.16 Advertisement for DSM

Figure 6.17 Advertisement for Akzo Nobel

BASF INTERMEDIATES

World's Largest Formic Acid Producer:

On Purpose, On Spec, On Stream!

We're serious about formic acid. So serious that only BASF operates purpose-built production, using the proven BASF methylformate route to minimize unwanted by-products.

Since we produce formic acid on purpose, we are serious about our quality, offering the purest product on the market with the broadest line of grades—85%, 94%, 99%.

And we're serious about continuing to serve the market even as others close their doors. As the world's largest producer, with 100,000 metric tons of annual capacity on stream now, BASF recently announced plans to add 80,000 metric tons more of annual capacity by the end of 1995.

So if you're a serious buyer of formic acid, stick with the serious producer—BASF.

Call us!

Wolfgang Dietrich
800-526-1072
Ext.: 3979

Fax in USA
201-263-8772
Fax in Europe
0621-60-22666
Fax in Japan
03-3238-2290

**Creative Chemistry for
Creative Chemists**

BASF

Figure 6.18 Advertisement for BASF

6.3.5 Conclusion

This case clearly shows that it is possible for a company to opt for a gradual change in its corporate identity policy, even in the wake of consistently turbulent developments. In Akzo's case, following the merger with Nobel, a change of identity took place which was entirely problem-free (at least as far as the outside world was concerned). This gradual change has been under way from the introduction of the new logo in 1988 through to recent changes necessitated by the merger with the Swedish company Nobel. It goes without saying that much work remains to be carried out in order to achieve broader recognition among the target groups most important to the company. However, the company is on the right track, as demonstrated in the recent award for the best annual report and accounts of 1993 (for clarity of expression of strategy), excellent results in image research at home and abroad, and, last but not least, positive publicity in the trade and national press.

6.4 Fortis: cherishing business unit identity

6.4.1 Introduction

Since the late 1980s many mergers have taken place between companies providing financial services both in Europe and in the United States. Most of these mergers took place between banks or between insurance companies themselves. Fortis is one of the first companies to have achieved successful cooperation between insurance companies and banks. Fortis is not only one of the first 'bancassurance' institutions, it is also one of the few financial conglomerates of a cross-border nature.

On 2 April 1990 the Netherlands' NV AMEV (which had already long been present on the international market) and the Belgian insurer AG Group announced their intention to amalgamate their operational activities. They shared the same views with regard to 'financial services', and there turned out to be little overlap in the markets in which the two partners operated. Another reason was that they were aware of the need for a certain critical mass in order to be able to continue playing a part as an international service company in an integrated Europe.

6.4.2 Fortis: combined force in financial services

Fortis's structure

Fortis can best be described as the combination of the operational activities of AG and AMEV/VSB. The parent companies of Fortis are Fortis AG (was AG Group) of Belgium and Fortis AMEV (was NV AMEV) of the Netherlands. Both hold a 50 per cent interest in Fortis (see Figure 6.19).

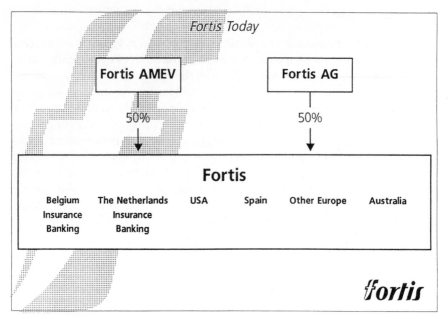

Figure 6.19 Structure of Fortis

On account of legal difficulties it was impossible to enter into a formal merger between the two companies. Fortis is therefore not a company but a group of companies comprising a large number of enterprises in Europe, the United States and Australia. There are no Fortis shares. The shares of Fortis AMEV and Fortis AG are traded on the Amsterdam and Brussels stock exchanges respectively and on SEAQ International in London.

Because there are hardly any overlaps between the two companies from the geographic point of view, complicated integration procedures right down to the shop floor were virtually unnecessary.

Management of Fortis

Fortis is managed by a Supervisory Board and an Executive Board. The Supervisory Board provides the link between the Executive Board and the boards of the parent companies and between the boards themselves. The Supervisory Board discusses important issues such as strategy, acquisitions, divestments and financial results.

The Executive Board formulates Fortis's strategy and takes the key decisions deriving from that strategy. Four members of the Executive Board, including the two joint chairmen, make up the Coordinating Committee (Coorcom). In addition, those holding primary responsibility for the activities of Fortis in Belgium, the Netherlands and the United States also have a seat on the Executive Board. The Executive Board further numbers members who are responsible for the other geographic areas and for functional areas of focus. The Coorcom is responsible for general planning and control of the group's activities. The management structure of Fortis is based on central direction combined with decentralized operation, which allows the operating companies a large measure of responsibility (see Figure 6.20).

Fortis's activities

Fortis is one of the first companies to have successfully implemented the principle of 'bancassurance'. The merger between NV AMEV and VSB Group was the first in the Netherlands between a bank and an insurance company. This was followed in 1990 by the first instance of cross-border cooperation between financial institutions for the Netherlands. At the end of 1993 a controlling interest was acquired in ASLK-CGER-Bank and ASLK-CGER-Insurance in Belgium. Thus, Fortis's services in the Benelux are made up of both insurance products and banking services. In addition, Fortis is active in niche markets in a large number of European countries, Australia, Asia and the United States.

Fortis's home base lies in Belgium and the Netherlands, where VSB and AMEV (the Netherlands) and AG 1824 and ASLK-CGER (Belgium) work on the principle of 'bancassurance'. In Belgium Fortis leads the market in the field of financial services. The group markets a large number of insurance products

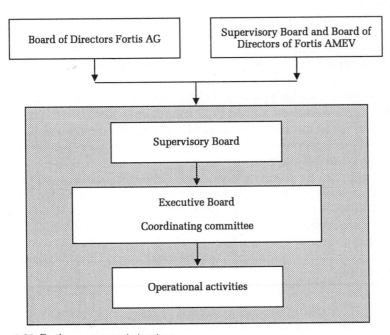

Figure 6.20 Fortis management structure

for companies and individual customers. It does so through independent intermediaries (AG 1824) and through the branch offices of ASLK-CGER. In addition, Fortis has a strong presence in Belgium in the market for banking and other financial services. These banking activities are mainly directed at individual customers and small and medium-sized enterprises. In all, 14,447 people work for Fortis in Belgium and total income amounts to 2,054.2 million ECU[1] (as at August 1994).

In the Netherlands Fortis occupies a strong position in the field of insurances, banking and other financial services. AMEV Nederland, with a wide range of insurance products, focuses on individual customers and businesses through independent and tied consultants and the branches of VSB Bank. VSB Group (which includes GWK, VISA and Top Lease) is an all-round financial institution which, with a wide range of financial services, focuses primarily on individual customers and small and medium-sized enterprises. Fortis has 9,931 employees in the Netherlands and a total income of 3,472.7 million ECU (as at August 1994).

In the United States the 'Fortis Banner' companies are active in the markets for health insurance, long-term disability insurance and group life insurances and to an increasing extent in individual life insurances and investment products as well. Added to this, Fortis is developing a niche strategy in a number of specialized markets. Fortis has 5,845 employees in the United States and total income amounts to 2,682.9 million ECU (as at August 1994).

Together with Spain's largest savings bank 'la Caixa', Fortis is striving to build up a position in Spain which is comparable as regards range of products and size with the position that the group holds in its two home markets. To this end, Fortis in 1992 set up the joint venture CAIFOR together with 'la Caixa'. Its activities include life insurance, non-life insurance and mortgages. Fortis employs 780 people in Spain (including Seguros and Bilbao) and its total income amounts to 494.1 million ECU (as at August 1994).

Fortis is further active in the Republic of Ireland, the United Kingdom, Denmark, Luxemburg, France, Singapore and Australia. Figure 6.21 gives an idea of its geographic spread.

In its entirety, the group numbers over 32,000 employees. In 1993, Fortis achieved total revenues of 9,552.5 million ECU and a profit of 476.2 million ECU, an increase of 14 per cent as compared with 1992. In the *Fortune* 'Global 50 largest diversified financial companies' Fortis was consequently given an excellent ranking. Thanks to the controlling stake in ASLK-CGER Fortis climbed, as regards total assets, from the twenty-seventh to the tenth place (summer 1994).

---

1. The number of employees includes the employees of ASLK-CGER-Bank and ASLK-CGER-Insurance (10,576). No figures for ASLK-CGER have as yet been incorporated in the profit and loss account of Fortis for 1993.

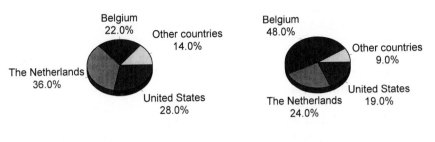

(a) excluding ASLK-CGER

Belgium
22.0%

Other countries
14.0%

The Netherlands
36.0%

United States
28.0%

9.553 million ecu

(b) including ASLK-CGER

Belgium
48.0%

Other countries
9.0%

United States
19.0%

The Netherlands
24.0%

14.471 million ecu

Figure 6.21 Total income/geographic spread for 1993, in percentage

Fortis's strategy

Fortis's strategy is aimed at playing a leading part in the field of financial services by achieving profitable growth and reinforcing its market positions. In its home markets, the Netherlands and Belgium, Fortis has focused on offering a wide range of financial services and on cooperation between the insurance and banking sectors: 'bancassurance'.

Fortis is likewise endeavouring to build up a position in Spain similar to the one it holds in the Netherlands or Belgium.

Through the combining of its activities and its recent acquisitions Fortis has achieved one of its central aims, namely to become one of the major parties in Europe in the financial services market. Although new acquisitions that would increase its size remain possible, if it is focusing on the reinforcement of the companies in their markets and not on expansion in a geographic sense priority will be given in the next few years to the further building up of the group's internal structure and to cooperation between the various parts of Fortis themselves. This also includes the further fleshing out of Fortis's policy on communications.

6.4.3 Communications policy

The companies working together in the Fortis group opted from the start for a cautious policy with regard to the intensity with which the group should be introduced to the public, as its policy was aimed at retaining as much freedom as possible for the individual operating companies. This also meant as much freedom as possible for the operating companies in the field of communications.

Communications on 'Fortis', which is the common denominator for the group of participating insurance companies and banks, focused in the early years primarily on financial target groups and the group's own employees. *Fortis Magazine*, which is published four times a year in English, Spanish, French and Dutch, was created for the last-mentioned group (32,000 copies). This is shown diagrammatically in Figure 6.22.

Figure 6.22 shows a DIY kit for creating a box. Each open box has a bottom and four sides. A strong box has five (six, actually, if you include the cover) equally constructed sides (including the bottom). As the whole is more than the sum of its parts, one needs to be aware of the interdependence between the holding level and the BU level. A strong holding gives power to the BUs and vice versa. In the life cycle of Fortis (which this year has been in existence four years) empowerment was mainly created by the BUs. The recent acquisition of ASLK-CGER and the increasing awareness among important corporate shareholders (especially financial ones) of Fortis as a group is gradually changing the balance of empowerment in the direction of the group. This is shown, for example, by the high score given in the image ranking of the *Financial Times*/Price Waterhouse survey (see p. 100–1).

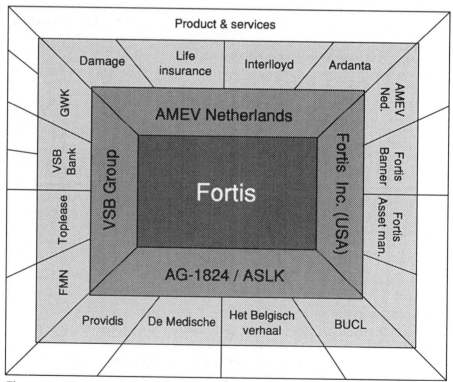

Figure 6.22 Corporate identity structure: Fortis

Communications policy until now

The following steps, which gave shape to the identity of Fortis, were covered. First, thought was given to a common name and logo which would reflect the strength of the new group. Wolff Olins thought up the name and the logo in Figure 6.23.

This name and logo were mainly used for typical group activities such as financial and internal communications. Further, the following agreements were made on the use of the Fortis name and logo by the operating companies. AG 1824, AMEV Nederland and VSB Group consistently use the endorsement 'a Fortis company' – but in small letters – on almost all their official communications, apart from exceptions like sponsoring. Not all operating companies make use of the Fortis name in the same way. The American branch of Fortis (6,000 employees), for example, decided in 1991 to use the name for the majority of its companies. In a large marketing operation, known as the 'Fortis Banner' strategy, the name Fortis has been used since that time in America for both the company (Fortis Inc.) and its products. In short, Fortis USA, unlike the other operating companies of Fortis, uses a strong form of endorsement in the sense of parent visibility. In imitation of this Interlloyd Verzekeringen of the Netherlands and AG 1824, who both focus on the industrial market, in 1993 altered their product names to Fortis Industrial, thus introducing the name Fortis to the end-user in Europe for the first time.

The VSB Bank (the Netherlands), on the other hand, developed a new – fully VSB-coloured – house style fairly soon after the house-style operation in America. In this operation, the name VSB Bank was clearly advanced as a uniform brand. GWK Bank also underwent an autonomous change in its house style. In the latter company – contrary to the VSB Bank – no reference is made to Fortis at all. The reason for this is fairly simple: the GWK Bank is not a 100 per cent Fortis company, but is partly owned by the Dutch railways.

As regards financial communications, the following choices were made with respect to the publishing of the annual report and the way in which the results are communicated to the target groups. The group first furnishes information through a bundle of three annual reports which have the same house style and, above all, a consistent content. After the Fortis annual report, the annual report containing the results of Fortis AMEV and an annual report with the results of Fortis AG follow the annual reports of the various operating companies, which communicate their own financial results to their specific target groups but in a less detailed manner.

Figure 6.23 The Fortis logo

Parent visibility

In choosing the degree to which the name Fortis is used in the communications of the operating companies, two issues play a part. In the first place, the principle of subsidiarity (everything that can be dealt with by the operating company should not be dealt with at head office) is a characteristic feature of Fortis policy. The operating companies retain as much of their freedom and identity as possible. Second, the choice of the degree to which the name Fortis is visible in the communications of the operating company appear to be dictated mainly by the question of which choice will benefit the marketing efforts of the operating company most. In broad outline, a choice has been made within Fortis for the endorsement model (see Figure 6.24). However, it is possible for an operating company to depart from this if market and/or organizational features justify this departure.

Fortis's communications policy shows that it is not necessary for a company to have to stick closely to one of the identity models for the entire organization. If circumstances justify it, it is and has to be possible to depart from the model chosen. Thus, Fortis's operating companies can be placed in various positions on the 'parent visibility' and 'substantive control' system of Cartesian coordinates (Figure 6.25).

Future communications policy

At the initial stage the identity of Fortis was principally a reflection of the operating companies. Communications at group level were limited mainly to internal and financial communications. The name of Fortis is increasingly being pushed into a more prominent position, however. A sign of this is the two parent companies changing their names to Fortis AMEV and Fortis AG (see Figure 6.26). The use of the name Fortis in America (as a product name), but also in the Netherlands and Belgium by Fortis Industrial, for example, indicates that the name Fortis is becoming increasingly important.

In the initial period the image of Fortis mainly acquired strength through its size and the group's profit figures. Now that the group is becoming more and more visible, it will need to provide greater clarity in the near future, just as all other big players in the financial services sector have done, about the nature of the common starting points of the group, in other words about the nature of the message concerning the Fortis group that they want to disseminate. At the moment the following features have been chosen:

- International insurance and banking group
- Healthy, strong financial position
- Good risk profile, stable, trustworthy
- Competitive advantages in the markets served
- Lot of growth potential, strong prospects for the future

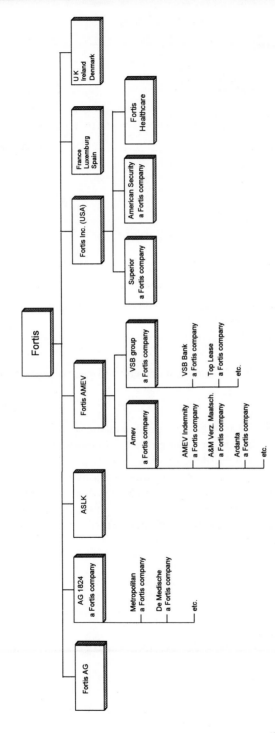

Figure 6.24 The endorsement model and Fortis

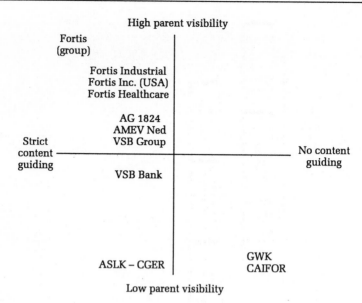

Figure 6.25 A possible fleshing out of 'parent visibility' and 'substantive control' coordinates system for Fortis

- Good payout
- Knowledgeable, forthright management who will give both good and bad news

Final remarks

The Fortis case shows clearly that companies in the second half of the 1990s no longer need to opt purely for 'uniformity' (pure monolithic) or 100 per cent 'variety'. The mixed form employed by Fortis and above all the dynamism in the nature of the way in which total communications policy for the group is being given shape is in my view typical of the developments that will characterize corporate communication in the near future. All this can be briefly summarized as 'unity and agreement are good starting points, but uniformity is not always advisable'.

AG Group and N.V. AMEV become Fortis AG and Fortis AMEV. What will that change?

Everything.

— **The names, of course.** And that's a symbol of a fundamental change. Fortis was created by its parent companies - N.V. AMEV from the Netherlands and AG Group from Belgium - to build a strong international insurance and banking group.

— **The names of the shares.** AG shares become Fortis AG shares and AMEV shares, Fortis AMEV. Now, investors and shareholders will follow Fortis AG share quotations in Brussels and Fortis AMEV share quotations in Amsterdam that reflect the value and success of all the companies within Fortis.

— **A clear corporate structure.** Through a better identification with Fortis, further confusion will be avoided with "AG 1824" in Belgium and "AMEV Nederland" in the Netherlands, both major insurance companies in their home countries. Next to these two companies, there are more than 100 other companies on four continents sharing a vision for the future that will benefit clients, investors and personnel. The name of this vision? Fortis.

And nothing.

— **Each Fortis company remains the same.** They retain their own identity, their own products and services. In every country, their individual brand names and logos will maintain a strong presence on the market as they continue to build their reputation for excellence.

— **Our service remains the same.** Brokers and other professionals will continue to work with local Fortis companies whose quality products and services they have come to rely on. Clients will perceive no change whatsoever in their individual accounts or policies: whether they are with AG 1824, AMEV Nederland, VSB Bank, ASLK-CGER, Fortis in the United States or any other company of the group.

— **The challenge remains the same.** Now, more than ever, each company within Fortis will continue to strive to play a leading role in its own market. And the 32,000 people worldwide who take on that challenge every day at local level, will know that they are part of a wider, international family. It's name? Fortis.

fortis AG
Boulevard Emile Jacqmain 53.
1000 Brussels, Belgium.

fortis AMEV
Archimedeslaan 10.
3584 BA Utrecht, the Netherlands.

Figure 6.26 Advertisement for Fortis, placed in the international press on 17 and 21 June 1994

Bibliography

Aaker, D.A., 1991, *Managing Brand Equity: Capitalizing on the value of a brand name*, The Free Press: New York.

Aaker, D.A. and J.G. Myers, 1982, *Advertising Management*, New York: Prentice Hall.

Aberg, L., 1990, 'Theoretical model and praxis of total communications', *International Public Relations Review*, 13 (2).

Abratt, R., 1989, 'A new approach to the corporate image management process', *Journal of Marketing Management*, 5 (1), 63–76.

Adema, R.L.A. and C.B.M. van Riel, 1991, 'Management van communicatie bij Nederlandse ondernemingen', working paper, Corporate Communication Centre: Erasmus University Rotterdam.

Adema, R.L.A., C.B.M. van Riel and B. Wierenga, 1993, *Kritische Succesfactoren bij het management van corporate communication*, Eburon: Delft.

Allen, R.K., 1977, *Organizational Management through Communication*, Harper & Row: New York.

Alvesson, M., 1990, 'Organization: From substance to image?', *Organization Studies*, 11 (3), 373–94.

Antonoff, R., 1985, *CI-Report 85: Identität und Image excellenter Unternehmen, Verbände, Städte: Analyse-Projekte*, Trench: Frankfurt.

Ashforth, B.E. and F. Mael, 1989, 'Social identity and the organization', *Academy of Management Review*, 14 (1), 20–39.

Association for Environmental Education (SME), 1991, *Annual Report*, Utrecht.

Ban, A.W. van den, 1982, *Inleiding tot de voorlichtingskunde*, Boom: Meppel.

Bantje, H.F.J., 1981, *Twee eeuwen met de Weduwe, Geschiedenis van De Erven de Wed. J. van Nelle N.V., 1782–1982*, Van Nelle NV, Rotterdam.

Barwise, P. and T. Robertson, 1992, 'Brand portfolios', *European Management Journal*, 10 (3).

Bauer, R., 1964, 'The obstinate audience', *American Psychologist*, 19 (5), 319–28.

Bavelas, A., 1960, 'Leaderships: Man and function', *Administrative Science Quarterly*, IV(4).

Beijk, J. and W.F. van Raaij, 1989, *Schemata: Informatieverwerking: beïnvloedingsprocessen en reclame*, VEA: Amsterdam.

Bennis, W., K. Benne, R. Chin and K. Corey, 1976, *The Planning of Change*, Holt, Rinehart & Winston: New York.

Bernstein, D., 1986, *Company Image and Reality: A critique of corporate communications*, Holt, Rinehart & Winston: Eastbourne.

Biggar, J.M. and E. Selame, 1992, 'Building brand assets', *Chief Executive*, July/August, 36–9.

Birkigt, K. and M.M. Stadler, 1986, *Corporate Identity, Grundlagen, Funktionen und Beispielen*, Verlag, Moderne Industrie: Landsberg an Lech.

Blauw, E., 1994, *Het Corporate Image, vierde geheel herziene druk*, De Viergang: Amsterdam. (4th rev. edn. First published 1986.)

Blauw, E. and O. Maathuis, 1994, 'Corporate communication; de stand van zaken in de praktijk, verslag van den telefonische en quete', working paper, Corporate Communication Centre, Erasmus University Rotterdam.

Bloom, N., 1989, 'Why research a company's image?', *Industrial Marketing Digest*, 125–31.

Bömer, M., 1991, 'De PR-manager is zo goed als hij wordt geïnformeerd', *ELAN*, Themanummer Communicatie, September.

Boorstin, D., 1961, *The Image, or What Happened to the American Dream*, Atheneum: New York.

Bosch, F.A.J. van den, 1989, 'Over de grenzen van organisaties, Bedrijfskunde, organisatie, strategie en omgeving', Inaugurale Rede, Erasmus Universiteit Rotterdam.

Bosma, T., 1993, 'Corporate Communicatie is voor communication based consultants', *Nieuwstribune*, 4 January.

Boulding, K.E., 1956, *The Image*, Ann Arbor: University of Michigan Press.

Brinkerhof, J.D.F., 1990, 'Corporate image als concurrentiewapen', *Holland Harvard Review*, 22, 46–54.

Brounts, H.M.J. and P.L.C., Nelissen, 1985, *Een nieuwe TIJD-geest*, Het Spectrum BV: Utrecht.

Cambell, A. and K. Tawadey (eds), 1990, *Mission and Business Philosophy*, Butterworth Heinemann: Oxford.

Carter, D.E., 1982, *Designing Corporate Identity Programs for Small Corporations*, Art Direction Company: New York.

Censydiam (Centrum voor Systematische Diagnostiek in Marketing), 1988, *Voorstel: Fundamenteel motivationele studie naar de behoefte aan en gebruik van "banken" en "bankdiensten" in het algemeen en de Postbank in het bijzonder*, z.p.

Chajet, C., 1989, 'The making of a new corporate image', *The Journal of Business Strategy*, May/June, 18–20.

Chandler, A.P., 1962, *Strategy and Structure*, Cambridge, Mass.: MIT Press.

Cheney, G., 1983, 'The rhetoric of identification and the study of organizational communication', *Quarterly Journal of Speech*, 69, 143–58.

Chernatony, L. de and M.H.B. McDonald, 1992, *Creating Powerful Brands: The strategic route to success in consumer, industrial and service markets*, Butterworth and Heinemann: Oxford.

Cock, G. de., R. Bouwen, K. de Wilde, J. de Visch, 1984, *Organisatieklimaat en cultuur: Theorie en praktische toepassing van de Organisatie klimaat index voor Profit Organisaties (OKIPO) en de verkorte vorm (VOKIPO)*. ACCO Leuven: Amersfoort.

Corporate Image Barometer 1990, Bonaventura/De Telegraaf: Amsterdam.

Corporate Imago-onderzoek en de photosort-techniek, FHV/BBDO/Industrieel: Amstelveen, 1986.

Cozijnsen, A.J. and W.J. Vrakking (eds), 1986, *Handboek voor strategisch innoveren: een internationale balans*, Kluwer: Deventer.

Cramwinckel, M. and P.L.C. Nelissen, 1990, 'Corporate Image Barometer, Research en Marketing BV', in C.B.M. van Riel and W.H. Nijhof (eds), *Handboek Corporate Communication*, Van Loghum Slaterus: Deventer.

Cuilenburg, J.J. van and G.W. Noomen, 1984, *Communicatiewetenschap*, Coutinho: Muiderberg.

Cutlip, S.M., A.H. Center and G.M. Broom, 1994, *Effective Public Relations*, Prentice Hall: Englewood Cliffs.

Daems, H. and S. Douma, 1989, *Concurrentiestrategie en concernstrategie*, Kluwer: Deventer.

Datta, D.K., 1991, 'Organizational fit and acquisition performance: Effects of post-acquisition integration', *Strategic Management Journal*, 12, 281–97.

Diefenbach, J.M., 1987, 'Design considerations', in M. Simpson (ed.), *Corporate Identity: Name, image and perception*, highlights of a conference, Report No. 989, The Conference Board, New York.

Dijk, R.J. van and C.B.M. van Riel, 1991, *ICPS, Integraal communicatieplannings systeem, Definitiestudie*, working paper, Corporate Communication Centre: Erasmus University Rotterdam.

Dowling, G.R., 1986, 'Managing Your Corporate Image', *Industrial Marketing Management*, 15, 109–15.

Downs, C.W. and M.D. Hazen, 1977, 'A factor-analytic study of communication satisfaction', *Journal of Business Communication*, 14 (3), 63–73.

Ellemers, N., 1991, 'Identity management strategies: The influence of sociostructural variables on strategies of individual mobility and social change', PhD dissertation, University of Groningen, The Netherlands.

Engel, J.F., R.D. Blackwell and P.W. Miniard, 1990, *Consumer Behavior*. The Dryden Press: Chicago.

Enis, B.M., 1967, 'An analytical approach to the concept of image', *California Management Review*, summer 1967, 51–8.

Erickson, G.M., J.K. Johanssen and P. Chao, 1984, 'Image variables in multiattribute product evaluations: Country-of-origin effects', *Journal of Consumer Research*, 11, 694–9.

Fahey, L. and V.K. Narayanan, 1986, *Macroenvironmental Analysis for Strategic Management*. The West series in strategic management, St Paul.

Falcione, R.L., L. Sussman and R.P. Herden, 1987, 'Communication climate in organizations', in F.M. Jablin, L.L. Putnam, K.H. Roberts and L.W. Porter (eds), *Handbook of Organizational Communication*, Sage: Newbury Park, 195–228.

Fauconnier, G., 1988, *Het imago als placebo: niet ernstig, maar het werkt*, Kongresboek Ondernemen Deel II.

Fayol, H., 1949, *General and Industrial Management*. Pitman: New York.

Fenkart, P. and H. Widmer, 1987, *Corporate Identity: Leitbild, Erschienungsbild, Kommunikation*, Orell Fuessli, Zürich.

Fishbein, M. and I. Ajzen, 1975, *Belief, Attitude, Intention and Behavior*, Addison-Wesley: Reading, Mass.

Floor, J.M.G. and W.F. van Raaij, 1993, *Marketingcommunicatie-strategie*, 2nd edn, Stenfert Kroese: Houten.

Fombrun, C. and M. Shanley, 1989, 'What's in a name? Reputation building and corporate strategy', *Academy of Management Journal*, 33 (2), 233–58.

Ford, R.P., 1987, 'The importance of image', *The Bankers Magazine*, September/October, 72–5.

Frank, A. and J. Brownell, 1989, *Organizational Communication and Behavior: Communicating to improve performance*, Holt, Rinehart & Winston: New York.

Franzen, G., 1984, *Mensen, produkten en Reclame*, Samsom: Alphen a/d Rijn.

Franzen, G. and F.F.O. Holzhauer, *Het merk*, deel I, 1987 t/m deel VII, 1990, Kluwer Bedrijfswetenschappen: Deventer.

Freeman, R.E. 1984, *Strategic Management*, Pitman: Boston.

Fryxell, G.E. and J. Wang, 1994, 'The *Fortune's* corporate 'reputation' index: Reputation of what?', *Journal of Management*, 20 (1), 1–14.

Gagliardi, P. (ed.), 1990, *Symbols and Artifacts: Views of the corporate landscape*, Aldine de Gruyter: New York.

Garbett, T.F., 1988, *How to Build a Corporation Identity and Project its Image*, Lexington Books: Massachusetts/Toronto.

Gent, B. van, 1973, *Andragologie en voorlichtingskunde*, Boom: Meppel.

Geursen, G., 1990, *Een hazewind op gympen. Conceptontwikkeling in de reclame*, Stenfen Kroese Uitgevers: Leiden/Antwerpen.

Goldhaber, G., 1986, *Organizational Communication*, Wm C. Brown Publishers: Dubuque.

Goldhaber, G. and E.M. Rogers, 1979, *Auditing Organizational Communication Systems: The ICA communication audit*, William C. Brown Publishers: Dubuque.

Gorb, P. (ed.), 1990, *Design Management: Papers from the London Business School*, Architecture and Technology Press, LBS: London.

Gray, E.R. and L.R. Smeltzer, 1985, 'SRM Forum: Corporate image – an integral part of strategy', *Sloan Management Review*, summer 1985, 73–7.

Greenbaum, H.H., P. Clampitt and S. Willihnganz, 1988, 'Organizational communication: An examination of four instruments', *Management Communication Quarterly*, 2 (2).

Grunig, L.A., 1989, 'Horizontal structure in public relations: An exploratory study of departmental differentiation', in J.E. Grunig and L.A. Grunig (eds), *Public Relations Research Annual*, vol. 1, LEA Publishers: Hillsdale, 175–96.

Grunig, J.E. and T. Hunt, 1984, *Managing Public Relations*, Holt, Rinehart & Winston: Fort Worth.

Guilford, J.P., 1954, *Persönlichkeit*, Weinheim.

Gusseklo, W.G., 1985, 'Reclameplanning', in *Handboek Reclame, 1984–85*, Samsom: Alphen aan den Rijn.

Halbband, *Marktpsychologie als Sozialwissenschaft*, Verlag für Psychologie: Goettingen, 402–71.

Handy, C., 1992, 'Balancing corporate power: A new federalist paper', *Harvard Business Review*, 70 (6), 59–72.

Hannebohn, O. and S. Blöcker, 1983, 'Corporate communications', *Werbeforum*, May.

Henrion, F., 1980, 'Corporate communication in der Praxis', *Werberforum*, 5 (80), 17–19.

Higgins, R.B. and J. Diffenbach, 1989, 'Communicating corporate strategy: The payoffs and the risks', *Long Range Planning*, 12 (3), 133–9.

Hinterhuber, H.H., 1989, *Der Stand der corporate-identity-politik in der Bundesrepublik Deutschland und west-Berlin, in Österreich und der Schweiz, eine Untersuchung über die strategische Bedeutung von Corporate Identity in Industrieunternehmen*, Dr. Höfner Management Software Gmbh: Munchen.

Holzhauer, F.F.O., 1991, 'Corporate image en brand image', in C.B.M. van Riel and W.H. Nijhof (eds), *Handboek corporate communication*, Van Loghum Slaterus: Deventer.

Ind, M., 1990, *The Corporate Image: Strategies for effective identity programmes*, Kogan Page: London.

Ingen, J. van, 1991, 'Van strategie naar conceptontwikkeling, Hoe worden abstracte uitgangspunten concrete ideeën?', in C.B.M. van Riel and W.H. Nijhof (eds), *Handboek Corporate Communication*, Van Loghum Slaterus: Deventer.

IPM, 1989, *Betekenis Structuur Analyse. Nieuwe ontwikkelingen in kwalitatief onderzoek ter ondersteuning van positionering, segmentatie en produktontwikkeling*, IPM: Rotterdam.

Jackson, P., 1987, *Corporate Communication for Managers*, Pitman: London.

Jefkins, F., 1983, *Dictionary of Marketing, Advertising and Public Relations*, International Textbook Company: London.

Jemison, D.B. and S.B. Sitkin, 1990, 'Corporate aquisitions: A process perspective', in *Mergers and Acquisitions: Organizational and cultural issues*, working document, Centre for Organizational Studies: Barcelona.

Johannsen, U., 1971, *Das Marken- und Firmenimage: Theorie, Methodik, Praxis*, Duncker und Humbult: Berlin.

Johnson, G. and K. Scholes, 1989, *Exploring Corporate Strategy, Text and Cases*, Prentice Hall, Hemel Hempstead.

Jonge, J.A. de, 1976, *De industrialisatie in Nederland tussen 1850 en 1914*, Nijmegen, SUN, reprint van uitgave Scheltema & Holkema, 1968.

Kammerer, J., 1988, *Beitrag der Produktpolitik zur Corporate Identity*, SBI-Verlag: München.

Kapferer, J.N., 1992, *Strategic Brand Management*, Kogan Page: London.

Keller, I., 1987, *Corporate Identity, Elemente und Wirkungen*, inaugural dissertation, Universität Mannheim: Stuttgart.

Keller, I., 1990, *Das CI-Dilemma. Abschied von Falschen Illusionen*, Gabler Management Perspectiven: Wiesbaden.

Keller, I., 1993, 'Conceptualizing, measuring and managing customer based brand equity', *Journal of Marketing*, 57, January, 1–22.

Kennedy, S.H., 1977, 'Nurturing corporate images: Total communication or ego trip?', *European Journal of Marketing*, 11 (1). 120–64.

Klaassen, L.E.O. and G.L.F.M. Mutsaerts, 1993, 'De relatie tussen opdrachtgever en bureau', in C.B.M. van Riel and W.F. Nijhof (eds), *Handboek Corporate Communication*, Bohn Stafleu Van Loghum: Houten.

Knapper, W., 1987, *De VEA op het Vinketouw, I en II*, onderzoeksverslag, BvA en VEA: Amsterdam.

Knecht, J., 1986, *Zin en onzin over images en reclame*, Toespraak tijdens corporate image/identity symposium, georganiseerd door ESPRIT/MOTIVACTION: Amsterdam.

Knecht, J., 1989a, *Geïntegreerde communicatie*, BvA en VEA: Amsterdam.

Knecht, J., 1989b, *SRM Syllabus Corporate Communication*, SRM: Amsterdam.

Knecht, J. and B. Stoelinga, 1988, *Communicatie begrippenlijst*, Kluwer Bedrijfswetenschappen: Deventer.

Kotler, P., 1988, *Marketing Management: Analysis, planning, implementation and control*, Prentice Hall: Englewood Cliffs.

Kundera, M., 1990, *Onsterfelijkheid*, Ambo: Baarn.

Lancaster, K.M. and H.E. Katz, 1989, *Strategic Media Planning*, MTC Business Books: Lincoln Woods.

Leyer, J., 1986, *Corporate Communication in de Strategie van Ondernemingen in Beweging*, BvA-congres, mei: Amsterdam.

Lilli, W., 1983, 'Perzeption, Kognition, Image', in M. Irle and W. Bussman (eds), *Handbuch der Psychologie*, 12. Band, 1.

Little, J.D.C. and L.M. Lodish, 1966, 'A media selection model and its optimization by dynamic programming', *Industrial Management Review*, 8, Fall 1966, 15–23.

Littlejohn, S.W., 1989, *Theories of Human Communication*, Wadsworth: Belmont, California.

Luscuere, C., 1993, 'Organisatiekunde: het zoeken naar variëteit', in C.B.M. van Riel and W.H. Nijhof (eds), *Handboek Corporate Communication*, Van Loghum Slaterus: Deventer.

Lux, P.G.C., 1986, 'Zur Durchführung von Corporate Identity Programmen', in K. Birkigt and M. Stadler, 1986, 515–37.

Maathuis, O.J.M., 1993, *CIPaC: Corporate image, performance and communication*, Eburon: Delft.

McGuire, W.J., 1976, 'Some internal psychological factors influencing consumer choice', *Journal of Consumer Research*, 2. March, 302–19.

Mackiewicz, A., 1993, *Guide to Building a Global Image*, The Economist Intelligence Unit, McGraw-Hill Inc.: New York.

McLeod, J.M. and S.H. Chaffee, 1973,'Interpersonal approaches to communication research', *American Behavioral Scientist*, 16, 469–500.

Mael, F. and B.E. Ashforth, 1992, *Alumni and their alma mater: A partial test of the reformulated model of organizational identification*,' Journal of Organizational Behavior, 13, 103–23.

March, J.G., 1988, *Decisions and Organizations*, Basil Blackwell: Oxford.

Margulies, W., 1977, 'Make the most of your corporate identity', *Harvard Business Review*, July–August, 66–72.

Martineau, P., 1958, 'The personality of the retail store', *Harvard Business Review*, January–February, 47–55.

Meffert, H., 1979, *Praxis des Kommunikationsmix*, BDW: Münster.

Merkle, W., 1992, *Corporate Identity für Handelsbetriebe, Theoretische Grundlagen und Realiserungskonzeptes*, Göttinger Handelswissenschaftliche Schriften eV: Göttingen.

Min, R.A.Q., van, 1990, 'Corporate identity with Akzo, guest lecture, Department of Economics, Erasmus University Rotterdam, October.

Minekus, G., 1989, 'Geïntegreerde communicatie', *Reclame en Onderzoek*, 1, 3–14.

Mitchell, P., 1988, *Advertising Agency-Client Relations*, Croom Helm: London.

Morgan, G., 1986, *Images of Organization*, Sage: London.

MORI, 1993, 'Meaning of corporate identity in several European countries', study commissioned by Henrion, Ludlow and Schmidt, London.

Mowday, R.T., R.M. Steers and L.W. Porter, 1979, 'The measurement of organizational commitment', *Journal of Vocational Behavior*, 14, 224–47.

Muir, N., 1987, *Rebuilding Equity, The Standard Oil Company, Corporate Identity: Name, Image and Perception*, The Conferencc Board, Washington.

Mulder, S., 1991, 'Trends in klant-bureau-relaties: een overzicht van onderzoek', deel I, *Nieuwstribune*, November.

Napoles, V., 1988, *Corporate Identity Design*, Van Nostrand Reinhold: New York.

National Investor Relations Institute, *Brochure*, USA.

Olins, W., 1970, *The Corporate Personality*, Thames & Hudson: London.

Olins, W., 1989, *Corporate Identity: Making business strategy visible through design*, Thames & Hudson: London.

Olsen, R.A. and M.F. O'Neill, 1989, 'The image study: A worthwhile "investment" for the small retail securities firm', *Journal of Professional Services Marketing*, 4 (2), 159–71.

Oxenfeldt, A.R., 1974, 'Developing a favorable price-quality image', *Journal of Retailing*, 50, 8–14.

Paivio, A., 1971, *Imagery and Verbal Processes*, Holt, Rinehart & Winston: New York.

Petty, R.E. and J.T. Cacioppo, 1986, *Communication and Persuasion: Central and Peripheral Routes to Attitude Change*, Springer Verlag: New York.

Pfeffer, J. and G.R. Salancik, 1978, *The External Control of Organizations: A resource dependence model*, Harper & Row: New York.

Pieters, R.G.M., 1989, 'Een nieuwe ontwikkeling in segmentatie- en positionering-sonderzoek: laddering', *Interface*, October, 30–41.

Pincus, J.D., A.P.R. Robert, A.P.R. Rayfield and J.N. DeBonis, 1991, 'Transforming CEOs into Chief Communications Officers', *Public Relations Journal*, November.

Poiesz, T.B.C., 1988, 'The image concept: Its place in consumer psychology and its potential for other psychological areas', paper presented at the XXIVth International Congress of Psychology, Sydney, Australia.

Porter, M.E., 1985, *Competitive Advantage: Creating and sustaining superior performance*, The Free Press: New York.

Prahalad, C.K. and G. Hamel, 1990, 'The core competence of the corporation', *Harvard Business Review*, 68 (3), 79–91.

Prakke, H.J., 1968, *Kommunikation der Gesellschaft. Einführung in die funktionale Publizistik*, Verlag Regensberger: Münster.

Prince, R.A., 1989, 'Image management: A source of strategic advantage', *Bank Marketing*, 21 (10), 28–30.

Pruyn, A.T.H., 1990, 'Imago: een analytische benadering van het begrip en de implicaties daarvan voor onderzoek', in C.B.M. van Riel and W.H. Nijhof (eds), *Handboek Corporate Communication*, Van Loghum Slaterus: Deventer.

Quin, J.B., H. Mintzberg and R.M. James, 1988, *The Strategy Process: Concepts and cases*. Prentice Hall: London.

Raaij, W.F. van, 1984, *Affectieve en cognitieve effecten van reclame*, VEA: Amsterdam.

Raaij, W.F. van, 1986, *Impressie Management: Het Communicatiebeleid van de Onderneming, Tekst uitgesproken tijdens de Industriële Communicatiedag van de Bond van Adverteerders*. Erasmus Universiteit: Rotterdam.

Raaij, W.F. van, 1994, 'Onderzoek naar de effecten van corporate communication', in Riel, C.B.M. van (ed.), *Handboek Corporate Communication, Geselect-eerde artikelen voor het Hoger Onderwijs*, Bohn Stafleu Van Loghum: Houten/Zaventem.

Raaij, W.F. van and T.M.M. Verhallen, 1994, 'Domain specific market segmentation', *European Journal of Marketing*, December.

Ramanantsoa, B., 1988, *Stratégor: Stratégie, Structure, Décision, Identité: politique générale d'enterprise*, InterEditions: Paris.

Rappaport, A., 1986, *Creating Shareholder Value: The new standard for business performance*, The Free Press: New York.

Rasberry, R.W. and L.F. Lemoine, 1986, *Effective Managerial Communication*, Kent Publishing Company: Boston.

Ray, M.L., 1982, *Advertising and Communication Management*, Prentice Hall: Englewood Cliffs.

Rebel, H.J.C., 1993, 'Images, Imago's, Identiteiten en Idealen', in J. Katus and A. van der Meiden (eds), *Jaarboek voor Public Relations en Voorlichting*, Coutinho: Muiderberg.

Redding, W.C., 1972, *Communication within the Organization: An interpretive review of theory and research*, Industrial Communication Council: New York.

Reitter, R., F. Chevalier, H. Laroche, C. Mendozá and P. Pulicani, 1991, *Cultures d'Entreprise*, Vuibert: Paris.

Rekom, J. van, 1992, 'Corporate Identity, Ontwikkeling van concept en meetinstrument en de betekenis ervan voor concern-positionering', in C.B.M. van Riel and W.H. Nijhof (eds), *Handboek Corporate Communication*, Van Loghum Slaterus: Deventer.

Rekom, J. van and C.B.M. van Riel, 1993, 'Corporate communication: van geïntegreerde communicatie naar integrerende communicatie', *Bedrijfskunde*, 2, pp. 157–71.

Rekom, J. van, C.B.M. van Riel and B. Wierenga, 1991, 'Corporate Identity. Van vaag concept naar hard feitenmateriaal', working paper, Corporate Communication Centre: Erasmus University Rotterdam.

Reynolds, T.J. and J. Gutman, 1984, 'Advertising is image management', *Journal of Advertising Research*, 24, 27–37.

Reynolds, T.J. and J. Gutman, 1988, 'Laddering theory: Method, analysis, and interpretation', *Journal of Advertising Research*, February/March, 11–31.

Rice, F., 1991, 'Champions of communication', *Fortune*, 123, 3 June, 111–20.

Riel, C.B.M. van, 1986, 'Overheidsvoorlichting en intermediaire kaders', doctoral dissertation, Eburon: Delft.

Riel, C.B.M. van, 1990, 'Corporate communication: een plaatsbepaling', in C.B.M. van Riel and W.H. Nijhof (eds), *Handboek Corporate Communication*, Van Loghum Slaterus: Deventer.

Riel, C.B.M. van, 1992, *Identiteit en Imago, een inleiding in de corporate communication*, Academic Service: Schoonhoven.

Riel, C.B.M. van 1994, *Balanceren tussen variëteit en uniformiteit in het corporate communication beleid, inaugurale rede*, Erasmus Universiteit Rotterdam. Bohn Stafleu van Loghum: Houten.

Riel, C.B.M. van and M.J.E. van den Broek, 1992, 'Besluitvorming over concern-communicatiebudgetten bij twintig Nederlandse beursgenoteerde ondernemingen', *Massacommunicatie*, 4, 267–86.

Riel, C.B.M. van and R.J. van Dijk, 1991, 'CPS, Communication planning system', working paper, Corporate Communication Centre: Erasmus University Rotterdam.

Riel, C.B.M. van and J. Nedela, 1989, *Profiles in Corporate Communication in Financial Institutions*, Eburon: Delft.

Riel, C.B.M. van, A. Smidts and A.T.H. Pruyn, 1994, 'ROIT: Rotterdam Organisational Identification Test', working paper, first Corporate Identity Conference, Department of Marketing, Strathclyde University, Glasgow.

Rinnooy Kan, E.A. and J.H. Knaap, 1988, *Syllabus Middelenplanning*, SRM: Amsterdam.

Rock, M.L., 1984, 'A value for corporate image?', *Mergers & Acquisitions*, 5, winter.

Roberts, K.H. and C.A. O'Reilly, 1973, 'Some problems in measuring organizational communication', paper prepared for US office of Naval Research, US Department of Cornmerce.

Rogers, E.M., 1983, *Diffusion of Innovations*, Free Press: New York.

Roode, H. de, 1986, *Public Relations, Interne en externe communicatie voor organisatie en beleid*, Kluwer: Deventer.

Rossiter, J.R. and L. Percy, 1987, *Advertising & Promotion Management*, McGraw Hill: New York.

Russell, D.A. and D.L. Starkman, 1990, 'Measuring the emotional response to advertising: BBDO's Emotional Measurement System and Emotional Photo Deck', *Reclame en Onderzoek*, 1, 15–26.

Scholten, M., 1993, 'The meaning of choice alternatives: Attitudes and images', dissertatie Katholieke Universiteit Brabant, 15 January.

Schultz, D.E., S.I. Tannenbaum and R.F. Lauterborn, 1994, *Integrated Marketing Communications: Pulling it together and making it work*, NTC Business Books: Chicago.

Selame, E. and J. Selame, 1975, *Developing a Corporate Identity: How to stand out in the crowd*, Wiley: New York.

Selznick, P., 1957, *Leadership in Administration: A sociological approach*, Row, Peterson and Company: Evanston.

Shelby, A.N., 1993, 'Organizational, business, management, and corporate communication: An analysis of boundaries and relationships', *Journal of Business Communication*, 30 (3), pp. 241–67.

Sikkel, D., 1991, *Natural Grouping*, Computerprogramma Research International Nederland: Rotterdam.

Smythe, Dorward and Lambert, 1991, 'The rise to power of the corporate communicator', a study of the current and future role of the UK's inhouse PR professionals, London.

Sobol, M.G. and G. Farrelly, 1988, 'Corporate reputation: A function of relative size or financial performance?', *Review of Business & Economic Research*, 24 (1), 45–59.

Spiegel, B., 1961, *Die Struktur der Meinungsverteilung im sozialen Feld*, Verlag Hans Huber: Stuttgart.

Sullivan, M., 1990, 'Measuring image spillovers in umbrella branded products', *Journal of Business*, 63 (3), 309–29.

Tafertshofer, A., 1982, 'Corporate identity: Das Grundgesetz des Unternehmensideologie', *Die Unternehmung*, 36 (1), 11–25.

Tagiuri, R., 1968, 'The concepts of organizational climate', in R. Tagiuri and G. Litwin (eds), *Organizational Climate: Exploration of a Concept*, Harvard University Press: Boston.

Tanneberger, A., 1987, 'Corporate Identity. Studie zur theoretischen Fundierung und Präzisierung der Begriffe Unternehmenspersönlichkeit und Unternehmensidentität', Dissertation Universität Freibourg, Switzerland.

Tedeschi, J.T. (ed.), 1981, *Impression Management Theory and Social Psychological Research*, Academic Press: New York.

Thayer, L.O., 1968, *Communication and Communication Systems*, Irwin: Homewood, Illinois.

Thomas and Kleyn, 1989, *Communicatiebegrippen voor dagelijks gebruik*, Thomas and Klein: The Hague.

Timm, P.R., 1986, *Managerial Communication: A finger on the pulse*, Prentice Hall: Englewood Cliffs.

Topalian, A., 1984, 'Corporate identity: Beyond the visual overstatements', *International Journal of Advertising*, 3 (1), 55–62.

Toth, J.C., M.C. Valk and J. Keip, 1988, *Corporate Image Onderzoek Onder Marketingbureaus: enige hoofdlijnen*, Motivaction Amsterdam BV: Amsterdam.

Troy, Kathryn, 1993, *Managing Corporate Communications in a Competitive Climate*, Conference Board: New York.

Verbeke, W., A.P. Mosmans and M. Verhulp, 1988, *Communicatiebeleid binnen Nederlandse Ondernemingen*, Erasmus Universiteit Rotterdam.

Verhage, B.J. and W.H. Cunningham, 1989, *Grondslagen van de Marketing*, Stenfert Kroese: Leiden.

Verhallen, T.M.M., 1988, *Psychologisch Marktonderzoek*, Inaugurale Rede, Katholieke Universiteit Brabant, Tilburg, 7 October.

Walsh, J. and G. Ungson, 1991, 'Organizational memory', *Academy of Management Review*, 16 (1), 57–91.

Wathen, M., 1986, 'Logomotion: Corporate identity makes its move into the realm of strategic planning', *Public Relations Journal*, May, 24–9.

Westendorp, P.H. van and L.J. van der Herberg, 1984, *The CS Technique: More value from image research for less money*, ESOMAR Congress Proceedings: Amsterdam.

Wiedmann, K.P., 1988, 'Corporate Identity als Unternehmensstrategie', *Wist*, 5, 236–42.

Wierenga, B. and W.F. van Raaij, 1987, *Consumentengedrag, theorie, analyse en toepassingen*, Stenfert Kroese: Leiden.

Wiio, O.A. and M. Helsila, 1974, 'Auditing communication in organizations: A standard survey, LTT communication audits', *Finnish Journal of Business Economics*, 4, 305–15.

Williams, C.J.F., 1989, *What is Identity?*, Clarendon Press: Oxford.

Winsemius, P., 1985, 'Communicatie en overheidsbeleid', *Lezingencyclus Adviescommissie Rijksdienst*, 13 May.

Woerkum, C.M.J. van, 1984, *Massamediale voorlichting, Een werkplan*, Boom: Meppel.

Young and Rubican, 1994, 'Brand power study', internal report, New York.

Index